DATE DUE

FEB 1 4 2017

Muslim Women Activists in North America

Speaking for Ourselves

Edited by Katherine Bullock

University of Texas Press
Austin

First edition, 2005

Requests for permission to reproduce material from this work should be sent
to Permissions, University of Texas Press, Box 7819, Austin, TX 78713-7819.

(∞) The paper used in this book meets the minimum requirements of ANSI/NISO
    Z39.48-1992 (R1997) (Permanence of Paper).

Library of Congress Cataloging-in-Publication Data

Muslim women activists in North America : speaking for ourselves / Edited by
Katherine Bullock.— 1st ed.
      p.   cm.
Includes bibliographical references.
ISBN 0-292-70631-6 (cloth : alk. paper)—ISBN 0-292-70666-9 (pbk. : alk. paper)
1. Muslim women—North America—Biography.   2. Social action—North America—
Case studies.   3. Voluntarism—North America—Case studies.   4. Women in Islam—
North America—Case studies.   5. Women social reformers—North America—
Biography. I. Bullock, Katherine, 1967–
HQ1170.M8472 2005
305.48'697'09227—dc22
2004027056

*In memory of the first Muslim women, whose
belief, strength, courage, and determination
inspire Muslim women to activism today.*

Contents

Contents

Preface

I decided to put together a book about Muslim women activists after the tragic events of 9/11. The mainstream reaction in the United States and Canada at the time was, naturally, to question a religion that could inspire such carnage against innocent civilians. This was understandable given Osama bin Laden's blessing of the attacks and his argument that this kind of terrorist act was an Islamic duty for all Muslims. Most Muslims reject his viewpoint, and 9/11 has been a setback for the Muslim community in North America, which has struggled for many years to overcome the negative stereotypes of Islam as an oppressive and violent religion. Though there was a lot of outpouring of support from concerned non-Muslim citizens in both the United States and Canada, hate crimes have increased, and there has been a rise in anti-Islamic literature and speeches, even at the highest level of the U.S. government. Muslims are now a community under siege, as their civil liberties come under attack in the name of national security.

In all of this it was apparent to me that no one seemed to be aware of the thousands of Muslim women (and men) who devote themselves, often at great personal and financial sacrifice, to what the Victorians called "good works." And that they did so not in spite of their religion, but because of it—because of their belief that Islam mandates that Muslims work for the betterment of their fellow human beings. In his first State of the Union address after 9/11, President Bush called on Americans to devote themselves to volunteerism. I smarted under that call, since I knew firsthand how many devoted Muslims were involved in the kind of volunteerism he was advocating, and yet no one outside the Muslim community seemed to be aware of this volunteerism. Rather, Muslims continued to be maligned as suspect, as a people committed to "un-American" or "un-Canadian" values. Some of the best-selling books on Amazon.com at the time were (and still are) Muslim-bashing diatribes about the threat Muslims represent to Western civilization. I found the positive reader reviews of these books almost more frightening than the books themselves because they showed how ignorant people could be taken in by the scaremongers whipping up hatred against Muslims.

Thus it seemed urgent that a book about Muslim volunteerism be on the market, available to as a wide an audience as possible. I started out by e-mailing Muslim women activists that I had either worked with personally or had heard of in Canada and the United States, explaining my idea for a book and inviting them to contribute. I asked them to write a short autobiographical narrative that focused on their life story as an activist (i.e., not a general life story) and to talk about their challenges, mentors, motivations, and successes/failures. Many women felt honored to have been asked, but modestly (and falsely in my opinion) replied that they hadn't done that much, and suggested "so and so," whom I would subsequently e-mail. In this way, I invited well over fifty women to contribute, and received in the end seventeen essays. There are nine contributors from Canada (including myself), and eight from the United States.

I gave these writers a free hand in how they wanted to present themselves, giving only some general guidelines: What motivates you to do activism work? What do you think Islam says about activism? How would you describe your ideal society (i.e., what is the vision behind your activism)? What is the history of your activism? And so on. This is why some stories focus on the here-and-now and others on life history. I felt that it was important that each author present herself as she wished, and not according to a formula that I had given. This allows the essays in the book to express the originality and uniqueness of each person.

I wish I could have included more stories. *Muslim Women Activists* is the story of eighteen Muslim women across the United States and Canada who devote themselves to some kind of activism in addition to their other life activities—being a wife, a mother, a student, a worker, and so on. They are only eighteen voices out of literally thousands of Muslim women across North America (indeed the world) who dedicate themselves to working for the betterment of their communities. From big cities like New York, Chicago, San Francisco, Vancouver, and Toronto, to small country towns dotted all over the countryside, Muslim women are active in a myriad of ways. I hope that this collection serves as an honoring of all them. May God guide us, forgive us our sins, and bless our endeavors.

Katherine Bullock
Toronto, Canada

Acknowledgments

This book has been a joy to put together. My thanks go first of all to the wonderful women who responded to my invitation to contribute to *Muslim Women Activists in North America*. It hardly needs to be said that without their stories, this book would not exist. I am grateful they agreed to share their personal stories with the public. It has been a pleasure to work with them on this book, and their stories continue to inspire me.

I am blessed to have a wide circle of family and friends who are a constant source of support and encouragement. I wish I could acknowledge everyone by name, but that would be a long roll-call! Please consider this a thank you to everyone who is a part of my life.

A few people should be acknowledged by name, and I'd like to start with my parents, who have endured my living overseas with good humor and who have continued to nurture and encourage me across the seas.

I am indebted to Jasmine Zine, my friend and colleague of many years, for her always excellent critical feedback on parts of the manuscript, and for her unflagging professional and personal support for my career. Thanks also to my husband for his continuous encouragement about the book, his firm support for my activism, and his always reliable advice about how to manage the challenges both have thrown my way. May God give you both good, in this life and in the next.

Special thanks must also go to the women who have taken care of my little son, Zakaria. Their warmth, caring, and expertise while he was with them gave me the peace of mind I needed to focus on preparing the book: to Muzhgan, Khala (Aunty) Zakia, Rebecca, Sabra, Khala (Aunty) Zaina, and Khala (Aunty) Saleema, many, many thanks.

I am also deeply grateful to Jim Burr at the University of Texas Press, whose interest in and encouragement of the book as it was taken through the early stages of review and approval was crucial; and also to Wendy Moore, who then took over from Jim, for her expertise and support in assisting me through the editing and publication process. Thanks also to Sue Carter for her expert copyediting of the manuscript, which improved its quality, while retaining its heart.

And to close: a traditional Muslim invocation to God, the Creator, the Sustainer, the All-Merciful, to whom all praises belong. May this book be accepted and counted amongst my good deeds.

Introduction

Katherine Bullock

Throughout the centuries, Muslim students have been known to travel great distances to learn from renowned scholars. One scholar whom students used to seek out, often undertaking long journeys in order to do so, was Ai'sha bint abd al-Hadi (723–816), a woman scholar considered to be one of the most knowledgeable of her time about the *hadith* (the sayings of the Prophet Muhammad [peace be upon him]).[1] One of her students was Ibn Hajar, famous for his book on *hadith, Fath al-Bari.* In fact, Ibn Hajar records having had fifty-three women teachers.[2]

Imam ash-Shafi'i, one of the greatest scholars of Islamic law, used to attend the lectures about *hadith* given by the renowned woman scholar Nafisa bint al-Hasan (d. 208/024)[3] in al Fustat (Cairo). Shuhda bint Abi Nasr Ahmad al-Ibari (d. 574/1178), who was described by biographers as "the calligrapher, the great authority on *hadith,* and the pride of womanhood,"[4] used to lecture to large audiences in one of the main mosques in Baghdad.[5]

These days, if a Muslim woman takes to the podium, it is not usually to teach others as an authority on the Islamic sciences. More likely, it is to give a lecture about the "rights of Muslim women," among which she might mention a "right" to education. Such is the decline of the status and role of Muslim women in many contemporary Muslim communities that female education is something that needs to be *argued* for.

Knowledge of the *hadith,* which represent the collected sayings of the Prophet Muhammad (peace be upon him), is one of the most important branches of knowledge in the Islamic sciences. As a source of Islamic law and guidance, the *hadith* are second only to the Qur'an (which is considered by Muslims to be the divine word of God). There is an important connection between being able to acquire and pass on this knowledge and women's role in the community in other capacities. For to be an authority on one of the most important sources of sacred law is to be an equal partner in the maintenance and (re)production of a community at its most foundational level—preserving a political, social, and cultural community; its way of life, formation, and identity. To remove women from this aspect of community maintenance is to signal their subservience to men, and then to give this subservience religious sanction by maintaining that women have no part to play in this, the most important of roles.

As the title of this book signifies, *Muslim Women Activists* is not a book about contemporary women scholars of *hadith,* though I wish it were. Rather, it is a book about Muslim women who seek to restore their position in the community, as equal partners in its maintenance and (re)production with men.

The North American context renders the link between becoming an authority on an Islamic science and becoming an activist somewhat different from what it might have been in the premodern Muslim world, and also from what it might be in other contemporary Muslim communities, especially Arabic-speaking ones. For to become an authority in the religious sciences, a scholar needs first of all to be fluent in Arabic. Acquiring Arabic in the North American context is a challenge for most Muslims, even if one is a child born to Arabic immigrant parents. The next challenge is to find instructors qualified to teach Islamic sciences, and a further hurdle is to find the time to study the Islamic science—always an "extra-curricular activity" here, since in the Western context, one must acquire the schooling and the career path guaranteed to reproduce life here.

But civil society in the West provides a lot of avenues for people to be involved in activities outside the dominant ones of work and family. Some people involve themselves in sports or hobbies, and others devote themselves to some kind of volunteer activity aimed at helping someone or improving something. Still others dedicate themselves to more political causes, and join Greenpeace, Amnesty International, or a political party. Muslim women are no different from their non-Muslim counterparts in this regard, and it is Muslim women's activism that is the subject of this book.

"Activism," as Rose Hamid reminds us in her essay, carries with it a negative connotation in mainstream North American society. So too in Australia, where I grew up. I used to be leery, as many people still are, of "activists"—they were the ones who were "troublemakers," "complainers," or "fringe radicals" out to destroy the fabric of decent society. My involvement in various causes for justice has changed the way I perceive activism, and in this book, I mean by activism something positive, good, and decent. While it is true that sometimes an activist has to be a "troublemaker," it is also true that to stand up for what is right requires making trouble for those perpetrating injustice. How could it be otherwise? I think of activists as people committed to a "cause," to something they believe will benefit humanity and that requires struggle and self-sacrifice (of time and resources). I see activism as doing something concrete for the sake of a social good. One of the blessings of living in the West is its open political and cultural environment; there are an infinite number of causes to which people have the freedom to devote themselves. Indeed some of these causes are contradictory—the right to life versus the right to abortion being a stark example.

In contemporary Western societies, Muslim activists have tended to focus their energies inward rather than outward. The center of attention has been maintaining an Islamic identity for the community and resisting the powerful centripetal force of assimilation into a largely secular environment. Thus fund-raising to build places of worship and then Islamic schools has been a priority. This has been changing over the last ten years, however. Converts, the second generation, and African Americans (whose practice and maintenance of Islamic communities in North America predates the large immigrant influx of the 1960s)[6] are joining together for more outward focused activism: media and political advocacy, and social services. Having grown up in North America, these groups tend to understand the context better than the first generation of immigrants, and they have a confidence that allows them to contemplate activism outside their subcultural, subreligious milieu. Of course, the commitment to Islam held by the younger generation, coupled with the growing presence of converts in the Muslim community, is testament to the success of the efforts of immigrant and African American groups to preserve and pass on Islamic identities: the focus on mosque and school building was an essential ingredient that has paved the way for activism in other fields.

The relatively unchanged nature of the negative stereotypes of Muslims held by mainstream Americans and Canadians and perpetrated in the main-

Katherine Bullock

stream media has compelled Muslim activists to reach out to their neighbors, colleagues, and fellow citizens to impress upon them the decency of Islam as a religion and the positive contribution the activists believe Islam can make to the fabric of North American societies. This has been especially necessary after the public demonizations of Islam and the rise in hate-related anti-Islamic crimes and Islamophobia in the United States and Canada since the tragic events of 9/11. Sadly, too much energy is spent by Muslims combating and dealing with negative stereotypes rather than working toward alleviating more pressing issues of social justice, like the poverty, homelessness, and drug addiction that plague most modern cities in North America.

Why focus on Muslim women activists? There are countless men as well as women who spend precious time and resources for various Islamic causes. My focus on women is deliberate, though not meant to deny or sideline activist work by Muslim men. But Muslim women find themselves in a "special" position in North American society that their male counterparts do not. First, the negative discourse about Islam as religion invariably targets the religion's supposed oppression of its women. The traditional religious dress of Muslim women, the *hijab* (misnamed in the West as a "veil") is the symbol of this supposed oppression. "The veil" comes to be a shorthand for the alleged backwardness and inability of the entire Muslim community to adapt to "modern" ways of life. Thus Muslim women who wear a headscarf (and the minority in North America who wear a face veil) are targets every time they step out into public space in a way that most Muslim men are not. (The men who wear the traditional Muslim head-cap may face similar public scrutiny, but their headgear is not held up in public discourse as a symbol of oppression.) Thus Muslim women, especially those who cover, face discrimination and harassment that is unique to them. Even those Muslim women who do not cover suffer from the negative stereotype of Muslim women: first their identity as a "non-scarf" wearing woman is effaced by the ubiquitous image of "the veiled woman," and second, they are guilty by association: even if they dress like a "modern woman," the mere fact of their being Muslim makes them suspect. Hence it is important to disrupt the negative stereotype of "the veiled Muslim woman," the one who is supposed to be silently suffering due to her religion. What better way to do this than to invite activist Muslim women to speak about themselves and tell their own stories?

Another reason to focus on the narratives of Muslim women is that, again unlike their male counterparts, Muslim women face barriers to their activism from inside their own community. As my opening has suggested,

Muslim women have lost their public roles as intellectuals, and along with this has been a restriction to the private sphere of the family. Such restriction has not necessarily resulted in the total subservience of Muslim women to men. As anthropological studies of different Muslim cultures highlight, women have retained a strong role in the community through their command over the extended family.[7] Nevertheless, the loss of a more public role is to the detriment of women's ability to contribute more fully to their community and to be consulted over issues pertinent to its well-being. Unfortunately, as the narratives will reveal, many women waste far too much energy combating negative pressures from their own communities—about the right to speak publicly, to be involved in community decision making, and to participate in activities outside the home. One of the premises of this book, as of the women activists themselves, is that the denial of a more public role for women is one of the reasons the Muslim community is in a stagnated state of decline and mess. All the women contributors to this book reject restrictive interpretations of their role as Muslim women. They believe that the Qur'an and the teachings of the Prophet Muhammad (peace be upon him) envisage a positive and active role for women outside their family and emphasize the importance of working hard to improve the world around them. They are reclaiming the heritage of the women in the first Muslim community: women like A'isha, who was consulted by all for her religious verdicts; like Ruqqayah, who set up a tent in the *masjid* to treat the wounded; and like Nusaybah, who sustained thirteen wounds to her body while defending the Prophet (pbuh) from attack. Thus the book presents the stories of women who have overcome (crucially often with the support of a father or husband) the patriarchal pressures that exist to keep women in the more private sphere of the family. I have given several speeches about this book to Muslim groups, and they—especially the young women—are all fascinated, captivated, and inspired by the authors' stories. The importance of this book for providing role models for an ultra-marginalized group cannot be underestimated.

Autobiography is one of the best ways to break down stereotypes. Autobiography presents the life stories of individuals. Each one of us is unique and has a different life story to narrate. In the West, as I have mentioned, there is a generic image of what it means to be a Muslim woman—oppressed, silenced, subservient—the placard of "the veiled woman" that serves to efface individuality and uniqueness. The autobiographical narratives of the seventeen women presented here in this book challenge this singular image, because they illuminate the women's unique struggles, dreams, goals,

Katherine Bullock

triumphs, and challenges. In short, autobiographies by Muslim women individualize and humanize the ubiquitous poster image of "the oppressed Muslim woman." It is not our intention, though, to claim to "speak for" other Muslim women. Studies of Muslim women in North America highlight the diversity among Muslim women, their different ethnic and linguistic backgrounds, their different understandings of Islam, and the role they want it to play in their lives (if at all).[8] Autobiography here serves to illuminate the possibilities and life stories of a few Muslim women. The narratives highlight the different ways it is possible to be Muslim and female in North America, drawing attention to the diversity of the female experience of Islam, while not claiming to be the definitive or authoritative version of such a female experience. Everyone has her own unique life story. One of the most important aspects of *Muslim Women Activists in North America* is that it is virtually the only book on the market that is a collection of first-person narratives from Muslim women: voices that are rarely heard in North America.

As the narratives will reveal, the book is also documenting a social history of Muslims in North America that has hardly been recorded elsewhere. The stories of the older activists are a record of the founding of institutions, such as the Muslim Student Association, that are now well established and well known. Some of the younger activists have grown up viewing the MSA as a venerable organization, even though, as Muniza's story shows, the MSA is still in foundational mode in campuses across the country.

Many of the women activists in this book wear many "hats," working where needs arise. Most of them are not professional writers, just women activists who agreed to share their stories with a general reading public. Some of the authors have achieved local or national prominence; others are working tirelessly out of the spotlight for the good of their communities. I hope that *Muslim Women Activists* helps open a channel for constructive dialogue between mainstream society and the now-maligned Muslim community.

Notes

Note on Transliteration: Since this volume is meant for the general reader, the transliteration of Arabic words into English has been simplified. The transliteration follows loosely the standard set by the *International Journal of Middle East Studies,* with some exceptions. Diacritical marks and the initial and terminal hamza have been left off. Sometimes the spelling of the Arabic word follows the more phonetic usage common in the Muslim community.

Only the specialists will notice this, and we hope for their indulgence for the sake of the non-specialist reader.

1   Muhammad Zubayr Siddiqi, *Hadith Literature: Its Origins, Development and Special Features* (Cambridge, U.K.: Islamic Texts Society, 1993), p. 119.

2   The Islamic calendar began with the Prophet Muhammad's (pbuh) escape from Mecca to Medina, in the year 622 A.D.

3   A'isha Bewley, Islam: *The Empowering of Women* (London: Ta-ha, 1999), pp. 13–14.

4   Siddiqi, *Hadith Literature,* p. 119.

5   Bewley, *Islam,* p. 12.

6   See Aminah Beverly McCloud, *African American Islam* (New York: Routledge, 1995).

7   See, for example, Janice Boddy, *Women, Men, and the Zar Cult in Northern Sudan* (Madison: University of Wisconsin Press, 1989), and Uni Wikan, *Behind the Veil: Women in Oman* (Baltimore: Johns Hopkins University Press, 1982).

8   See Shahnaz Khan, *Muslim Women: Crafting a North American Identity* (Gainesville: University Press of Florida, 2000).

Katherine Bullock

Muslim Women Activists in North America

1

Silent Revolution of a Muslim Arab American Scholar-Activist

Nimat Hafez Barazangi

Where are you from?

After thirty-five years of living in the United States, every time I meet a new person, I am asked: "Where are you from?" My own personal, political, and scholarly journey along with that of some of my cohorts engaged in search for answers to this and similar questions has shaped my silent revolution. It is a revolution against the way Muslim Arab girls have been raised unprepared to experience their identity autonomously. It is a revolution against the social systems that abuse and stereotype Muslim Arab women—be it the Muslim, the Arab, or the American systems—chiefly because of their dress code. The goal of this revolution is to ignite the flames for social change, reinterpreting the Qur'an in order to retrieve its dynamics that originally intended to establish gender justice. In my search for answers to the question "Where are you from?" I weave back and forth between two distinct periods during my three and a half decades in the United States—first as a foreign student, and then as a permanent resident and a citizen.

In the late 1960s, I answered the question in my usual honest, straightforward manner: "I am from Syria." More often than not, the questioner could not locate Syria on his/her "mental" map, so I would add "from Damascus, the biblical city that St. Paul and Peter passed by during their travels." Whether the questioner made the connection or not, his/her next question would be: "Is this your national costume?" (because I was dressed modestly, with a head-cover). My reply has always been: "No, I am a Muslim." By then, the questioner was confused enough to simply nod and move on to another subject. On a rare occasion, if the questioner happened to be a reader of the *New York Times* or the *Washington Post,* he/she would lament, "Oh, yes, isn't it sad that those women are suffering under illiteracy (1960s), that they are subject to polygamy and divorce (1970s), that they are forced into seclusion (1980s), that they cannot drive (1990s), and that they are stoned and beaten in the streets (2000s)." These different, pathetic descriptions changed chronologically along with world events. With the eyes of a scholar-activist, I noticed that the majority of my Muslim women friends and colleagues did not dwell on similar situations.

Later, I started answering the same question sarcastically: "I am from Ithaca, New York," or "American." But the unconvinced questioner would persist, adding: "No, I mean originally, where do you come from?" I would still say: "I am a Muslim!" (with an *s* sound), and the questioner would add, "Oh, Moslem!" (with a *z* sound).

So who am I, and why do I identify with Islam? Why do my fellow American citizens still insist on identifying me as an "outsider," and why do I still insist on identifying myself as a Muslim (with an *s*) when this identity, along with every expression related to Islam, has been associated with many negative connotations?

When I left my native country, Syria, after finishing my formal university education in Islamic philosophy and ethics, and after the 1967 Middle East war, I was determined to be identified as a Muslim first. Primarily, I chose Islam as a belief system and a worldview, the main goal of which is social change and, in particular, enhancing gender justice. Being born and raised in an Arabic/Muslim culture, and because Arabic is also the language of the Qur'an, I feel Arabism to be part of my heritage. Ironically, these meanings of "Islamicity" and of "Arabism" crystallized for me only after years of self-searching, self-learning, and self-identification while living in the United States. In this anthology, I reflect on my experience in the context of the uneven sociohistorical and political exchange between the Arab, the Muslim, and the American peoples, as affected by the different governing bodies and world events, during the late 1960s through the early 2000s.

When I first arrived in the United States, I thought that by adhering to the Islamic article of faith, "there is no god but God (Allah in Arabic), and Muhammad is the last Messenger," and by following what is known as the "Islamic dress code," I would secure my Islamicity, and I would defy the

Madison Avenue mind-set that sees girls only through their clothes. There are problems, unfortunately, with understanding the meaning of the Muslim head-cover, which at base is an expression of modesty. For one thing, the term *"hijab,"* which literally means "curtain," or "physical divider," increasingly took on the meaning of complete segregation between the sexes as Muslim male elites began imposing more restrictions on women and reading these restrictions back into the Qur'an.[1] What I did not realize when I first came to the United States was that in practice, a Muslim who self-identifies with Islam as a way of life is one whose thoughts and actions are shaped by the dynamics of *tawhid.* That is, God is the only source of knowledge and value, in addition to being the Creator. Although I was living by the basic ethics of Islam, such as honesty and respect for others, these traits were overlooked, by both Muslims and non-Muslims, because of a preoccupation with many loaded words: *hijab, seclusion, oppression, modernity, liberation,* and so on.

How did you become concerned with Muslim women's status?

I realized that identifying with Islamic ideals only as a philosophy or a political ideology, and with Arabism as ethnic heritage or a nationalistic sentiment, was not enough for me to endure the true test of being perceived as an "outsider" in the American society. Hence, I began my self-search that also shaped my scholarly-activist strategies. I delivered my first talk about Muslim women three months after arriving in New York City, armed with a meager knowledge of English because I thought that I needed to defend Islam. ("Yes," "No," and "Thank you" were my early companions. My husband had encouraged me to write my talk in Arabic. He translated it into English. Then I read the English with a "nice" Arabic accent). I discovered later that I was neither convincing, nor convinced, because I did not really address the realities of Muslim women. Instead I was talking about the ideals of Islam and justifying the predominant male interpretations and practices of Islam. Not feeling comfortable with being continuously on the defensive, I reversed my course of action by becoming my own questioner. I moved from justifying my way of dress—claiming that it is not as oppressive as it may seem—to studying the Qur'an in order to understand the Islamic view on public appearance. Instead of explaining my cultural background—asserting that people in Damascus use shoes and do not walk barefooted—I began reading about the history of a civilization that existed for an entire millennium before colonization. Rather than being nostalgic about the revival of this part of history through different authoritative governments and elites, I decided to participate in changing history. In the process, I realized that the above questions and the defensive replies were not unique to me, or to Muslim women in general, but are common among many middle-class, "educated" people from the developing world awakening from colonial and missionary confusion.

What makes my experience somewhat unique is that I chose to pursue my identity to the point where I became "an outsider" even to my Arab and Muslim cohorts, both male and female. By departing from the usual road to activism—protesting, petitioning, rallying, and so on—I was going through my silent revolution alone. After joining many Muslim and Arab organizations, mainly preparing and serving food in holiday gatherings, teaching their children Arabic and some basics of Islam, and listening to the predominantly male rhetoric about the "Western, secular immorality," or "the imperial, capitalist injustice," I decided to start my own activism by changing myself first. Studying and learning about the Western education system, and in the process, searching for what "Islamic" and "Arabic" mean in practice, and why Muslims and Arabs lost their civilization despite the *madrasa* system, which preceded and helped shape the creation of residential colleges like Oxford, Cambridge, Harvard, and so on. During my studies at the University of Damascus, the Islamic philosophy of thinkers such as Al-Kindi, Ibn Sina, Ibn Miskawayh, Ibn Al Arabi, and Ibn Khaldun, side by side with ancient Greek and contemporary European philosophers, helped me see how the action-oriented Muslim thinkers were in dialogue with others. Hence, my action research approach—seeking collaboration with other Muslim women researchers to further their grassroots movements, as well as with my academic feminist colleagues—has been an attempt to revive this lost dynamism of Islamic philosophy, ethics, pedagogy, and activism. I observed how other Muslim women researchers developed their own research questions, while seeking to solve some of their local problems and not stopping until they made sure that others benefited.

Who is your mentor or role model?

Less than a week after arriving in New York City, I discarded my *jilbab,* the heavy coat, and my *khimar,* the heavy head-cover that I chose to wear when I left Damascus, persuaded—but not convinced—by interpretations of "Islamic" dress codes as being similar to the headgear of nuns, or similar to the black *'abaya* or *chadoor*. I originally wore the *jilbab* as a revolt against my mother, who preferred a moderate perspective. Despite her practice of modest clothes and wearing of a headscarf, she did not want me to practice the heavy coat, as—in her opinion, and, in retrospect, rightly so—it represented an extreme interpretation of *"jilbab."* My instincts for surviving the cultural shock of New York, along with some convincing evidence provided by my husband and a few Arab and Muslim friends who happened to be scholars of Islamic *shari'ah*, made me decide to face the new culture by immersing myself in it. I reverted to the modest clothes (sans headscarf) that I had worn for twenty-four years in Damascus, those of the average "modern" woman on the streets of Damascus or the streets of New York in the 1960s, but I revolted against the traditional role of the Muslim Arab woman who joins her husband on his study abroad to develop himself. I took many volunteer and low-paying jobs (secretarial work and baby-sitting) to improve my English. A year later, I took up a job at Columbia University that would help me both supplement my husband's graduate fellowship and gain free tuition to further my formal education. After two years, I was admitted to the master's program at Columbia's Teachers College. By earning a master's in educational psychology and early childhood education, I thought that I had fulfilled my intellectual needs and that I was ready to fulfill my maternal desires and duties by having a child. The real challenge started with the arrival of my lovely daughter in 1973. She drew me back to my early days in the United States. I realized again that I still did not know what identity to instill in her. "How could I teach her Arabic in an English environment? Would I be able to shape her character Islamically in a society that was biased against both Islam and Arabism?" I used to ask myself.

The rationale that persuaded me to take off my *jilbab* during my early days in the states was that I would lose many opportunities if I remained confined by the long coat and the heavy head-cover.[2] So, after receiving a degree in higher education, along with my self-study of Islam, I thought I could answer any question and respond to cultural misunderstandings, not realizing that crossing the road over again would be more difficult than before, as I was not only questioning my own identity, but also the would-be identity of my daughter. Apparently, my intellectual growth further flamed my curiosity and dissatisfaction, especially at the time when the feminist movement and women's studies programs on university campuses were at their peak. I wondered then why feminists were revolting against the traditional Western family, which did not grant women minimum civil rights, such as voting, while bashing the "oppressive" Islamic religion, which had given women the right to vote more than fourteen centuries ago. Meanwhile, I also wondered about the unjust practices that were, and still are, taking place in the Muslim and the Arab world against women's rights to vote and the right to be elected to public office. Thus, another phase of my scholarly-activist revolution began.

While looking for resources to study bilingualism and language acquisition for the sake of safeguarding my daughter's Arabic language and Islamic development, I accepted a research position at Cornell University in comparative psycholinguistics, with Arabic as one of the languages under study. I volunteered, paying my own expenses, to travel twice to my native Damascus in order to collect data among preschool children between 1974 and 1978. These trips reunited me with a Syrian women's study group with whom I had corresponded. These women were ordinary housewives, nursery school teachers and administrators, MDs and PhDs who decided to study the Qur'an and apply this learning in their daily lives. They were also attempting to regain their liberation—not by joining women's organizations, but by searching for their own identity. I did not believe then that it was possible for these women to be liberated from the local social customs, considering both the political conditions and my own perceptions that the women had been "indoctrinated" by their male relatives. But, when I saw the results of their silent activism and the changes that they have enacted in their private lives and those who were in their social circle, I was convinced that if those women were able to maintain such a strong identity under a socialist one-party government, then I could do the same under a democratic multi-party government!

Nimat Hafez Barazangi
Photo courtesy of
Nimat Hafez Barazangi

How could you move between the multiple identities?

Being convinced that I could exercise my self-identity without losing many opportunities, as I was warned in the 1960s, I decided to test the American democratic system in the early 1980s. Dressed in modest, loose, long clothes and a headscarf, I thought that I would be accepted and understood, now that I had proved that I was not the "illiterate, oppressed" Middle Eastern woman. Personally, I was convinced that I could no longer live as a hypocrite—dressed in Western clothes in the classroom and the lecture halls, while changing into my *jilbab* and headgear to go to Friday prayers and Muslim gatherings. Hence, I adopted an intermediate style: a practical, modest long-skirt suit and a headscarf, clothing that would be inconspicuous to Western eyes and also meet the criteria for prayer.

Given my political stance during those testing times for Muslims and Arabs (attempting to demystify Islam in the aftermath of the Iranian revolution), I found myself once again questioned, this time by the research group that I had been working with for five years. This questioning period intensified during the year when I enrolled once again as a graduate student, this time to pursue a PhD. At the end of that year, I was denied a renewal of my graduate research assistantship as well as the qualification to continue my PhD program by the same professor who had earlier highly recommended my admission to the program. This same professor, with whom I had worked as a research specialist and who had awarded me the graduate research assistantship, told me that my "English was not strong enough to qualify me for writing a dissertation." I had to take a one-year leave from graduate school, fighting my case through the University Ombudsman. I was able to retain my status as a graduate student, but I decided to change my major.

I was dismayed with Muslim parents' lack of enthusiasm about their children learning Islam and Arabic in the Sunday school that I voluntarily ran, and I decided to focus my dissertation project on the parenting of American Muslims. I wanted to understand their perception of Islam and their view of passing the Islamic identity to their children, in order to use the results as a foundation for building a multicultural, multilingual curriculum.

Prior to enrolling in the PhD program at Cornell University, I took a lecturer position in 1978–1980 teaching at King Abdul Aziz University Girls College in Jeddah, Saudi Arabia, while maintaining my relations with the research group and collecting data about Arab children's cognitive development. During these two years I had the opportunity to reexamine, through discussion with a number of religious scholars and educators, the Islamic belief system and its stance on women's identity. Meanwhile, I was observing the discrepant practices of sex segregation, the differentiated curriculum of girls and boys, and women's identification with Islam.[3] I realized then that the only way for Muslim woman's emancipation is through reeducating herself in Islam, in order to defy the social customs behind those discrepant practices. Hence, I began deconstructing the "Islam" that was practiced by

Nimat Hafez Barazangi

Muslim societies and studied in Western universities, with the goal of recovering the Islam whose guidance is in the Arabic Qur'an.

I remember vividly a conversation that took place in my office at the Girls College with two young Saudi seniors who were deeply convinced that Islam had a lot to offer. They were well versed both in the Islamic traditional sciences and in modern Western education, more so than average Muslim women I met in the states. Their families, and other families of close Saudi colleagues, were learned, valued education, and were willing to send their daughters abroad for higher education. The only obstacle, as I learned, was that the authorities did not allow women to travel alone without a male relative as a companion *(muhram)*, stretching the meaning of *muhram* to mean a "moral guardian."[4] This conversation and similar ones with Saudi females highly learned in Islamic knowledge encouraged me to interview some Saudi authorities for my articles on women's and children's education, which I was writing for the English edition of the *Saudi Gazette.* I learned then that there was no law prohibiting women's travel or driving, but that social customs dictated such practices. Whether we were American or Saudi citizens, we were to abide by these customs, despite the fact that these customs had no basis in Islam. Even after the Saudi government reversed its policy, allowing girls to continue their higher education in Western countries, the government insisted that these young women be accompanied by a *muhram.* Several Saudi women faculty members and I, led by Fatina Shaker, a professor of sociology and a graduate of Purdue University, organized a panel to discuss this issue with the authorities before they passed the ruling, but the entire event was canceled at the last minute by the Ministry of Girls' Education. Currently, women are allowed to earn higher degrees from Western universities, but mainly through correspondence.

Fueled by my findings that many social customs have no basis in Islam, I recharted my course of action to reaffirm my chosen identity, and that of my colleagues, as Muslim Arab women who identified with the Qur'an. I began defying some of these customs, such as refusing to wear the black *'abaya* because black clothes were—according to a Prophetic tradition— the most repugnant to Islam. I even ended up arguing with a *mutaw'a* (a religious "police officer," an idea that contradicts one of Islam's basic tenets that there is no coercion in religion [Qur'an, 2:256]), who tried to prevent me from entering the Prophet's mosque because I refused to use the *'abaya.* Sadly, the *mutaw'a* chastised my husband, who maintained that my long, wide dress and head scarf were enough for me to enter the mosque, by telling him that he (my husband) would be accountable for my behavior in the Hereafter. Such pronouncements made me even more angry because they implied that I was not an autonomous entity responsible for my own behavior—spiritually, religiously, or legally.

As I searched the Qur'an and early Islamic sources, not readily available in libraries, I became more convinced that I should further my formal education and informal Islamic higher learning in Islam (Islamic higher learning means deeper knowledge of Islam, not attaining a higher academic degree in Islamic studies). I thought then that by going back to the states I could both pursue my formal higher education and live freely in the "democratic pluralistic" society of America, where there was no "religious police" and no pressure of the local customs. My perceptions proved accurate to a certain extent. Without any doubt, I had more freedom of movement than when I was in Saudi Arabia, more leverage in defying social customs than when I lived in Syria, and more access to Islamic literary sources than what was available in either country. Yet, in reality, I had less freedom in asserting my identity, not just because of my different physical appearance but mostly because I lacked the deep knowledge of the Qur'an. This realization triggered the "Self-Identity with the Qur'an" project that eventually led me to work with two groups of Muslim women scholar-activists. One group is in Damascus, Syria; the other is in North America.

As I became more outspoken, publicly expressing my intellectual and political views and making critical statements about intellectual and political double-standard practices within both the Muslim Arab and the American systems, I found myself lacking knowledge of the evidence that would support my intuitive feeling that those practices must be contradicting the Qur'an. In the fields of both education and women's liberation, I could expose the contradictions to the constitutional amendments of equal access and equal opportunity, but I did not have the basis to expose the patriarchal Muslim/Arab elites' claims to the exclusive authority on Islam. I was able to convince the Ithaca school district authorities, for example, with my argument analyzing how to comply with Title Nine and the 14th Amendment, allowing women equal participation in sports, along with the affirmative action for equal access to education. The school administration, after more than a year of my research, lecturing, and negotiation, provided separate space and time for Muslim girls' swimming activity. Yet, some Muslim community leaders and some families refused to allow their daughters this privilege, because it was foreign to their social customs. Since swimming was a required course for safety instruction in Ithaca public schools, I explained that Muslim parents should allow their daughters equal access, as they did to their sons, instead of withdrawing them from sports classes, but to no avail. Hence, I intensified my undeclared revolution against the gender bias in these Muslim communities by responding to several invitations to become an active member of different Muslim organizations and committees.

Despite the claim to the Islamization of knowledge that was charted by the late Isma'il al Faruqi in the early 1980s, some American Muslim male elites were authoritarian and gender biased to the point of making me more convinced that I had to resume my journey alone. I was one of the early female lecturers about Muslim women education at the Islamic Society of North America's (ISNA) Women's Committee, chaired by Khadija Haffajee, the first female member of the ISNA Majlis al Shura (consultative council). In 1988, after finishing my PhD dissertation, titled "Perceptions of the Islamic Belief System: Muslims in North America," I was also invited to become a member (the only woman) of the ISNA Education Committee, on which I served for three years, concluding with the First Islamic Education Conference and, later, the formation of the Council of Islamic Schools. In 1978 the late Isma'il Al Faruqi invited me to give my first lecture at the newly founded Association of Muslim Social Scientists (AMSS) on early childhood Islamic education, which in 1980 was published in the *Journal of Islamic Studies.*[5] He later agreed to be an ad hoc member of my PhD dissertation committee, but sadly was assassinated before the thesis was defended. For several years after the passing of al Faruqi, I continued to be actively involved with AMSS and the International Institute of Islamic Thought (IIIT), which was also founded by him, and to serve as a contributor and a reviewer of papers for the *American Journal of Islamic Social Sciences,* in addition to serving as an occasional participant in and contributor to the monthly AMSS seminars and annual conferences.

Unfortunately, after several attempts to sensitize some of the leaders of these groups to gender issues, I became convinced that women's participation in the decision-making process in such organizations was still a foreign concept to most of them. The situation improved in the American Muslim Council (AMC) and the Center for the Study of Islam and Democracy (CSID). In 1997, I was nominated and elected to serve as a member of the AMC advisory board for three years, during which time I participated in few important events, including lobbying Congress and the First National Muslim-Christian Interfaith Conference at the National Cathedral (1998), where I also conducted a workshop on Muslim women's self-identity. In 2001, I was nominated and elected as a member of the board of directors of the CSID, and at the 2003 annual conference, I spoke on the role of women and gender in the governance of Muslim states, with a focus on women's participation in religious and secular *ijtihad* and decision making and in the political discourse to secure human dignity and religiosity.[6]

How was the ideal Islam transformed by Muslim Arab practices?

Arabs and Muslims take it for granted that their children will learn the Arabic language of the Qur'an and their Arabic and Islamic heritage through emulating their parents, by hearing the spoken language, or by eating *"halal"* food and following Arabic/Muslim customs. Realizing that a language may not become enriching to one's identity unless one is able to read and write it, I was interested in studying language acquisition. I wanted to secure my daughter's upbringing in Arabic and at the same time pursue professional training in psycholinguistics. I felt that without the knowledge of Arabic, my daughter might despise Islam, particularly because the translation of the meanings of the Qur'an is very much compromised by the English language, especially with respect to gender-laden expressions (for example, the Arabic "Ya ayuha al Naas" (Oh, people) is typically translated as "Oh, mankind." Also, without reading and understanding Arabic poetry and prose, I thought, my daughter might be deprived of a meaningful appreciation of Arabo-Islamic cultural and literary traditions. Personally, I embraced Arabism, as it is the cradle of Islam and the rich environment in which the Islamic civilization and its people were nurtured from early on and for many centuries up to this date. I am, nevertheless, concerned about Arabism as a manifestation of nationalistic sentiments; such nationalism is imported and is an alien concept to Arabs and Muslims. Despite its many proponents, I believe that the concept of nation-state is one of the plagues inflicted on Arabs and on Muslims in general; the nation-state has failed to liberate Arabs and Muslims from colonizing cultures and created instead a deep division and confusion of identity among Arabs and Muslims.

My activism further intensified as I faced the exploding stereotyping of Islam, Muslims, and particularly Muslim women after the Iran revolution. Having been involved in Islamic and Arabic studies and education, as well as in interfaith dialogue through the Cornell Campus United Religious Work, I responded to several invitations to lecture on these subjects. When

Nimat Hafez Barazangi

my Muslim colleagues and I suggested in 1986 that a conference be held about the concept of justice in Islam, several departments supported and sponsored the conference. After a university press expressed interest in the subject, I ended up developing the conference proceedings into an edited volume. The book challenged the prevailing geopolitical rhetoric, and publishing it took several years. I continued to pursue the project, giving it priority over the publication of my dissertation, because, in addition to its timeliness, it contained my first essay on gender justice.

I graduated with a distinction, receiving the Glock Award for my PhD dissertation, and I thought that my age might be a barrier in my search for an academic position. I never thought that my being a Muslim woman who wears the head-cover would be an obstacle. I have no doubts that my head-scarf diminished my chances, because potential job offers disappeared every time after I went for an interview. Therefore, I decided to focus on my research and accept a courtesy academic appointment. In my forthcoming book on women's identity and the Qur'an,[7] I explain how the predominantly male interpretations of a modest public appearance transformed the Islamic ideals of gender justice into the unjust use of Muslim women's dress.

To whom do you see yourself being accountable in your scholarly and political work?

I am often asked how I could be a responsible American citizen if I believe in a divine source as my primary guide. Approaching the question from the perspective of a self-identified Muslim Arab woman, I see the clarity of my identification with Islam and my accountability as embedded in Islam's central concepts of *tawhid* and *taqwa*.[8] Many Muslims may not realize this self-identity; all Muslims are not of Arab descent, and not all Arabs adhere to the faith of Islam. In light of this situation I examine my compounded identity at the level of various underlying assumptions and consider my political and scholarly accountability from within the Islamic principles, instead of seeing it as part of the Muslim-Arab social milieu. These Islamic principles include, in part, some of the basic tenets of the American constitution, such as conscientious choice and religious liberty. As a matter of fact, historically, the Islamic social structure included something that would not become one of the American constitutional civil rights until the twentieth century—women's right to vote and to exercise freedom of choice.

Within the framework of the Islamic worldview, I proceeded by asking what in a particular practice contradicts the Qur'anic guidelines, and what in the Muslim intellectual psyche led to the stagnation of Islamic dynamism. Then, I sought an alternative course of action and determined the skills that could bring me closer to *taqwa*. As a scholar-activist Muslim-Arab woman wanting to bring a sustainable and fair change to the Arabo-Islamic cultural view of women through education, I began working with other women's activists and scholars to bring further awareness on the issue of self-identity with Islam. The first conference to establish the North American Council for Muslim Women (NACMW) in 1992 set the stage for my contact with about 150 Muslim women activist leaders in different communities, some of whom I had already worked with during my dissertation field research. I conducted an informal survey to record their interests and aspirations. As a founding member, and having been elected a member of the advisory board, I maintained a close working relationship with a good number of these women, particularly NACMW's first president, Sharifa Alkhateeb, a very good friend and highly respected, nationally renowned activist, interfaith and intercultural educator, and political advocate for Muslim women and against domestic violence. (Sadly, Sharifa Alkhateeb died October 21, 2004.)

In 1993–1994, I was awarded a visiting fellowship from the Oxford University Centre for Islamic Studies, based on my research on Islamic education and the education of Muslim women. Arguing my model of women's trusteeship *(khilafah)*, as the Qur'an intended (30:2), I explained how extreme stances on the status of Muslim women, resulting from the endless interpretations of verse 4:24 in the Qur'an—usually translated as "men are responsible for women because God made the ones excel the others"—contradicted the basic premise of *khilafah*. *Khilafah* means that (a) no human being is superior to another, except as different individuals fulfill the meaning of *taqwa* (Qur'an 49:13 and 3:73) and (b) God's intent is to create variation and not sameness among human beings (Qur'an 16:17), where equality does not require sameness. My experience at Oxford—meeting different Muslim scholars and communities and encountering different perspectives on Muslim women's development—also made me more persistent in arguing for understanding Muslim women's issues from a Qur'anic perspective. During the same year, pressure to adopt an universalistic version of feminism mounted in preparation for the Beijing Conference (the Fourth World Conference on Women); participants hoped to ratify the Convention on the Elimination of All Forms of Discrimination against Women (CEDAW) document.[9]

In September 1994, the Sisterhood Is Global Institute held a conference entitled "Religion, Culture, and Women's Human Rights in the Muslim World." When I read the preliminary program, I realized that there was no representation of the American Muslim women's grassroots groups. I contacted Sharifa Alkhateeb, Maysam al Faruqi (professor of Islamic and religious studies at Georgetown University), and Azizah al-Hibri, (professor of law at the University of Richmond), to identify an appropriate person to represent this wide-ranging group. By the end of the first day of the conference, it was clear that the focus was neglecting Muslim women speaking from the Islamic perspective. The conference organizers responded by opening the discussion to a town hall meeting format, getting input from all groups. Only few weeks later, Maysam al Faruqi joined efforts with Sharifa Alkhateeb and NACMW to launch the Muslim Women's Georgetown Study Project to discuss the Islamic perspective on women's human rights vis-à-vis the Western position. We began with the intent that we would interpret the Qur'anic perspective on Muslim women's human rights. I focused on Muslim women's right to higher Islamic learning, asserting that without such learning, women may not be able to consciously identify with Islam. Kareema Altomare, a liaison from the American Muslim Council who was coordinating AMC support of NACMW's efforts toward sending a delegate to Beijing, also helped in communication and administration. In 1998, Sharifa Alkhateeb and I accepted First Lady Hillary Rodham Clinton's invitation to the White House Eid celebration, joining the other forty Muslim women's scholar-activists and their families.

Feeling uneasy about the evolution in my ideas and my simultaneous inability to effect broad social change due to the forces of conservatism and secularism, I expanded my search to the Middle East. After receiving a grant from the International Council for Adult Education, I conducted a collaborative action research with Pakistani and U.S. adult women literacy groups. Having also received a three-year Fulbright scholarship to Syria to develop a computerized curriculum in the Arabic environment, I revived my working relations with the Syrian women group I had left in the late sixties, while pursuing political empowerment of Muslim Arab women. By then I had broken away from sentimental Islam (my nostalgic memories of a Muslim society), and I worked from within the Islamic framework toward a change in both my own attitude and the negative outlooks on Muslim Arab feminism, all in accordance with my scholarly findings about the rights of women in Islam. Numerous other activities followed, among them the 1995

Middle East Studies Association (MESA) annual conference panel on Muslim women's self-identity. Well received by the audience, we were encouraged to publish our papers, which addressed both the Islamic view and practical solutions to reinstating women's human rights by reinterpreting the Qur'an. Gisela Webb, who moderated the panel, accepted the challenge of editing these papers and would later become part of *Windows of Faith.*[10] In 1999 I wanted to further the collaborative work with the same contributors and other North American Muslim women scholar-activists, but the dominant trend of the Christian Right religious conservatism in North America was unfavorable to this enterprise. However, I was able to expand my work with the Syrian women's group during my tenure as a United Nations Development Program Scholar in 1999 and 2002.

Epilogue

Muslim Arab women's political assertion and accountability need to be discussed on two levels before we can assess their various manifestations. On the philosophical and policy-making level, it is a question of who legislates and who applies the legislation, not merely a question of the ideal and the practice. This level is basic to understanding the Islamic principles of religious identification and worth for both men and women, wherein neither may legislate for the other, but each has the right and responsibility to interpret and apply Qur'anic guidance according to his/her disposition of free reasoning, or *ijtihad,* and within the procedural framework stated in the Qur'an (33:36).

On the psychological and pedagogical level, it is a question of how new ideas and procedures foreign to the Islamic worldview can be introduced without distorting or changing the ontology and epistemology (or the view on human relations to nature and to Divine Knowledge) as the bedrock for Islamic principles and teachings. New ideas and procedures could be introduced to Muslims and Arabs in a way that enables them to modify their perception and attitude about the role of women while maintaining their identity with Islam and Arabism. This level helped me determine which skills I—and perhaps each individual Muslim—need to be a qualified interpreter of the Qur'an, specifically, a reader of new meanings in time and place. The Qur'an itself supports the right to knowledge and the means for understanding Qur'anic teachings (6:50, 34:6, 96:3). My personal accountability lies in questioning those who claim that their authority approaches the level of God's authority, be they male or female.

Notes

1   Syed Abul A'la Maudoodi (*al-Hijaab,* Beirut: Daar al-Fikr, 1967) and H. Al Banna (*Al Mar'a al Muslimah,* compiled and edited by Muhammad Nasir al-Diin Al Albani, Cairo: Daar al Kutub al Salafaiyah, 1983) extended the meaning of *hijab* as in Qur'an (33:53) to the form of modest clothes for all Muslim women, resulting in two misconceptions: (1) referring to the woman's head-cover *(khimar)* as *hijab* and confusing the word *jilbab* (Qur'an 33:59) in reference to women's outer garment or cloak with *hijab;* (2) extending the use of *hijab* from mere respect for the privacy of Prophet Muhammad's wives to implying complete segregation between the sexes among all Muslims.

2   Ironically, the occasion that prompted me to wear the *jilbab* before I clearly understood the Qur'anic basis and its implications, and a discussion about this among members of a Syrian women's study group of which I was a member, became the subject of a book published by the well-known Syrian thinker/philosopher Jawdat Sa'id. That book, *al-Tawazun al-Ijtima'ai* (The Social Balance), was published in 1980 in response to questions raised by my Syrian colleagues about the phenomenon of Muslim women's shedding their *jilbabs* when they go to Western countries. Sa'id argues that these Muslim women, as well as men who shed their Islamic practice in foreign countries, do not understand the ideas behind the practice, so they are unable to defend it in the face of social pressure. I agree with Sa'id, but I would add that more often than not Muslims memorize the ideals of Islam, but do not understand how to translate these ideals into practice in different social contexts. In essence, Muslims, and particularly women, generally follow "Islamic teachings" as customary practices without understanding the principles behind the interpretations and practices, and without questioning whether or not these practices fulfill the intended principles.

3   It is worth noting here that during my tenure at King Abdul Aziz University in Jeddah, two other important and relevant events took place: the Great Mosque in Makkah (Mecca) was occupied by an armed group that was thwarted with the help of a special French squad; and the Iranian revolution took place, a movement whose ideals lived a short life before the radical conservative Mullahs took over and started imposing the *chadoor* and seclusion on women.

4   Aside from "husband," *muhram* (from Arabic) refers to a person who is not in a marriageable category, such as father, brother, uncle, and so on, as specified in the Qur'an (24:31).

5   Nimat Hafez Barazangi, "Islam and Early Childhood Education: Implications for Women's Education," *Al-Ittihad* (Journal of Islamic Studies) 17, no. 1 (January–March 1980): 33–38.

6   Nimat Hafez Barazangi, "Domestic Democracy: The Road to National and International Democracy," *Center for the Study of Islam and Democracy, Fourth Annual Conference Proceedings,* Washington, D.C., May 16, 2003 http://www.islam democracy.org/4th_Annual_Conference-Barazangi_paper.asp. Accessed September 16, 2003.

7   Nimat Hafez Barazangi, *Women's Identity and the Qur'an: A New Reading* (Gainsville: University Press of Florida, forthcoming).

8   *Taqwa* (from Arabic), often translated as "piety," refers to the individual's conscientious balance of her autonomy with social heteronomy/hegemony and her interaction with natural and divine laws. It is also the only criterion that distinguishes individuals from one another (Qur'an 49:13).

9   United Nations, *Covenant for the New Millennium: The Beijing Declaration and Platform for Action,* Fourth World Conference on Women (Santa Rosa, CA: Free Hand, 1996).

10 Gisela Webb, ed., *Windows of Faith: Muslim Women Scholar-Activists in North America* (Syracuse: Syracuse University Press, 2000).

2

Allah Doesn't Change the Condition of People until They Change Themselves

Ekram Beshir

The hot sun beat down on me as I hurried to the tram stop tightly gripping my hefty textbook in one arm and holding my bag in the other. I made my way through the crowded streets and reached the steps of the tram just before it started to move. People were still streaming in and out of the doors as the tram began to move, but as the speed picked up the last few jumped on or off, and the door was left clear until the next stop. The tram filled up quickly and you were lucky if you could find a place to stand, let alone an empty seat. I noticed several girls from my class grasping piles of overflowing notes and skimming through them nervously. I silently went over the chapters in my head. It was 1971 and I was a third-year medical student in Alexandria, Egypt, about to take an exam.

The exam hall was even busier than the tram that day. It seemed like an ocean of students sat in wave after wave of desks, everyone hustling around. I found my assigned seat and prepared myself to write yet another exam. The examiner's voice boomed through the hall and I knew that was my cue. I turned over my booklet and entered another world. Three hours later, as I looked over my last answer and handed in my paper, I could hear a storm brewing just outside the doors of the hall. I met up with my friend and she filled me in on what all the commotion was about. One of the girls in our class had been suspended from taking her exam for two years because she was caught cheating. As I walked home that afternoon, I struggled to contain my frustration. Cheating was one of those things I had absolutely no tolerance for. It was just so unfair that one person would spend so much time and effort on studying and not necessarily get the best marks while another person could be completely unprepared beforehand and be guaranteed to get the right answers. But despite my anger, I had a feeling that something just wasn't right with this whole situation. It hit me soon after. The girl who'd been caught was someone I had dealt with before and she didn't seem at all like the type who would ever cheat. As a matter of fact, I knew for certain that she would never cheat and what really happened was suddenly clear as glass. The most common method of cheating at the time was simply bringing in the answers on a piece of paper that was folded a billion and one times. And the most common method of making sure you weren't caught cheating was by throwing that paper onto someone else's desk when you no longer needed it. A supervisor had found the paper on this girl's desk and had concluded that she cheated—but anyone who even remotely knew this girl soon realized she had been framed. I began to think about the girl and how this would put her whole life on hold for two years. What if that had been me? What if they dismissed her case without even looking into it? I decided I had to do something about it, and the next day there I was, nervously walking down the unfamiliar hall with two of my friends. My heart was pounding like an army drum and I could feel the palms of my hands beginning to sweat. I'd never met the dean before; I didn't even know what he looked like. He wasn't the type of man to introduce himself to the students or take walks around campus; he was a distant figure, and so what my two friends and I were planning to do was unheard of at that time. When we reached the secretary's desk, she looked up at us curiously. I can imagine how strange it was for her to see three young women standing in front of her when she was used to seeing only big executives and important professors. She pushed her glasses all the way to the top of her nose to make sure she was seeing correctly. After a moment of silence in which she was obviously trying to figure out what we were doing there, she questioned us bluntly. My two friends looked at me, so I figured I should say something in reply. My heart beat faster…

"C-can we please make an appointment to see the dean?" The lady looked stunned, even more stunned than when she first saw us. "Let me get this right," she announced. "You girls"—she waved her hand in our three faces—"want to speak to the dean?" I wondered why that was so difficult for her to understand and nodded my head. But apparently that still wasn't clear enough for her, so after asking us the same question a few more times, she finally got up to see if the dean was available. When, at last, we got into the dean's office, I could feel my knees quivering. The dean was also quite surprised to see that it was three students who were requesting a moment of his time, but he let us in anyway. As I piped up in my shaky voice and began explaining to him why we were there, the dean looked down at me in stupefaction. After I finished my spiel, he said, "Did you say you were in third year *medical* school?" "Yes," I replied. "Well, you should have gone to law school," he said. He told us he'd look into the case, and the next minute we found ourselves walking back through the empty hall. I don't remember what became of the girl who was framed or what the dean decided in the end; all I knew was that I couldn't keep silent about what had happened. I had to try to help, actively.

I guess you could say my activism was with me since I was a child. As the oldest girl in my family, I often had to watch out for my younger twin sisters. I was never the passive type and if you asked anyone I went to school with, they would tell you that I was always asking questions, always had my hand up in the air. It helped that my Dad used to discuss and converse with me a lot from a young age. As a child of seven years old I was already being exposed to talk of revolutions and wars. I was surrounded by it, at school, on the radio, at home. I still remember the cool nights when guards would roam the streets of Cairo, blowing their loud whistles, warning us to turn off all our lights and keep our voices to a whisper so that our house wouldn't be the next target of the fighter planes flying overhead. Living through these events drove me to think of major issues from a young age. Even the games I played as a child reflected the state of affairs my country was in. We often role-played war scenes. I would act as a nurse attending to sick and wounded soldiers. Even when my older brother pulled out of the game, we pronounced him as a war casualty.

But it wasn't until after a series of events that took place later in my life that I realized my mission: a series of events that left me wondering what the purpose of my life really was. In my third year of high school, during a very stressful period of study, my mother had a sudden stroke, which brought back the memories of when my aunt was diagnosed with multiple sclerosis and her health began to deteriorate rapidly. Added to this was the fact that Israel kept declaring war on Egypt and other surrounding countries. I didn't know what to make of everything going on and I was confused and scared. Suddenly, the teenage life I was living seemed so frivolous. Why was I concerning myself with petty dreams and trivial matters when there were so many more serious things in this world to contemplate? I think medical school played a big role in how I felt at the time because day in and day out I was so intimately exposed to all sorts of sicknesses and illnesses that forced me to look at life from another angle. It got to a point where I couldn't go on living with this feeling that something pivotal was missing in my existence. And I wasn't alone. One of my friends confided in me that she was also searching for an explanation for life. I still remember sinking into the plush couch in her living room, with a clipboard and pen in hand ready to reflect on the changes that had taken place in our lives that might be responsible for how we were feeling. After a long conversation, pages of messy notes (we were, after all, medical students), and several cups of tea, we had narrowed our list of changes down to two things—gym class and religion class. Both had been cast off in hopes of focusing better on medical school. It was possible, we reasoned, that our malaise was due to the absence of activity in these two areas. We approached the problem scientifically. The next day after our lectures, we went to the gym and signed up for tennis lessons. We continued our tennis regimen for about two weeks to see if, after exercising and playing, our feelings of confusion about the meaning of life would vanish. And of course, they didn't. That could only mean one thing… we were missing religion.

Alhamdulillah, my friend's father was a professor and knew a colleague who was willing to teach Islamic education classes. It was then that I got my first taste of taking the initiative for an Islamic purpose. If we wanted these classes, my friend and I would have to organize the whole thing. This was quite an extensive duty at the time as there were no systems in place and no Muslim Student Association to turn to. We were on our own. But *alhamdulillah,* as they say, necessity is the mother of invention and, with Allah's aid, we leapt over the numerous hurdles we encountered. I looked forward to Thursday evenings from the day our lessons began; attending became a basic necessity for me. It nourished and fostered me, but most of all it enlightened me. It was as if I had woken up one day with my mouth parched, my body dehydrated, and my heart yearning. Yearning for what I didn't know. Until I sat in the lecture hall full of curious students that first Thursday evening and felt the aching begin to disappear. I had found it. Every Thursday after that, I took a sip and I kept taking sips until my lips were no longer dry and my body was no longer drained. I began to learn the real meaning of life.

I remember, thinking one Thursday evening as I walked up the steps to my house, "Yes, this is it, life makes sense." It was an incredible feeling, one that was well worth waiting for. I learned for the first time what it was truly like to be a Muslim and I saw for the first time how beautiful Islam was, if understood properly. The professor who taught us didn't focus on what we should and shouldn't do; in fact he hardly used the terms *halal* (permissible) and *haram* (forbidden) at all. Instead, he worked on building belief in our hearts. He had the right approach to Islam and I thank Allah for the opportunity to learn from him.

I think that Islam is all for activism. I believe it's everyone's job to promote Islam and do *da'wa* (spreading the news about Islam) in whatever form they are capable of. Islam is not an individualistic religion; as a matter of fact, it's at the opposite end of the spectrum. There's a lot more to Islam than locking yourself up in the local mosque and praying 24/7. Prayers and pure rituals are not ends in themselves, but they are prescribed to train and prepare us to fulfill our responsibilities in life. Islam is about community, cooperation, and support. And I could tell my professor understood that. At first, I wondered why a busy man like him would give up his valuable time and volunteer to teach us. He wasn't a sheikh or an imam so it wasn't even his job to teach Islam, he just loved doing it because he understood how important it was. In a sense, that was almost better for me because I could relate to him so much more. I believe *da'wa* is a big component of worshipping in Islam. For if all the knowledgeable Muslims out there isolated themselves for worship, how could they ever pass on their knowledge? How would I have ever discovered the true Islam? *Alhamdulillah,* I found what I was looking for; my thirst was quenched after a rigorous sequence of trial and error. Now it seemed undoubtedly clear to me that I had to help others find what they are looking for, help show them what they're missing out on. In my mind, it was simple really— if everyone passes on the message, everyone will be happy. It was then that I adopted a new lifestyle: that of a Muslim committed to action.

Nine months into our classes, a young man of twenty stood up to address the audience. He was one of the students that attended regularly and it was obvious that he was eager to discuss an issue. The professor gave him the go-ahead to begin and the man took a deep breath; something was evidently upsetting him. "Why are our Muslim sisters not wearing *hijab* (head-cover)?" he demanded. "The Qur'an distinctly asks Muslim women to wear *hijab* for their protection and modesty [at this point he cited the *ayat* (verses) that

Ekram Beshir

mention *hijab*], so why aren't they wearing it?" His strong voice echoed through the hall. I looked around the full room and saw a sea of brown and black hair staring back at me, my head among them. That was the first time I heard that *hijab* was a requirement for Muslim women, so I didn't quite understand what the young man was talking about. But when I went home that night, the first thing I did was open my Qur'an to the *ayat* he mentioned, and there, indeed, I found the same lines the young man had recited earlier that evening. I no longer had an excuse, I thought to myself, for now I knew. *Alhamdulillah,* my level of *iman* (faith) had reached the point where I could say... I hear and I obey you, Allah.

"The answer of the believers, when they are summoned to Allah and His apostle, in order that he may judge between them, is no other than this: They say, "We hear and we obey" (Qur'an 24:51). In fact, that's what I did. Within a week I was wearing *hijab.* Suddenly people stared at me as I walked down the street. Actually, it was more like gawked. I had spent a couple of days shopping for appropriate clothes, but hadn't had much luck, so I decided to make do with what I did find. I'd also spoken to my father about it. I sat down beside him at the kitchen table as he ate his breakfast and announced, "Baba (father), I'm going to start wearing *hijab.*" "Okay" he replied calmly, and that was it. To this day I don't know what was running through my father's head when I told him. He neither protested nor encouraged my decision. I remember asking my father one time, after I'd been wearing *hijab* for a couple of trying months, to stop me if I ever wanted to take my *hijab* off. He looked at me and said, "Ekram, how can I ask you not to take your *hijab* off, if I never asked you to put it on?" He had a point.

It was during the *microjupe* (miniskirt) era, and Egypt had mostly adopted European culture. The university was flooded with Egyptian women wearing painted faces and Western-styled hair—and then there was me, I wore *hijab.* I wasn't the only one in Alexandria wearing *hijab* at the time, but out of the several million people, it was a very rare sight. It was definitely a new thing, new and quite controversial. In my family, I got many different reactions. My immediate family was mostly neutral, but my extended family was definitely surprised, and after the surprise wore off, disappointed. My aunt would often question why I was acting so silly and how such a pretty young woman could ruin her beauty the way I had. My uncle expressed a deep concern for how I would ever get married looking the way I did. I replied that if God created me to think like this, he had probably created a man who thought like this too.

If it wasn't a family member protesting about my *hijab,* then it was someone on the street. I had a professor who always had to make some sort of comment about it. As I was leaving campus, one hot summer day our paths crossed yet again. He shook his head at me and declared loudly, "Poor you, Ekram, in a scorching day like today, why are you doing this to yourself?" (He had made a point of learning my name because it came in handy at times like these.) Then he stopped and said, "Why do you wear that thing on your head anyway?" "Because I'm Muslim and Allah asks Muslim women to…" He interrupted before I could finish, "I'm Muslim, my wife's Muslim, they're Muslim!" he motioned to the people in the busy campus. "So, you're questioning how faithful we are now too?" He shook his head furiously and walked away. I went home that evening barely containing my tears and opened my Qur'an. And *subhan'allah* (glory to Allah), Allah was comforting me as right in front of me I saw the *ayat* that talked about the rewards that Allah gives for those who follow his commands and are patient.

Another time, as I was riding the tram, an elaborately clad young woman sat down in front of me. She looked me up and down disapprovingly and then said, "Haven't you read what the latest feminist wrote?" I looked over at her and responded, "Haven't you read *surat al Noor* (chapter al Noor)?" In time, I got used to these types of situations, for they happened quite often. The Qur'an was my comfort and a great solace. It seemed like I always opened up to the right page at the right time, *subhan'allah.*

As time went on, some people began to get used to my newfound way of life, though not all. I tried to be a good daughter, sister, and friend, and to represent my idea of Islam well so that my siblings and mother would want to learn. One summer, I invited my sister to join the unofficial study circle my friends and I had organized. All it was really was a bunch of friends who wanted to learn more about Islam getting together in someone's apartment and discussing a book we'd read. We didn't even have a teacher, *Alhamdulillah,* after that summer, which was two years after I first put on *hijab,* my younger sister decided to do the same. As time went on it also became increasingly apparent to me that I didn't want to marry the traditional man of that time, a man whose main focus in marriage is to have a freshly cooked meal every day and a spotless house. I wanted someone who would encourage and share with me a life of learning and working for Islam. I wanted someone who had the same priority as I, somebody who knew that Muslim women are responsible for spreading Islam just like Muslim men. *Alhamdulillah,* I found that man and I thank Allah everyday for such a big blessing.

I would definitely say that wearing *hijab* helped me be more active, especially since it was such a big effort to go against the accepted culture and tradition of the time. *Hijab* stopped me from doing the little bad things that can add up. I would tell myself, if you've gone so far as to wear the *hijab,* why would you sleep without praying Isha (the night prayer) or why would you backbite? I laugh when I hear someone say that *hijab* limits women, because it has always only enhanced my productivity. It's also a great form of *da'wa,* whether in Egypt or in Canada: when you wear the *hijab,* you're no longer just representing yourself, you're representing Islam. No matter where you live in the world, people will always question what is different. Wearing *hijab* definitely makes me different. I learned not to get offended when asked about my way of dressing; people are just trying to understand, and it's every Muslim's job to help them understand. So, instead of getting defensive, encourage their questions, invite them to ask more. Give them the benefit of the doubt; maybe they really don't know what you're all about, so it's your job to teach them.

When my husband and I got married in 1974 we pledged to base our lives and the lives of our future children on Islam. When I joined my husband in Canada in 1975, we pledged to *keep* our pledge, no matter how difficult it would be. One thing we soon found out was that to properly serve Islam we must first acquire knowledge, so my husband and I tried to soak up all the knowledge we could get, whether it was by reading from authentic books, going to lectures, or going to knowledgeable people's homes and asking them questions. As a student in Canada, my husband was heavily involved in forming the first Muslim Students' Association (MSA) chapter at Carleton University in Ottawa. They arranged for a prayer area for Muslim students, and then organized and gave the *jumu'a khutbah* (Friday noon sermon). At that time the Ottawa mosque had just been opened so I began to go there and teach Arabic and Qur'an to adults. I also began attending conferences, lectures, and camps, where I would invariably pay close attention to the youth. While working with the youth I noticed a trend I didn't quite like. Many of these adolescents, though from strong Arabic backgrounds, struggled to utter their mother tongue, but worse yet, many of them struggled to maintain their *deen* (Islamic way of life). One thing was for sure, I didn't want my children to end up like that.

During this time, I was also studying for my medical qualification exam so I could practice medicine in Canada and had just gotten the news that I was pregnant with my first baby. By the time I finished all my qualifications, my daughter was almost two years old. Then, I was assigned my internship placement in Regina, a city very far from where my family lived. I couldn't imagine what my life would be like if I took that placement. My baby daughter and I would have to move far from my husband, who was still pursuing his postgraduate studies in Ottawa. This idea sounded absurd to me, so I decided to delay my internship, and I managed to get some training at a hospital in Ottawa instead. But after working there for a while, I couldn't fathom continuing to leave my baby all day and then come home to her feeling exhausted at night. I was missing out on too much in her life, so I decided to postpone pursuing my medical career and work full time instead in the best job in the world—motherhood. *Alhamdulillah,* in the years to come, my husband and I were blessed with three more wonderful children. From a young age, we got them involved, which meant getting involved ourselves, in Islamic *halaqas* (study circles), children's camps, and youth conferences.

There were many times that I thought of resuming my professional medical career. However, it was obvious to me that if I did this, I would need to stop all my community involvement and spend less time with my children. After thoroughly thinking it over, I decided that the time was not right to change my plans, as I felt it was too early to go back to work considering the age of my children. As years went by, I became completely convinced that what I was doing was much more valuable and needed. I have never regretted my decision not to pursue my medical career. All my studying and training did not go to waste in the end: the years I spent studying helped my personal growth, and being trained in medicine came in handy on many occasions. Looking back on it, it seems like a small price to pay for everything I gained and experienced through my work with my children and the community.

I also wanted to get involved in the public schools my children attended, but I was very hesitant at first. I hesitated not because I doubted whether or not I should do this, but because I didn't know what to expect. But then it hit me: if I, a grown woman, wasn't comfortable going there to volunteer, how would my kids feel? So I took the plunge, putting aside my fears, and began to volunteer during field trips and activity days. I also received permission from the teacher to come in during Ramadan (the month of fasting) and Eid (Islamic festival) and give the class a little presentation about these Islamic festivities, along with complimentary goodies for the students of course. I was soon a familiar face around the school. I don't regret for a minute volunteering my time with the public school system because it gave me an insight into the environment my kids were learning in, the culture they were surrounded by, and how the public school system worked. It also showed me when to shelter my kids and when to let them share in social activities.

It was so important to my husband and me that our girls wouldn't lose their Arabic, as it is the language of the Qur'an. To ensure that this would not happen, I taught my two eldest daughters Arabic and Qur'an at home. However, when it came time to teach my two younger ones, I thought, why not establish something that will educate them *and* other kids at the same time? At this point I felt confident enough to take on this challenge, and with the help of other community members, we established a Saturday school that is designed to make children love learning about their religion and their language. Rahma School started off with only forty-three students, but doubled every year after that. It's now in its seventh year, *alhamdulillah*, with over four hundred students. In the year 2000, by the will of Allah, I was presented the Director's Citation Award from the Ottawa Carleton District Board of Education in recognition of the school's success.

Not too long after, a bigger challenge came knocking on my door. Our community was in need of a full-time Islamic School. So, again with Allah's guidance, I and a few other community members set out to establish this new school, facing many challenges along the way. Tasks that had to be fulfilled and fulfilled quickly included planning the curriculum, finding and training suitable teachers, promoting the school, fund-raising, and finding a building to host the school. Through working day and night, *alhamdulillah*, things eventually began to progress in all departments, except for one; we couldn't find a building. We searched all over town: mosques, community centers, warehouses, unoccupied schools—you name it, we searched it. But nothing worked out. We were left feeling hopeless: you can't start a school without a place to host it. Just when we thought it was over, we found a community center that agreed to rent out four rooms to us between eight A.M. and four P.M. As relieved as we were, this posed a very big challenge. The main problem with this situation was that we had to set up the classes each and every morning and then, after school, take everything back down again since the rooms were used for other activities that were carried out in the evening. *Alhamdulillah*, our team was motivated to take on this challenge and we managed to survive the first year. It was a very tough year, and we faced numerous difficulties. Our resources were limited; we were working under tremendous pressure and learning how to deal with one another in a professional and Islamic way.

How did we make it through the year? Flexibility, dedication, patience, and a lot of *dua'a*. With the grace of Allah a great, united, and dedicated team of workers who believed in the Islamic education mission was formed during this year. Toward the end of our first year we found a treasure—a school for sale and at a reasonable price. By that time, *alhamdulillah,* we had already gained the trust of the community, which enabled us successfully to fundraise and pay for the building. *Alhamdulillah,* Abraar School is now in its third year and doing very well. It is providing a motivating and safe environment for over two hundred full-time students who feel proud to identify themselves with Islam.

In the course of raising our children and working with the schools, my husband and I became increasingly aware of the special challenges that young Muslims face growing up in North America. To prepare ourselves for the challenge of raising our children, we read many books on child psychology and family relations, and we talked with families who had had successful experiences raising their kids in North America. As time went on, my husband and I found ourselves accumulating experiences and knowledge about raising Muslim children in North America. Whenever it came time to make any decisions about what the children could and could not participate in, we made the decision based on Islamic standards, not cultural ones, and we would always explain these reasons to our children. The children began to model this behavior, and eventually they identified themselves primarily as Muslims. This was a growing process that each one of them went through on her own with our support. They may be Egyptians, Canadians, students, volunteers, swimmers, and tennis players, but first, foremost, and by choice, they are Muslims. We were asked to share our parenting experiences; "Just for Moms" and "Just for Dads" were the first two seminars we prepared and presented in our city. *Alhamdulillah,* they were well received by the community and later evolved into a full-day workshop about positive Islamic parenting skills. Soon after, my husband and I started receiving invitations from numerous communities in North America, as well as from other continents with Western cultures, to conduct these workshops in their cities.

After these workshops began, we often thought about writing a book about Islamic parenting. But it wasn't until one summer evening that we finally made a decision to do it. It was the evening of our daughter's graduation, and we were all gathered in the cafeteria after the ceremony enjoying refreshments and cake. My daughter's vice-principal happily approached us and said, "Keep sending good children like these to the school. Tell me: What's your secret?"

I laughed and replied, "We're just lucky."

"No," said the vice-principal, "You can be lucky with one or two children, but not with four. You must have done something right and I recommend that you share it with your community."

After that, we decided to document our *tarbiyah* (experiences) and from there we wrote our two books: *Meeting the Challenge of Parenting in the West: An Islamic Perspective* (Amana Publications, 1998) and *Muslim Teens: Today's Worry, Tomorrow's Hope* (Amana Publications, 2001). *Alhamdulillah, Meeting the Challenge* has sold out three editions, and the fourth edition has just been released. It has also been translated into Arabic, with three editions published so far, and is currently being translated into French, German, and Indonesian. Our workshops proved to be a great help in the development of the books. Through the workshops we met many families in different cities throughout North America, and these people helped us develop insight into the real challenges that are facing Muslim families today. With Allah's help and guidance, my husband and I then researched possible practical solutions for these real problems and included them in the books and the workshops.

In 2001, the Islamic American University, located in Detroit, Michigan, invited us to teach one course in Arabic and another in English on the subject of raising children in North America, and we gladly accepted.

As I look back on it now, I'm glad I took on these various challenges, though at the time I may have thought they were too big to tackle. I'm so grateful to Allah (swt) for making it possible for me to do this kind of work. I wouldn't have been able to do all of these things without my husband's proper Islamic understanding of women's status in society and his ability to turn his belief into a lifestyle. He was always the first one to encourage and support me, even when it meant eating leftovers frequently, helping out around the house, and watching the children when I had other commitments. My husband and I take immense pleasure in having happy, balanced, practicing Muslim children who know how to live their lives in North America as good Muslims, doing *da'wa* in their daily lives.

Many people helped me along the way, starting with my father and his willingness to spend endless hours listening to and discussing any ideas and concerns that I had. At a time when so many parents only ordered and children only obeyed, my father was unique in that he didn't only advise me and expect me to listen, but instead, he put me on an equal playing field on the debating table and we would discuss back and forth and back again. I could challenge his opinions and he would explain and vice versa until I was clear on the issues. This process that my father led me through made me a critical thinker and paved the road for me to look at different ways to meet challenges which may seem insurmountable. This, in turn, made it possible for me to do the work that I am doing now. There were also many school teachers who influenced me through their impressive high moral standards. The professor who voluntarily taught us religion classes with the proper approach when I was at the university, at a stage in my life when I was ready for the pure meaning of Islam, made a profound difference to me. There were also a couple of pious people who helped me actualize my belief and live my philosophy; I am particularly grateful for their patience and leadership. My husband, who set an example for me in many Islamic characteristics, encouraged me to continually improve myself, and supported me in the face of all adversity, has been wonderful for my morale.

All of these people were instrumental in directing me toward the straight path, but before and after everything, knowing the Prophet Muhammad (peace be upon him) as a role model was what gave me the strength to keep going in all circumstances.

3

War Zones
Anecdotes

Mariam Bhabha

Bosnia

I had entered Bosnia. However, it looked like Sarajevo airport was as far as I would get. It was the spring of 1994 and the Bosnian war was still raging. I was trying to deliver money and mail to central Bosnia, which had been cut off from the outside world for the past two years.

As president and one of the founding members of the Toronto-based Bosnian Canadian Relief Association, I had been to Bosnia on three previous occasions. I had visited refugee camps to assess the needs of refugees and others affected by the war. On one occasion I went to receive a relief shipment sent by BCRA from Canada and to supervise its distribution. This time, however, I was here on behalf of a Saskatchewan-based organization. I had conducted a speaking tour in Canada for the organization to raise funds for Bosnia. The organization then persuaded me to deliver the funds as I had contacts in Bosnia and would find it much easier to get around.

Bosnia held a special place in my heart. I had grown up in a small town in rural Quebec—a twelfth-generation Québécoise. We hadn't learned much about the outside world; I remember when we moved to Ontario when I was fifteen being surprised to meet Christians who were not Catholic! I converted to Islam in my early twenties and lived as a Muslim for twenty years without really knowing that there were Muslims in Europe.

There had been Muslims in Europe for over five hundred years. And when the war in Bosnia broke out in the spring of 1991 I felt choked. The faces of the people that I saw on TV were familiar to me. They were like me, European Muslims. The war in Bosnia also choked me because my dad had been in World War II and I had heard and read stories about that war. My grandfather, who had lived with us as I was growing up, had told me stories about World War I. I had never imagined that there would be a war in Europe again. That was the reason my dad had spent his twenty-first birthday in a concentration camp just outside of Munich: so we could have a good and safe life.

Getting into central Bosnia this time around was daunting, as the only entrance to the area was through an 800-meter tunnel in besieged Sarajevo, and the only way to get into Sarajevo was on a military flight operated by the United Nations Protection Force (UNPROFOR) from Zagreb, Croatia. A few days earlier, having made the rounds of various UN offices in Zagreb, I was able to convince the authorities that my humanitarian mission warranted space on a flight to Sarajevo and they issued the necessary papers.

On the appointed day I reported to the UN authorities at Zagreb airport wearing the required helmet and flak jacket. My seat was not guaranteed. I had to wait until the soldiers and supplies were checked in. Eventually I was told that I could board the plane. My bags were searched. In addition to the funds from Saskatchewan I had letters and money for families of Canadians in Sarajevo and central Bosnia. I was afraid that unscrupulous officials might confiscate the money from me, but they didn't.

We boarded the plane through a wide ramp under the tail of the plane through which military vehicles were also being boarded. We sat on small pop-down seats. The plane was not insulated so the one-hour flight was noisy, cold, and uncomfortable. Except for ten civilians the plane was filled with Dutch UN soldiers. I was the only woman on the plane.

On arrival at Sarajevo airport I discovered that there was no transportation to the city. UN forces from France were in command. I asked them for use of a telephone and was informed that the phones were reserved for military personnel. It was just as well because although people in Toronto had given me the name of a family, I knew that they did not speak English and we would have had trouble communicating.

Mariam Bhabha with her husband, Mohamed Bhabha, at their home in Oakville, Canada, August 2000.
Photo courtesy of Mariam Bhabha

Despondent, I walked out of the bleak, war-ravaged terminal and stood forlornly at the entrance, wondering what to do next. The airport was surrounded by Bosnian-Serb positions, cutting it off from the city of Sarajevo. Walking to Sarajevo was out of the question. I would never be able to cross the Bosnian-Serb checkpoints. Beyond the checkpoints was "Sniper Alley," the notorious stretch of roadway where Bosnian-Serb snipers passed the time taking potshots at anything that moved.

Just as I was contemplating the possibility of flying back to Zagreb, a UN personnel carrier pulled up in front of the terminal. The young soldiers swarming out of the vehicle stared at me with unabashed curiosity. One of them approached me and said, "As salaamu alaikum." I returned the greeting. He started to speak in Arabic. I explained that I did not speak Arabic.

Learning that the soldier was part of an Egyptian contingent, I told him why I had come to Sarajevo and asked him for help to get to Ploce Street, the address of the relatives of my contacts in Canada. After conferring with his colleagues the soldier told me that they were not supposed to do this but they would take me as far as the Holiday Inn. They warned me that the only road was under constant Serbian attacks and if we were stopped, UNPROFOR would not be able to protect me. As I struggled to clamber up and into the vehicle I remembered reading about a high-ranking Bosnian official who had recently been fatally shot after being stopped at a checkpoint with his UN escorts.

The pockmarked façade of the Holiday Inn with all its windows blown out was familiar to me from the television news. Entering the hotel I offered a silent prayer of thanks for being allowed to make it this far. There were a few men in the lobby, but one really stood out. He was a black man with his head covered in dreadlocks. As I sat down in the nearest seat to consider my options he came to me and said, "As salaamu alaikum." I returned the greeting and we started to talk. He told me that he was a student from the Sudan. The war had interrupted his studies so he was working as an English–Bosnian interpreter for foreign journalists and others. I told him that on my previous visits I had been helped by Br. A., a Sudanese medical student working for a foreign humanitarian organization. To my surprise and joy he informed me that Br. A. was in Sarajevo. I asked him to phone Br. A. right away and ask him to come and get me.

I had first met Br. A. in Split, on the Adriatic Coast, when he lectured me about the dangers of a woman traveling in a war zone. He counseled me to stay home in the future but provided me with a car, driver, and a female

Mariam Bhabha

guide to help me in my work. On my last trip I had met him in Zagreb. He was most annoyed that I had again ignored his advice. But with his generous nature he could not avoid helping me out by offering me the use of his office and transportation as needed.

Br. A. was incredulous when, half an hour later, he strode into the lobby of the Holiday Inn and saw me. "Sr. Mariam! What are you doing here in Sarajevo?" he exclaimed in astonishment.

Through Br. A. my prayers had been answered. He immediately drove me to Ploce Street. He told the family who I was and how their relatives had sent me to them. They welcomed me warmly into their family compound. Entering the enclosed courtyard I found myself engulfed by a beautiful feeling of safety. I was taken to the house of the patriarch, where I was to stay. The compound was located in a part of the city that dated back about four hundred years.

Br. A. asked me to rest up while he went to make arrangements for me to travel to Zenica in central Bosnia. I could not shower as there was no electricity, and what little water there was had to be brought up daily in bottles in a life-threatening routine of dodging Serbian snipers. I was used to living without all the conveniences of modern life. In our house in Quebec, the power would regularly go off every day around 5 P.M., and we were the only ones in our family to have a bath. On Saturdays my aunt would start boiling water on the wooden stove and fill a large galvanized steel container in her kitchen. Her kids, all six of them, would take turns washing.

Through sign language my Bosnian host family and I managed to communicate with each other. The grandfather told me that since the two granddaughters, ages eight and ten, could not attend school anymore, he was helping them memorize the Qur'an. This was his own form of *jihad* (struggle in the way of God). Muslims were being killed just because they were Muslims. By his teaching he was ensuring that Islam and the Qur'an would not be extinguished.

The next day Br. A. informed me that my travel arrangements had been made. I would have a female companion as well as a vehicle, driver, and bodyguard supplied by the Fateh Brigade of the Bosnian Army. This heroic brigade had successfully withstood the Serbian onslaught on Sarajevo and continued to help keep the Serbian Army at bay. The driver had been a high school mathematics teacher and was now a commander in the Bosnian Army. The bodyguard was a soldier and also the mayor of the area where the tunnel began. The entrance to the tunnel was through a trapdoor in a house. Work on the tunnel began in January 1993 when Sarajevo was under siege and cut off from all supply lines. The tunnel would connect Sarajevo to Bosnian-Muslim controlled areas of Bosnia. Under the advice of engineers, it was dug by volunteers working in shifts, using only picks and shovels. It took six months to complete and saved some four hundred thousand citizens from starvation, military defeat, and possible annihilation.

The journey from Sarajevo to Zenica would, under normal circumstances, be a pleasant one-hour drive through lush countryside. For us, however, the journey would have to be on foot and would have to begin at the tunnel after dark, as it was safe to do so only then. Within a few minutes of entering the tunnel we had to backtrack, as an injured Bosnian soldier was being brought in from the opposite direction for emergency treatment.

We resumed the journey. The tunnel was roughly 1.5 meters high. Crude wooden supports kept it from collapsing. The path was muddy and water-logged in parts. An electric cord was strung along the length of the tunnel to provide weak illumination. We had to maintain absolute silence in order not to alert the Serbian forces just a few meters above us. It was a terrifying experience, like being in a grave. The smell of earth and water was strong. It was with great relief that we emerged into the fresh cool air at the other end. At the end of the tunnel our driver, a Bosnian army soldier with a jeep, was waiting for us to continue our journey. We drove in the dark at very high speeds with no lights on to avoid being spotted by Serbian forces.

Memories of this trip in the tunnel always fill me with dread. Later, when I was in training for my trip to Palestine, we were doing an exercise where we had to be blindfolded and led by another team member through a series of obstacles. I did the exercise fine but afterward, during the debriefing, I broke down, and cried and screamed. I was back in that tunnel. I have even had trouble writing about this time in Bosnia.

It was only with the help of Allah that I was able to accomplish my mission. To do the seemingly impossible one needs to develop a strong faith and commitment. The fact that I was visibly Muslim was a great asset. For instance, in Sarajevo it was UN peacekeepers from the Egyptian army who saw me and came to ask if I needed help. They were the ones who agreed to take me in their armored vehicle into the city. I had also encountered similar kind treatment from a Malaysian Muslim peacekeeper at Zagreb airport before boarding the UN flight. I was also, as a Muslim woman, able to travel in the Bosnian war zone in a way that would not have been possible for a Muslim man. People treated me with respect, giving me safe passage and making my mission easier.

Soon I returned to Sarajevo to take a UN plane back to Zagreb and from there to fly to the safety and comfort of home. As for the kind people who helped me, Br. A. has completed his medical studies. He is now married to a woman from back home and is settled in Sarajevo. At the end of the war my driver was appointed Minister for Veterans' Affairs in the Bosnian government. And by the end of the war, the two granddaughters of the man on Ploce Street had successfully memorized the entire Qur'an.

Although many Bosnians died, more survived the war. Today, both Bosnia and Islam are still very much alive in the heart of Europe. I shall never forget all the kind people of Bosnia who helped me accomplish what seemed impossible.

Journey of Hope

A six-part narrative about my time in Palestine (September to December 2002) with the International Women's Peace Service (IWPS), an international group of women committed to the nonviolent defense of Palestinian villagers against the Israeli occupation

Part One: Jerusalem—The Starting Point

On my first morning in this city, from which Prophet Muhammad (peace be upon him) started his journey to heaven, I wake up to the call of the *adhan* (call by voice to prayer). I get up drowsily, perform *fajr* (the dawn prayer), and fall back into bed. It had been a long flight from Toronto to Tel Aviv via London. The fact that I had traveled to Israel on September 11, 2002, the first anniversary of the suicide bombings in the United States, didn't make it easier.

At Ben Gurion International, I was an object of immediate suspicion because I was in *hijab*. The Israeli officials became more suspicious when they learned that I was traveling on my own and was not being met by anyone at the airport. As a Westerner I found their attitude to be strange. As a Muslim I understood it perfectly. Their experience had taught them that Arab women do not usually travel alone and, if they do, they are met at the airport by a crowd of relatives and friends. It took them a while to accept that I was a harmless middle-aged woman traveling alone to visit friends and relatives.

No matter how irrational, attitudes, once hardened, are difficult to change. Back home, in Canada, there's an attitude among many Muslims that it's somehow sinful for Muslim women to engage in the type of activism that I find it necessary to undertake from time to time. During the war against the Bosnian Muslims, each time I went on a mission to Bosnia, I received the type of approbation that seemed to say, "What you're doing is courageous and helps Muslims but, as a woman, you should not be doing it, so it's not commendable."

Some of the things that I was able to do during the Bosnian war—such as going into the besieged city of Sarajevo when there was no way to get into the city except on military planes—would have been impossible for a man in my situation to have accomplished. Similarly, during the current intifada in Occupied Palestine, women of all races, nationalities, and religions—including Israeli women—are playing a leading role in helping Palestinians.

As the only guest at the cozy Notre Dame Hospice in Jerusalem—tourism has been a serious fatality of the current intifada—I am preoccupied by these thoughts. I take comfort in knowing that in the time of the Prophet (peace be upon him) women took an active role in the activities of the nascent *ummah* (community). They were on the battlefields as Muslims fought against overwhelming odds. Sometimes the women fought, but even when they did not fight, they would be exposed to the dangers of the battlefield. This did not deter them from working in support roles and tending to the injured.

I choose the Notre Dame because it is technically in West Jerusalem, on the Israeli side of the Green Line—the 1948 border. The hotel is within walking distance of the walled old city, which is across the Green Line, legally part of Palestine, but being increasingly Judaicized by the Israeli occupiers. I would have liked to stay in Occupied East Jerusalem, but I would not have been able to get a taxi directly from the airport to East Jerusalem, as many Israeli cab drivers are not willing to go into Palestinian areas, particularly at night. The logistics of traveling across the Green Line are complex, even though Israel is the effective ruler on both sides of the border.

No visit to the old city would be complete without performing *salah* (prayer) at Bait al Muqadis (the House of the Two Mosques, the Dome of the Rock, and Al-Aqsa Mosque). It is usually an ordeal for Palestinians to enter the sacred precincts. Most Palestinians cannot even travel to Jerusalem. Those fortunate few who are able to do so usually face a gauntlet of Israeli soldiers and police in order to pray at Al-Aqsa. I sailed past the Israeli military guards posted at the gates without being questioned. On my last trip, in 2000, no Palestinian men under the age of forty were permitted to enter the grounds. This time I saw younger men in the big crowd of worshippers.

Walking with a friend at the Damascus gate of the old city after *salah* (prayer), we witness an example of the humiliating treatment of young

Palestinians that is such a common feature of daily life under the particularly spiteful and mean Israeli occupation. A passing Palestinian youth is stopped and asked to produce his identification card. Then he is handcuffed and forced to wait while the Israeli border police make a call. For the next half-hour the youth stands meekly with his head down and arms bound behind his back as the border police lounge nearby. Palestinian shoppers rush about their business on the narrow cobblestone streets and watchful shop owners assume nonchalant, uninterested poses in the shadows of the ancient city walls. A man with professional camera equipment, who looks like a press photographer, noses around. The police order him to move along. Eventually, a police jeep arrives and the youth is taken away. At least they didn't beat him in the process, as they have been observed doing in the remote villages of the West Bank.

The shadows are lengthening and the sandstone ramparts of the old city, built by the Uthmaniya Calif, Suleiman the Magnificent, reflect the soft, rosy glow of the late afternoon sun. I have finished my preparations in Jerusalem for my three-month mission with the International Women's Peace Service (IWPS) in Hares, a village in northern Palestine, on land coveted by Jewish zealots.

There have been more than two hundred illegal colonies established in the West Bank on confiscated Palestinian land. Contrary to international law and against the objections of the UN, every Israeli government since 1948 has promoted the colonization of Palestinian land and settlement therein by heavily armed religious fanatics. The Zionists' greed for Palestinian land and resources is limitless. There are today about half a million Jews settled illegally in the West Bank. They are the cause of most Palestinian grievances and of much of the violence in Israel and Palestine. They are the reason for the formation of our all-women group of sixteen team members and many female volunteers from all over the world.

The IWPS house, rented locally, will be occupied at all times by four team members, each serving for three months each year. IWPS volunteers will join team members for one or two weeks at a time. Three members of our first team are already in place. I will be joining them tomorrow. Although each one of us has received two weeks of intensive training, we are inexperienced and apprehensive about our ability to be effective. My friend and I part, and I walk through the Christian Quarter to my hotel. My thoughts are focused on what I will have to do over the next three months to make a difference in this land that has been engulfed by so much violence and pain. I pray silently all the way back to the hotel.

About two thousand people live in the village of Hares, lying between Ramallah in the south and Nablus in the north. To the east is the coastal city of Tel Aviv, a fifteen-minute drive on highway 505, a road that Palestinian cars are prohibited from using. This costly stretch of black ribbon, cutting through prime Palestinian agricultural land, was built especially to serve the illegal Jewish colony of Ariel—the second largest settlement of its kind in Palestine—and is in sharp contrast to the rutted, dirt tracks that Palestinians are forced to use.

I arrived in Hares on September 13, 2002, to join two other women—one from the United Kingdom and the other from the United States—to form the first team of the IWPS. Because I was driven from Jerusalem in an Israeli car it took me only forty-five minutes. Had I used Palestinian transport, proscribed from using Israeli-only roads and subject to numerous roadblocks, it would have taken me at least four hours.

One of my first tasks as an international observer is to meet the people of Hares to learn about their lives under Israeli occupation, particularly since September 2000, when the Al-Aqsa intifada began.

My first stop is a small store a few hundred meters from our base. It is very basic and I've noticed that, before noon, there is a lone woman in the shop. This is a good time for me to stop and chat. Many of the items in the store, such as olives and olive oil, are produced locally. Some items, like hummus, baba ghanoush, and other salads, are prepared in the village. Other items are brought in from other parts of Palestine or imported from Israel and other countries.

The reality of the intifada is that the olives and the olive oil, which used to be sold internationally, can no longer be exported; the Israelis do not permit it. It is not easy to bring supplies into the village, either. The Israeli occupation forces have blocked off the main road leading into the village by bulldozing and dumping, at the entrance to the village, dirt, rocks, rusting cars, and whatever else gets in their way. Delivery trucks cannot drive into the village. Drivers have to leave their vehicles at the mound of dirt and carry their goods over or around it.

As I continue down the main road I meet a fruit seller, Khader Mansour, sixty-five, in his wagon, full of lemons, pulled by a donkey. Traditionally the people of this region owned and tended olive groves and grew fruits and vegetables. Since the beginning of the occupation in 1967 Israelis have built "bypass roads," such as highway 505, established colonies, such as Ariel, and developed industrial zones on land expropriated from the villagers. In the process, they have destroyed twenty-five hundred olive trees, some of them centuries old, divided family land, and, in some cases, cut off farmers' access to their lands.

Khader grows olives and lemons. His land lies next to the illegal Jewish settlement of Immanu'el. He is forbidden by the occupation forces from working his fields. If his fields lie fallow for a while they can be expropriated by the Israelis as abandoned land to allow for the expansion of their colonies.

Israeli settler colonies are heavily armed camps. They are a means for the Israeli government eventually to win land that they were unable to capture in 1948. They hope that by settling Jews on these lands they will be creating "facts on the ground." Then, when they are ready to make peace, they will be able to claim that the land belongs to them since it has been settled by Jews for so long.

Despite the dangers he faces from armed Jewish civilians and soldiers, Khader continues to assert his ownership of his land by working it. He has been beaten and shot at. He shows me a wound on his left calf where a bullet entered on one side and exited the other.

The Israeli occupation in 1967 changed forever the traditional lives of the farmers of the region. Many were forced by the new circumstances to work in Tel Aviv or other cities in Israel. Many also took up work in the new Israeli industrial zones and settler colonies.

Now, during the intifada, their lives have changed drastically again. Further down the road I talk to a group of men who gather every day under the olive trees. Abid, forty-five, father of twelve, used to work in a flour mill in Tel Aviv. He can no longer work because he has been prohibited from using the Israeli public bus that Jewish settlers use to go to work. It's the same for Ayid, thirty-eight, father of nine, and Lotuf Sultan, twenty-eight, father of four.

I see brutal signs of the occupation everywhere I walk in Hares. Windows shattered by rampaging soldiers. Doors dented by kicks during house-to-house searches. Bullet casings and empty gas canisters by the roadside, in people's backyards, and on rooftops. Two children, Raid A. Mageed Daoud, fourteen, and Mohamed Amin Daoud, sixteen, and an adult, Mohamad Ahmed Souf, twenty-seven, all unarmed civilians, have been killed in the first eighteen months of the intifada. Sixty unarmed civilians have been injured by soldiers shooting live bullets. Countless gas bombs, filled with irritating chemical agents that can cause death, have been fired, sometimes daily, into the village. I am told that, since September 2000, six women have had miscarriages that may have been caused by exposure to the gas.

The most affected by the brutality of the occupation are the children. It is a challenge for parents to get the children to school, particularly the boys. Some of the little ones refuse to be left alone and cry or run away from the school entrance. When asked why, they answer simply: *"Jesh"* (army). You tell them that there are no soldiers in sight. They reply, "But they will come."

Wire cages protect all the windows of the school because during the first year of the intifada tear gas canisters and sound grenades (grenades that make deafening noise, widely used to disperse crowds) were employed almost daily against the school. Even if all the children make it to school, there's no guarantee that the teachers will be there. Most of the teachers come from neighboring towns and villages. They are at the mercy of the Israeli occupying forces, who arbitrarily declare closures, whereby Palestinians are confined to their villages, or curfews, whereby they are confined to their homes for long periods at a time. The soldiers' actions are designed to humiliate and inconvenience the Palestinians. Perhaps the Palestinians will get fed up and leave their homeland. Finally, the Zionists will have a homeland all to themselves and the ethnic cleansing of the Holy Land will be complete.

Part Three: Fence to Some, Wall to Others

Shortly after my arrival in Jerusalem I received an invitation from B'Tselem, the Israeli Information Centre for Human Rights in the Occupied Territories, to visit, together with a group of international television and print journalists, a controversial wall that the Israelis had started building in June 2002 between the West Bank and Israel.

The "security fence," as the Israelis call it, is being built, according to them, "to protect Israel's population from terrorist attacks by suicide bombers." It will run the entire 360-kilometer length of the West Bank and will include electrified fences, trenches, and security patrols. The "apartheid wall," as some call it, will negatively affect the livelihoods of Palestinians, their access to their lands, and their freedom of movement.

Critics of the wall say that Israel is violating international law by enclosing illegal Jewish settlements and prime Palestinian lands within UN-mandated Israeli territory. By doing so Israel may effectively achieve what it has been attempting to do without success for over fifty years.

The international community has been curiously silent in the face of yet more flagrant violations of international laws by Israel. By organizing this outing B'Tselem was, presumably, attempting to generate some interest in what Israel is doing.

We are traveling to where the wall is being constructed between two villages—Metzer, a kibbutz on the Israeli side of the Green Line drawn by the UN in 1948 to create Israel, and Qaffin, on the other side of the line. The land here is lush with groves of pineapples, bananas, oranges, and, of course, olives.

The Palestinians from Qaffin reach across the dividing fence and shake hands with the Israelis from the kibbutz. They know each other. Y.M. tells me that he has lived in the kibbutz all his life. His father was Lithuanian and his mother Polish. The kibbutz was established in 1954.

Y.M. insist that there is no need for the wall. There has never been any trouble with the Arab neighbors. Actually there have been instances of close cooperation between them in times of need. The people from the kibbutz are adamant that if the wall has to be built, it should follow the Green Line and not annex any Palestinian land. The plans call for the annexation of thousands of acres of fertile Palestinian land. Y.M. tells me that kibbutz officials have already talked to Israeli authorities. They have even offered some of the kibbutz land for the wall.

M.E. from Qaffin says that Israel has already started cutting down olive trees on his land. There have been no discussions with him, nor has any compensation been offered. M.E. says that in 1948 Israelis stole his father's land to build the kibbutz. More of his land was grabbed in 1967 when Israel occupied Palestine. Now, what's left is to be taken away for the wall. He asks, "How am I going to feed my family? It is better for me to be dead!"

Y.M. is listening to M.E. He agrees. He feels that this is what causes people to become terrorists. There are more Arabs living in this area than Jews. Arabs work on the kibbutz. The kibbutz had always felt safe, but not anymore. The actions of the government are provocative and confrontational. Both men fear that it will fuel hatred between the two peoples. As we left at the end of the day I could not help wondering what the future will bring to the people of these villages.

The answer came sooner than expected. Two months later I visited Metzer again. For the third evening in a row Palestinians and Israelis have been sitting together mourning the loss of five Israeli lives—two women, one man, and two children—at the hands of a Palestinian gunman. There are about 150 people cramped into the common room of the kibbutz. Many are from the Arab areas of Um El-Fahm, Wadi Ara, and Baka al-Gharbiyeh.

The first to speak is the mayor of Um El-Fahm, Suleiman al Gharbiyeh. His message was of solidarity. He deplored what happened. He blamed it on the occupation. An end to the occupation and the establishment of a Palestinian state is the only solution to the bloodshed on both sides. Other Palestinian leaders present echo the message.

The Jewish message is that nothing could justify the killing of women and children. But they don't blame their Arab neighbors. The Arabs are told that their presence the past few evenings has given strength to the kibbutzim to face what happened. It gives them hope for the future. The Jewish voices also call for an end to the bloodshed on both sides.

What prompted the attack on Metzer? As the people of the kibbutz and the surrounding Arab villages say, there has to be a will to end the occupation, not a wall.

Part Four: At the Mercy of Israeli Justice

I had been in Hares for less than a week when my worst nightmare became a palpable, terrifying reality. IWPS' objective in the village of Hares was to establish an international presence in this district to provide a protective shield for the Palestinian residents against the brutal excesses of the Israeli military occupation. Our work would include the monitoring, documenting, and publicizing of human rights abuses and nonviolent interventions in such abuses.

My nightmare began shortly after noon on September 19, 2002. I was at IWPS headquarters in a rented home in Hares. Claire, a team member from California, was with me. Joan, an Irish woman who had just finished volunteering with the International Solidarity Movement (ISM) during her two-week vacation, was spending a few days with us before returning home. Suddenly, the sharp sound of gunfire broke the peaceful quiet of the day. Looking out of our window we saw Israeli soldiers shooting into the village from a road about 100 meters away. In accordance with our practice we rushed to the scene and asked the soldiers why they were shooting live ammunition into a residential area. They replied that some children had thrown stones at them.

There were no signs of any children or stones in the area; nor were there any signs of injury to the soldiers or damage to their vehicles. We asked the soldiers whether the alleged "stone throwing" warranted a response with live fire, which, according to the Geneva Convention, is permissible in self-defense only if there is a clear and immediate threat to life. The soldiers refused to respond. We asked if they had checked to see whether anyone had been hit. They continued to ignore us.

Then, a man got out of a jeep marked "POLICE." He aggressively denied that there had been any shooting. We pointed to over twenty spent bullet casings scattered around the soldiers' feet. He began picking up the casings and throwing them into the field by the side of the road. I said that he was destroying evidence. He became very angry and screamed, inches from my face, "Yes, I'm destroying evidence. So what?"

The policeman, whose name we later learned was Shimon Dahan, kicked the remaining casings under one of the jeeps and demanded to see our passports. He ordered us to stand in a line. At this point Rabbi Arik Ascherman, of Rabbis for Human Rights, was driving past. He stopped to ask if we needed help. He tried to intercede on our behalf, but Dahan ignored him.

Claire had been discreetly filming the events with a digital camera and Joan was secretly taking photographs. One of the soldiers noticed them and informed Dahan, who demanded that the cameras be handed over to him. They refused. By this time more police had arrived, and they began to surround us. Dahan threatened that if we did not give up our cameras he would arrest us. We asked him on what grounds, but he refused to tell us.

I had noticed that Dahan had been treating me more harshly than the other two women. He kept insisting, probably because of my *hijab*, that I was Arab and his behavior toward me was clearly racist. Now he demanded that I proceed to one of the police jeeps. I panicked at the thought of being separated from my teammates and refused to go. The three of us locked our arms in solidarity and insisted that we would stay together. Eventually Dahan relented and told us to get into the jeep together. We asked if he was arresting us. He said that we were in a military area and we had to follow his orders. We complied and were taken to a police station at the nearby illegal Jewish settlement colony of Ariel. Rabbi Ascherman followed in his car.

At the station we were told to wait in the reception area. We were being "detained," but Dahan refused to tell us on what grounds. We could not make any phone calls and we could not have legal counsel. The police demanded to see Rabbi Ascherman's passport. He was ordered to wait outside and not to speak to us. Dahan, accompanied by other police, demanded our cameras and cell phones. We refused, demanding to know why we had been brought here. They would give no information but insisted that we hand over our equipment. Eventually we were forced to comply. Two female officers then led us to a small bathroom where we were subjected to a humiliating strip search.

About an hour later we asked again to be informed of why we were being detained. Dahan told us to "shut up." He had the right to hold us for six hours without having to give a reason. Another policeman added, "twenty-four hours." Twenty minutes later Dahan called me up to the desk. He told me to sign a document that he had prepared. The document was in Hebrew with some parts written in Arabic. I told him that I did not speak Hebrew or Arabic. Dahan, hostile as ever, became extremely agitated. He accused me of lying since he had seen me reading an Arabic prayer book. I took the book, which was *Surat al Yaseen* (a chapter of the Qur'an) out of my bag to show him that it was also written in English. He snatched it from my hands. Shocked at his outrageous behavior I quickly grabbed it back from him. For the first time that afternoon, Dahan was briefly dumbfounded. He had never expected that an "Arab" woman would dare to stand up to his brutalizing behavior. Then his eyes hardened again as he composed himself and the hatred returned. I could not look into his eyes.

I continued to refuse to sign the document that Dahan was forcing on me, on the ground that I could not read it. Claire and Joan also refused to sign the documents they were offered. Shortly afterward Rabbi Ascherman was called in and we were led upstairs, where we were again told to sit and wait. Finally the rabbi was called into an inner office. When he came out he told us that he was not allowed to speak to us. Each of us was then called in separately. When I was called in a man introduced himself as Ami Baran. He said that he was the prosecutor. He informed me that my colleagues and I were being charged with (1) obstruction of police officers in the course of their duties and (2) incitement to riot because we had instigated stone throwing by some children in order to film the response of the soldiers.

Of course, we denied these ridiculously trumped-up charges. We asked Ami Baran to investigate seriously the unprovoked shooting by the soldiers that afternoon, which imperiled the lives of innocent villagers. He made notes but we knew that he was just going through the motions, because he asked no probing or follow-up questions. Finally he gave us two choices: (1) sign a paper agreeing to stay out of the West Bank for a specific period of time or (2) be transferred to a military holding unit pending deportation from Israel.

Mariam Bhabha

I asked for time to consult a lawyer and to talk to the Canadian Embassy. My request was denied. We had two choices. There was no other option. We opted for the first choice, as deportation would have meant being barred from Israel forever and not being able to continue the work for which we had been trained. Although we had all been charged with the same "offenses" we were, inexplicably, exiled from the West Bank for varying periods—Claire, 15 days; me, 30 days; and Joan, 180 days. Each of us signed the relevant documents, translated from Hebrew for us by Rabbi Ascherman. We were not allowed to have copies of any of the documents. We were told that we had to leave the West Bank immediately. We could not stop at the house in Hares to collect our belongings, not even a toothbrush, toothpaste, or overnight clothes. We would be driven directly to Jerusalem by Rabbi Ascherman.

We had been incarcerated for eight hours and denied fundamental human rights. We had been harassed and bullied and not allowed to communicate with anyone, not even each other. Our treatment at the hands of the Israeli police was tantamount to torture. But we were thankful that we were not Palestinians because we knew that for them torture has an entirely more chilling meaning.

Yet the Israelis claim that it is the neighboring countries that are despotic.

Part Five: Exiled from Palestine

We were despondent as we were driven out of the West Bank into Israel. Joan was scheduled to fly home to Ireland in a few days. But Claire and I were concerned about our ability to fulfill our commitment to serve with IWPS for three months. Our team was already shorthanded. Now Angie was left alone in the house in Hares that served as our home and office.

Mariam with her husband, Mohamed; her son, Faisal; and her daughter, Nadia, in Jerusalem, 2000.
Photo courtesy of Mariam Bhabha

In Jerusalem we were taken to the home of a supporter of IWPS. In the morning, over coffee, I discovered that we were in a beautiful old Arab house made of stone. This part of Jerusalem was occupied by Israel in 1967. The new owners were British Jews. Although sympathetic to the plight of the Palestinians, they were living in an "occupied house." Walking in the garden I could not help but wonder where the family was that owned this beautiful house. Perhaps in some refugee camp in Lebanon, I thought. I decided that I could not remain in the house. A family friend who has an apartment in Beit Safafa, a suburb of Jerusalem, offered us his flat as he was going away on business that day for a week. Joan and I gratefully accepted his offer.

Our first task in Jerusalem was to file a report about the shooting incident involving the Israeli soldiers and police in Hares that led to our arrest. We also filed a complaint about our treatment at the hands of the Israeli border police during our detention. Our reports were made to B'Tselem, the Israeli Information Center for Human Rights in the Occupied Territories. The agent who took our statement said that a copy would be sent to the Ariel police station. He added that in most cases you never hear back from them. He was also quite certain that the whole incident had been meant to scare us.

While in Jerusalem we were invited to join the weekly vigil held by the Women in Black in the heart of West Jerusalem to protest against the occupation. I was appalled by the vitriolic responses of passing cars and pedestrians to the vigil. The group of about one hundred women holding signs stood silently with great dignity as obscenities were shouted at them by people with frighteningly contorted facial expressions. Women in Black is an international peace network that was started in Israel in 1988 by primarily Jewish women protesting against Israel's occupation of the West Bank and Gaza. In Canada Women in Black holds vigils regularly in Ottawa, Montreal, Toronto, Calgary, and Vancouver.

As a Muslim woman in *hijab* I experienced some of the very real racism that is prevalent in Israel. As Joan, Claire, and I entered a supermarket, we had our bags searched, as is usual. However, I was the only one of the three who was followed by a security guard throughout the supermarket. At one point he stopped me to search my bag again. As I was walking up and down the aisles people stared at me as if they did not want me to be there.

Once, when Joan and I walked into a coffee shop, the server gestured to me to get out. On another occasion, as we were standing on the sidewalk waiting for a taxi, two policemen approached me, totally ignoring Joan, and asked me what I was doing there. I told them that we were waiting for a taxi. They checked my passport, searched my bag, and told me to move along. Our taxi arrived just at that moment.

One day Joan and I decided to go to Bethlehem. The Arab taxi driver told us that the city was closed and no one could get in. We insisted that he drive us to the checkpoint. He let us out about 100 meters from the checkpoint and waited while we walked toward the soldiers. It was midday and the sun was hot. We were nervous since both of us had been banned from the West Bank and crossing into Bethlehem could be a violation of the banning order. The young soldier barely looked at our passport and waved us on. We spent the day in Bethlehem, returning to Beit Safafa before dark. We realized then that it might be possible for us to sneak back into Palestine.

The next day we tried to go to Ramallah as a demonstration was being planned by a group of internationals. However, the West Bank had been sealed off by the Israelis so nobody could get in or out. So the day would not be a complete waste, we decided to visit the offices of LAW, the Palestinian Society for the Protection of Human Rights and the Environment, and the Women's Centre for Legal Aid and Counselling (WCLAC), whose offices were located close to the border on the road to Ramallah. LAW's main functions are research and legal advice on land issues, environment, and the monitoring of human rights. WCLAC provides legal aid services and does advocacy, training, and lobbying on women's rights. The two organizations are grassroots NGOs and provide an important service to Palestinians. It is important in our work to know what local organizations offer in order to refer cases to them. Especially in isolated rural areas, many Palestinians are not aware of service offered by NGOs.

I spent seven days of my thirty-day sentence in Jerusalem establishing contacts for IWPS and running errands. Once I had completed my work I decided to return to Hares, as I was needed there. My arrest, detention, and deportation, as well as my experiences in Jerusalem, had given me a small taste of the harsh and cruel realities of Palestinian life under Israeli occupation. Far from being intimidated, I believe that I was strengthened by my ordeals. I was no longer afraid of Israel's soldiers or police. I was convinced that my role as a witness and a voice for voiceless Palestinians was necessary.

I made arrangements with a supporter of IWPS to drive me back across the Green Line. The soldiers at the checkpoint waved us through without a second glance: the woman who drove me was Israeli, driving an Israeli car on a road reserved for Israelis, and I wore a hat to cover my *hijab*.

As there is no access into Hares from the "settler road," she parked the car on the roadside and we proceeded to cross the two-lane road to walk into Hares. Suddenly we saw a car bearing down on us on the highway. I hesitated a moment. My companion shouted to me to run, and I ran all the way to our house. My heart was pounding and my legs were shaking. My companion joined me shortly. She explained that a Jewish settler from the neighboring settlement of Rivava had tried to hit me as he thought that I was Palestinian and I shouldn't have been on that road.

Palestinians are routinely hit by settler cars. Many die as a result of such criminal acts. This made me realize how crucial it is for internationals to maintain a presence in the West Bank; but it is dangerous, for the Israelis have started targeting them as well. Since January 2003 the occupation forces have killed one twenty-one-year-old American woman and injured two men, one of whom is in a coma after being shot in the face and is not expected to recover. The other, also shot in the face, will need extensive facial reconstruction.

Part 6: Harvesting Olives

As my time in Palestine draws to an end, I reflect on the last three months. I have learned so much about nonviolent direct action. I've had some really scary moments, but I've also had wonderful times. As I travel in a crowded Palestinian shared taxi over dusty gravel roads and rutted donkey tracks I cannot help but feel that I am living a chapter in the long and eventful history of Palestine.

My first experience of picking olives was in Marda, about an hour's walk from Hares, our home base. Marda is an ancient village with beautiful flowers and very old olive trees. Some of the trees are called Roman trees because they are claimed to date back to the days of the Romans. Mardawis, as the people of Marda are called, are very proud of their heritage. They say that Salah al Deen traveled with his army through this village on his way to retake Jerusalem from the European Crusaders. Mardawis boast that seven thousand of their men joined Salah al Deen's campaign.

The fields in which we are working today belong to villagers from Marda and Jamma'in. Nearby Jamma'in is claimed to be the birthplace of the famous scholar of *fiqh* (law), Ibn Taymiyyah.

The twin villages lie in the shadow of Ariel, the largest illegal Jewish colony in the West Bank, which crowns the top of the hill. Highway 5, a smooth asphalt road built by Israel for the sole use of the Jews of Ariel, poses a huge barrier for the Mardawis, cutting them off from their olive groves and fields.

During the olive harvest the Mardawis are often harassed by Jewish colonists hurling verbal abuse and stones, or firing guns at them. The colonists want to keep the Mardawis from working their land so that they can steal it by claiming that it was abandoned. Today I am leading a group of volunteers from the International Solidarity Movement (ISM). We have come to "protect" the Mardawis as they attempt to exercise their right to harvest their crops.

Our "protection" consists of being there to witness settler violence and to call the Ariel police should the need arise. We can also try to prevail upon the soldiers and police to stop settler abuse and violence against the Palestinians, as the police tend to ignore them or accuse them of provoking the incidents.

As I look up at the red-tiled roofs of Ariel it angers me to think that many of the two hundred thousand illegal settlers in Ariel are recent immigrants from countries like Russia. They claim sole use of the road built on land stolen from the Mardawis while the Mardawis, who have owned the land for centuries, are denied access to it. In fact the Mardawis must be vigilant when crossing the road to access their olive groves and farmlands because they and their donkeys are frequent targets of passing settler cars. The harassment by the settlers is having the desired effect. Marda, which once boasted seven mosques, now has need of only one.

There are so many memories I will be taking back with me. Some I will cherish while others I will try very hard to forget. Like the one in the village of Deir Istiya. One day, having returned from the olive groves, I was monitoring a roadblock that Israeli soldiers had set up at the entrance to the village. They usually do this to prevent the villagers from taking a shortcut across the "settler" road. This time, however, they were targeting yellow Palestinian taxis. The taxis were being stopped for identification checks of occupants. A yellow stretch Mercedes pulled up and I saw an Israeli soldier walk over to it.

The roadblock was crowded with villagers returning home from a hard day's work in the olive groves. About fifteen minutes later, when there was a break in the traffic, I noticed that the Mercedes was still standing by the side of the road. I walked over to the driver. With the help of a passenger who spoke English I introduced myself and handed him my IWPS business card. The driver explained that the Israeli soldier had walked away with his identification papers. I volunteered to ask the soldiers what the problem was, as I knew that if any of the occupants tried to approach the soldiers they could get shot.

I went to the soldiers and asked if I could speak to someone about the waiting taxi. The officer in charge responded. He explained that not everyone in the car had proper identification documents. I reported back to the taxi what the soldier had said. The passengers all assured me that they had proper papers since they travel that route every day to work. I walked back to the soldier and informed him that all the occupants had proper papers. He asked to see them. I collected the papers and took them to him.

As the papers were being checked, I talked with the Palestinians. There were two women, who were students, and seven men. They were all apprehensive. I talked about the work of IWPS and handed out our business cards. Shortly, the soldier returned with the identification documents and gave the driver permission to proceed.

I wondered how long the taxi would have been kept waiting had I not intervened. As a ruse, only the driver had been asked for identification papers. This is one of the ways in which the Israeli occupation dehumanizes and degrades the Palestinians, slowly grinding them down with deliberate callousness and cruelty.

On another occasion I was in the village of Jayous with two fellow IWPS team members to take part in a demonstration organized by ISM. In contravention of international laws and the silent acquiescence of the international community, the Israeli government is systematically confiscating Palestinian lands and uprooting valuable olive trees—the only livelihood of thousands of Palestinians—in order to build a 350-kilometer wall between Israel and Palestine. On the pretext of "security" the Israelis are building this wall to achieve a de facto land grab. The only non-Palestinian opposition to these outrageous actions of the Israeli government is being mounted by small groups of Israeli and international activists. They are given attention in the international media only when one of their number is seriously injured or killed, as in the case of ISM activist Rachel Corrie.

ISM members had been in Jayous for a few days. There were about one hundred persons gathered in the olive grove when we got there. The bulldozer was some meters away doing its work, backed by Israeli occupation forces. As the work crew started moving toward our position, we formed a human barrier. I was assigned to monitor the situation from higher ground and given my provision of sliced onions, which was being distributed to all participants for protection against tear gas.

The Israeli soldiers were shouting orders to the Palestinian villagers to leave their lands and not to disturb the work that had to be done here. After much discussion and persuasion by the "internationals," the soldiers agreed to let the villagers stay, but only within a clearly demarcated area.

Mariam Bhabha

It was Friday. When the time came, all the men, women, and children gathered in the mud to listen to the *khutba* and to pray behind the imam. Standing shoulder to shoulder with the village women on this Friday in the month of Ramadan was a very moving and emotional experience for me.

After *salah,* as the crowd was dispersing, a stone was suddenly aimed at a military jeep. The Israeli soldiers responded with live bullets. There was total confusion as the village youth fled through the fields with the occupation forces in hot pursuit.

I noticed that a lone soldier had been left behind in the jeep. The soldier, fearing for his safety, emerged from the jeep with his right hand in the air, holding a grenade. I could see that he was very young. I could see the fear in his eyes. Afraid that he might panic and throw the grenade at the villagers I went to talk to him. I told him that I had a son about his age and that I understood how he felt. He kept telling me to shut up and go away. He was very agitated. I asked him to consider the consequences if he threw the grenade. I kept talking to him, softly reassuring him, until his comrades returned. I rejoined my group and, as the jeep sped away, I saw the young soldier looking directly at me. I wondered whether he would look at Palestinians in a new light or continue to view them as obstacles to the Jewish vision of a greater Israel.

I wonder too about the woman from Deir Istiya who has breast cancer. Will I be able again to drink *kahwa* with her the next time I come? What's going to happen to the imam's nineteen-year-old son, who has been arrested by the police? He is being held without charge and without access to any of the basic rights that we take for granted. I worry about them and many others as I prepare to leave Hares. An Israeli friend of IWPS will take me across the Green Line in her car. I pray that I will be in the safety of my home soon.

4

Activism as a Way of Life

Katherine Bullock

I ran down the street to the bus, heart pounding as I rounded the corner. If I was lucky, I would be in time to catch the early bus home… But not today. I slowed to a disappointed walk as I saw the bus pull away from the bus stop. "Hmmph!" I exclaimed as I waited for the next bus. I had packed up my school books at 3 P.M.—fully twenty-five minutes before the school bell would signal the end of another day—but the teacher had decided to give us some notes after this, so I had had to unpack my books and get out my file. How inconsiderate of her! My annoyance turned to real anger as the next bus to come by roared on past, packed to the brim with students from the schools before mine on the same road. This was the height of unfairness, and I decided then that I would have to do something about it.

This was at my high school, Presbyterian Ladies' College (PLC) in Perth, Western Australia. We used the public transit system, as unlike in the United States and Canada, we didn't have a dedicated school bus. Our school was the last in a line of four private schools all on the same street, and, all too often, the bus roared past our stop, clogged with high school students letting off steam after another day in school (pity the silently suffering general public). Missing this bus meant missing the connecting bus in Fremantle and not arriving home till nearly 5 P.M., an hour and a half of time better spent relaxing at home after a hard day at school.

Thus my first act as an activist was to get signatures from my school friends for a petition to the Metropolitan Transport Trust (MTT) for an additional bus at the end of the school day. Though I hoped for change, I was somewhat surprised that the MTT took me seriously enough to respond and to send an inspector to investigate. I had then a glimpse of the power and importance of group efforts to effect change. But as I rounded the corner to find the inspector there taking notes, I knew the whole project was doomed. I don't remember why now, but it was a day when there were fewer of us than usual catching the bus home. That afternoon we had no problem getting on the 3:35 bus, and that was the end of that. It was disappointing since I knew that the overcrowding would continue.

Maybe it was this early failure at lobbying, but I was a quiet person after that. Throughout my whole undergraduate years, I studiously avoided getting involved in campus politics. I had several friends who were activists, either writing for the student newspaper or working with various groups— the campus political parties, Greenpeace, the feminists—but I looked askance at them. Heaven knows why. I thought they were compromising their education by being involved in nefarious extracurricular activities. This seems strange looking back, especially since my intellectual passion, and my major, was *politics*. It wasn't that I didn't participate in extracurricular activities: I played netball, swam regularly at the local pool, played flute in an orchestra, and acted in the French plays. I was involved in an organization for returned Rotary Exchange students, even holding the position of president for one year. (I'd been on a Rotary youth exchange scholarship in 1984 to Mt. Vernon, Washington, U.S.A.) It seems that there was something in particular about politically oriented activities that I was avoiding. I must have been the typical apathetic, middle-class university student.

But I was an activist at heart, someone who felt the need to *do* something when confronted by an injustice, so every now and then I'd be roused from this slumber to join a group trying to promote positive change. I still recall the exhilaration I felt marching on Parliament (in Perth) to protest the proposed introduction of a student administrative fee. Until then our university education was free (to us, of course, not to the taxpayer), and the introduction of the administrative fee seemed like the-end-of-life-as-we-knew-it, the thin-end-of-the-wedge, the beginning of the dreaded U.S.-style-of-expensive-education, and so forth. The turnout for that rally was small (I guess there were a lot of apathetic students at university), and we failed to prevent the fee, but the satisfaction was of at least having *tried* to prevent the wicked outcome. Am I only involved in rallies for losing causes? This experience seems to have been replicated too many times since then.

After I graduated from university, I had the opportunity to stay on as a teaching assistant, to start some research, and to embark myself on an academic career. Now I was warming up to the fully fledged activism that would come to fruition during my master's year in Canada. But I get ahead of myself. Indignation spurred me to activism as I discovered the forgotten and trampled down history of women intellectuals who had penned interesting and important works of political and social theory. "The Canon" deigned not to recognize that there were any women theorists worthy of mention, and so it was a thrill and a shame to discover a solid five-hundred-year history dating back at least to 1405 with Christine de Pizan's *The Book of the City of the Ladies*. I campaigned to get the study of some of these theorists included in the undergraduate political theory course—to no avail, of course. There wasn't room to include more theorists; there were also important men not included in the survey course (so I suppose they'd have to be included before any woman was?); the women hadn't written anything original, otherwise they would be included already; they hadn't written anything as profound, or as related to politics, as had those male theorists of the Canon, and so on. Progress on this score finally reached the department while I was overseas (around 1996) and Mary Wollstonecraft was added. No thanks to me of course. I was long gone.

Gone to do my master's degree at Queen's University, Kingston, Ontario, Canada, a small university town, and the place that changed my life dramatically. Or, more accurately, the place in which my life was dramatically changed. My activism continued to bloom as I helped found an international students' association at Queen's University. International students needed an advocacy group, as well as a group to address the particular issues that face international students while they are overseas: homesickness, culture shock, language difficulties, and the like. There's nothing like another international student to understand the experience, and with whom to share the trials and tribulations. From there it was a natural step to try and found an International Students' Association at the University of Toronto, where I went to get my PhD after finishing my MA (and getting married to an engineer from Algeria along the way). The Ontario government's decision (in 1994) to stop giving provincial health coverage (which is free to Ontario residents) to international students (even though they were residents for tax purposes), helped give the ISA a kick start. I led a rally to the state parliament,

Katherine Bullock

Katherine Bullock, PhD Convocation, University of Toronto, June 1999.

conveniently located across the road from the university. The turnout was good. We even got press coverage, and after the local unions took up the cause, a meeting with the provincial health minister. But, again, since there were no big money interests backing the students, the project was doomed, and international students had to start paying for their health care (as well as paying taxes), though thanks to our efforts, pregnant women were grandfathered until they gave birth. The ISA, I am happy to say, has since flourished.

I wasn't Muslim yet, but when I did become a Muslim, it was natural to turn my energies to the Muslim community. I had never really considered my "extracurricular" efforts (as Mona Rahman puts it) to change and improve the world around me special, unusual, or anything like that. During my childhood and into my teenage years, my mum had been involved in, and sometimes president of, Riding for the Disabled, a nonprofit group dedicated to teaching disabled children to ride horses. When I was in primary school I used to go with her to the farm where the kids learned to ride. We used to host pool parties at our house in the summer for the disabled kids: that was an early lesson in life about both the possibilities and the barriers for disabled children, as well as learning to be grateful for the gifts of having a completely functioning body and mind. I don't recall any specific lessons from my parents about "being an activist"; I think it just seemed normal for people to be involved in groups that try to effect positive change. My parents were always supportive and encouraging of my efforts.

It was during the first year of my PhD (1994), when I was trying to change the health care policies of the Ontario government that it really dawned on me that "activism" is a way of life. More, that activism is a *necessary vigilance* on behalf of justice, justice that is constantly threatened by nefarious power interests. This realization was deepened in the first days of my becoming a Muslim woman who wore *hijab*. I experienced harassment and discrimination for the first time in my life. Becoming Muslim joined me to the minority perspective, which is frequently under siege in Canada. So

I understood full well the need to be an activist for the sake of improving the image of Muslims in the West, and more importantly, improving the quality of their lives. Activism had become a part of me, and Islam's encouragement of believers to act on behalf of social justice made the religion perfect for me.

I was plunged into activist work in the Muslim community quite early in my life as a Muslim, when Mariam Bhabha invited me to help her found a Muslim women's group. I had met Mariam when I was president of the International Students' Association. I was president of the ISA for two years, the first year as a non-Muslim, and the second year as a scarf-wearing Muslim. (I felt like a fish out of water once I put on the scarf, not to mention that international students like to meet at bars for their socializing.) The University of Toronto had organized a meeting for the presidents of campus clubs in relation to some international event that escapes me right now—maybe the Bosnian war in 1994—so I went. I met Mariam there (she was founder and president of a Bosnian relief aid agency); we were two scarf-wearing Muslim women in a room of non-scarf-wearing men and women and, as is normal, we gravitated to one another.

There followed some long and difficult work to bring into existence a Muslim women's group based in Toronto. Long, because when you get five headstrong women at the same table trying to agree on things an organization needs, like a name (two hours to discuss the various possible names...), a vision, a statement of purpose, a constitution, by-laws, and so on, well, you can just imagine. (We finally settled on the Federation of Muslim Women.) But it was an exciting time, and I felt honored to be involved. We were all practicing Muslims, convinced of the need for a women's group: as an avenue for active women to get involved, to help Muslim women form bonds of sisterhood, and to help immigrants and the next generation of Muslims cope with life in Canada, as well as darker issues like domestic violence. I say the hours were long and difficult, but we kept our mind on the goals and remembered our Creator at the beginning and end of meetings. We tried consciously to practice proper Islamic etiquette, politeness, generosity, and no backbiting, or gossip. I think we succeeded reasonably well.

My main tasks in the beginning were the constitution and by-laws, and formal registration as a nonprofit group in Canada; then followed the membership drives, the web page, a newsletter, and regular board meetings. We attended multicultural festivals and set up tables in shopping malls explaining Islam to interested passersby. We organized social events for Muslim women—I was particularly pushy on this point, having learned the hard way during my time as president of the ISA that many activists like to stick to political issues, and when they do, the organization stays small. Many people (like myself in my undergrad years) are leery of politics, and are also leery of having to make commitments to organizations, but they do like socializing, and will attend in great numbers well-organized social activities. I am not in Toronto anymore, but happily, this tradition has continued, and grows, with an annual *iftar* at 'Eid Al Fitr, an annual mother-daughter tea, and other events.

I'd like to mention three highlights of my time at FMW: our experience at International Women's Day, our involvement in a roundtable on domestic violence, and our involvement in a media-watch project.

International Women's Day was celebrated in a variety of ways in Toronto. One mainstay was a day at Ryerson University in downtown Toronto, where women from all different kinds of women's and related groups would set up booths to share their ideas and information with anyone interested. There were groups protesting the military, women's bookstores, groups promoting natural foods, and us, the Federation of Muslim Women, promoting the equality of women inside the spiritual framework of Islam and hoping to expel negative stereotypes of Islam's treatment of women. The first year we participated we were approached by a group of Iranian exiles who were dismayed to see us there, convinced as they are that Islam oppresses women. I had left around lunchtime, to learn later that there had been a kafuffle between some members of the Iranian booth and members of FMW. They had come to tell us we represented the oppression of women and had no place at an International Women's Day event. Our vice-president, Zubeda Vahed, handled the situation very calmly, telling them that they promoted respect of women, but she hadn't felt respected by their treatment of her, and that was that.

The next year, however, things came to a head. In the first place our tables were next to each other—whoever made that decision had a wry sense of humor. The Iranians had literature condemning Iran and Islam's treatment of women as oppressive. They had large dolls of women wrapped in black chadors with anti-Iranian/Islamic literature pinned to their clothing. Several passersby would stop at their table, learn how horrible Islam was for women, and then approach us, all women wearing headscarves... Perhaps things would have been OK, if it hadn't been for a new ingredient: in addition to our table, there was a new participant—a religious Shia women's group, based in Toronto, staffed by two young university students. They were also wearing headscarves and had literature from Iran on their table, including devotional sayings of the Ayatollah Khomeini. They also displayed pictures trying to show a positive reality of life for women in Iran—pictures showing women as doctors, dentists, teachers, and other professionals, an attempt to demonstrate that the media image of Iranian women as oppressed chattels was too simplistic. We had a kind of truce with the anti-Islamic Iranian group, but this new booth was apparently too much for them to handle. These young women were subject to heckling and yelling from this group, and again, after I left, one man eventually up-ended their table in disgust and anger. Security came and escorted the man from the premises. The two young women were then asked to take down their display and leave also, apparently because security couldn't guarantee their safety.

This event was the talking point of several left-wing e-mail discussion lists for a few weeks afterward. The presence of the two kinds of Iranian groups, FMW and the moderate Canadian Council on Muslim Women (CCMW), at International Women's Day highlights deep and important contradictions in the left and feminist movement's commitment to freedom and equality on the one hand, and indigenous rights and anticolonialism on the other. Is secularism the only path to freedom and equality? If Islam dignifies women but sometimes in ways different from secularism in the West, does that disqualify Islam from International Women's Day, or does it expand the meanings of freedom and equality? Iranian women may be oppressed in some ways from an Islamic point of view, and in other ways from a secular point of view, and in ways from both points of view, but can the complexities of the lived realities of women's lives be captured in anti-Iranian, anti-Islamic exiled groups, with their ignorant Western leftist supporters? What does it mean, then, to be anticolonial and also supportive of voices from the South? Especially if those voices embrace non-Western ways of life? Different groups at the IWD obviously answer these questions differently, and the organizers of the IWD event at Ryerson should be credited with their broad-minded openness to the range of groups. But I and other FMW members were disturbed by Ryerson's security response to the event (asking the women to leave, while allowing the anti-Iranian/anti-Islamic group to stay). I was also disturbed by the racism and Islamophobia of many on the left during their subsequent discussions of this event.

FMW and the young women from the Shia group met with Ryerson's president and security officers later on. I don't recall everything from that

Katherine Bullock

meeting, only that I was disappointed with the president's inability to see that there had been anything wrong with asking the women to leave. I began to suspect that there were other agendas behind the scenes, based on anti-Islamic or anti-Iranian sentiment. We also met one of the IWD event organizers, who expressed her concern and apologies to us. One of our concerns was the anti-Islamic diatribe coming out of this Iranian group. I felt they had crossed the line from legitimate critique of Islam to hate mongering. Does an Iranian exile who was born a Muslim but who detests the religion after negative experiences in Iran with religious fanatics have more right than others to define "Islam" and to criticize other Muslims for their commitment to the faith? To engage in racist and anti-Islamic hate mongering? We tried to discuss these issues, though I felt that the woman's ignorance of Islam and the complexities involved in the whole "women's status in Islam" debate prevented her from really understanding what was going on. Nevertheless, the organizers were still committed to free speech and for FMW's presence at IWD. We tried to strategize for the following year and were invited to join the organizing committee. I think we sent a representative when it came time, but it was a moot point, because the Ryerson president decided not to host the display that year. I don't think the organizers found another venue, and so since then this great meeting of women's organizations has not taken place. This is a great loss to the women's movement in Toronto and a great shame.[1]

The kafuffle also shows that Muslims must not be naive about their involvement in non-Muslim events; they must know how to respond to hecklers and other hostile passersby. I had had enough encounters with hostile questions at display booths on Islam to know the potential, but I hadn't realized that things could go that far. Muslims who sit at information tables need training in how to respond to questioners politely, calmly, and to learn how to diffuse effectively an angry interlocutor.

A different kind of meeting of Muslim organizations took place when I was involved on behalf of FMW in co-organizing a meeting with Isabel Bassett, minister of citizenship, culture, and recreation, to discuss how her office could assist Muslims in combating domestic violence in our community. I don't remember how this got started, but I was meeting with Gul Joya Jafri (Afghan Women's Organisation), Maliha Chisti (ISNA-Canada), and Yasmin Zine (Muslim, Education Network, Training and Outreach Service), and we formed a loose coalition called the Muslim Women's Community Coalition to address the issue of domestic violence. I was particularly concerned for FMW to try and work toward assisting Muslim women in domestic violence.

It is appalling that anyone calling themselves a Muslim would beat or abuse his wife. The Prophet Muhammad (pbuh) condemned this behavior, and God commanded men to treat their wives kindly (Qur'an 4:19). I wanted Muslim women to be free of abuse and to live in families that practiced Islam properly. I had a friend who worked as a domestic violence counselor and was disturbed by her reports that Muslim women were having problems in the shelters in Toronto from shelter workers who believed that Islam allowed (even encouraged) men to beat their wives. According to her, Muslim women were being ridiculed for wearing headscarves, for being Muslim, for fasting during Ramadan, and they were not given access to *halal* food. What a double whammy—to be abused by your husband and then by the place in which you seek shelter. Clearly something had to be done. There were efforts in the Muslim community to address the issue; I focused on Muslim interaction outside the community—with government and shelters.

Minister Bassett met with representatives of the Muslim community in a room in City Hall. There were Muslim women social workers, able to share firsthand their experiences, and Imam Adbul-Hai Patel on behalf of the Council of Imams. We had prepared a position statement and had it approved by the Council of Imams:

> Islam does not condone violence against women. Husbands and wives are counselled to live together in mutual love, respect and harmony. Disagreements should be settled peacefully with respect and wisdom. Any resort to threats, verbal abuse or physical violence is condemned in Islam.

I think the meeting was effective in terms of raising issues for the minister and clarifying things from the Islamic perspective, but I am not convinced we really achieved anything concrete. I left Toronto soon afterward, and Bassett lost in the next election. Now we would have to start again with the new minister. FMW did manage to make links with a shelter, though, and raised funds at its annual Ramadan Iftar in 1999. This connection has probably been more useful than the meeting with the minister, but it is still important for Muslims to have access to, and to meet with, the politicians, even if it's only a talkfest. While slow, talkfests do eventually have an effect, even if it's just dispelling stereotypes personally for the minister and her staff.

The project that I enjoyed the most during my time at FMW was the media advocacy project spearheaded by the Afghan Women's Organization of Toronto. They had managed to get funding from Canadian Heritage and Status of Women Canada for a project about Muslim women in the media. The project was coordinated by Gul Joya Jafri and I was invited to be part of an advisory panel that included a representative of the media and Muslims from other grassroots organizations in Toronto. The project was launched at the AWO office in west-end Toronto. The minister for the status of women at the time, Hedy Fry, met with about thirty Muslim women over morning tea one Saturday morning. I mounted a wall display of the shocking and negative images of Muslim women that had appeared recently in newspapers across Canada and the United States. This was an effective visual reminder of what we were up against as far as the representation of Muslim women in the media goes.

The next stage was a series of focus group sessions with Muslim women from all different backgrounds. These were taped and transcribed, and included in the report written by Gul at the end of the project. Her report, "The Portrayal of Muslim Women in Canadian Mainstream Media: A Community Based Analysis," was a study of newspaper articles about Muslim women in Canadian newspapers between 1993 and 1997. An appendix listed media watch groups and other organizations Muslims could get involved in to try and change the negative image of Muslim women in the media. Gul and I wrote a short article about this project that was published in a special issue of *Canadian Woman Studies*, an academic journal. It was particularly gratifying to have this article accepted in a mainstream academic journal, and I hope it serves to highlight the problems facing Muslim women in the media.

One of the things I learned during my time on this media project was just how difficult it is for Muslims to have their perspectives understood by a well-meaning, but ignorant, press. One of the members of the advisory board, who had to leave before the project finished, was a representative of the mainstream media. Two things she said have stayed with me. The first was in regard to Muslim complaints that their voices are ignored and unrepresented in media. She said in a rather frustrated tone that she had tried on several occasions to call a mosque or Muslim organization to get their perspective on a news event related to Muslims, only to find that phone messages were never returned or people unable to speak in articulate English. One time, she said, she was told that the person she wanted to talk to was too busy to talk to her! She was flabbergasted at this. Imagine missing an opportunity to have your voice put forth in the media. Muslims do seem to be inept at maintaining professional relationships with institutional members of the outside world—even among ourselves. Of course she is not the first to have a message on an answering machine go unanswered.

I took this criticism to heart when I moved to a small town in California and have made sure all the phone messages at the *masjid* are answered. Remote access and a phone message log book makes this easy. At no time has this commitment been more important than after September 11, when our *masjid* was flooded with calls from people wanting to help, to invite us to talk, and so on. We sent a speaker to the local YMCA annual Martin Luther King interfaith breakfast, and the organizer told me how happy has was to have us on board. The year before they'd called and left a message on our machine, which, predictably, no one had returned.

The second point the media representative made during her time on the advisory panel for the AWO media project was in response to our complaint that Muslims are always painted as violent or terrorist. She was genuinely perplexed at this, and mentioned a recent event where Muslims had killed innocent civilians (I think it was the Luxor killing of tourists in Egypt). From her perspective, all the media was doing was describing violent events committed by Muslims in the name of Islam. Her reaction was an eye-opener for me. Here was a yawning gap in perspective based on insider-outsider experiences. Where we saw crazy people committing crimes, she saw *Muslims.* Muslims complain, with reason, about their representation in the media, but we don't often see things from the outsider's perspective. And sadly, often we are not usually as vocal about condemning the actual act itself, being more preoccupied with the image and way it is reported in the West. We decry the reporting of stories where Muslim women have acid thrown in their faces, but how loudly are we protesting to our fellow Muslims this kind of treatment of women?

Some Muslims are afraid to criticize Muslims publicly in the West, because this is to air "dirty laundry" in public and also because it may feed into the already existing racism against our community. The media has a nice way of using a Muslim who is critiquing her own culture and turning her into an anti-Islamic spokeswoman. But I think it is time we got past this. The West also respects and appreciates anyone who speaks out loudly for justice; Archbishop Tutu is a good example. Let us become this kind of respected role model for the West, and a lot of the criticism against Muslims will be put in a different context. Of course, if we could stamp out unjust practices among our fellow Muslims, that would be an even more significant step. After

Katherine Bullock

all, the media wouldn't be able to report stories of injustice in the name of Islam if we had created a good society in which people, men and women, flourished and prospered.

Moving to a small town has been a whole new experience: challenging, enriching, and frustrating. We moved in 1999 to a small town on the northeast edge of the San Francisco Bay Area. It is a "bedroom" community, with many people owning houses here but working in San Francisco or south in Silicon Valley. Many men and women spend three hours daily commuting; you can imagine the impact that has on community and family life. When we arrived there wasn't really a Muslim community centered around a mosque the way we were used to in Toronto. Most of the Muslims here are Afghan refugees, many of whom have been unable to continue in their professions of teacher, civil servant, or farmer, due to language and other barriers in the United States. While the children attend school/college, many of the men work long hours in low-wage jobs at gas stations, or as taxi drivers. The rest of the community are mostly middle-class Pakistanis, and a few scattered Arabs and hangers-on like me. There was a tiny room being rented for a mosque. On Fridays it housed about thirty men for prayer. I was nearly the only woman attending for a whole year. Sometimes a woman would come for prayer, and I'd never see her again. At 'isha (evening prayer) it was often only myself and my husband and maybe one or two other brothers.

There was a little Islamic school on the weekends, where the children were learning to read the Qur'an. We went to visit on our second weekend and were asked if we could help out! I'd never worked with children before, but there was clearly a need, so the next week I found myself in a room with about seven teenage girls, all of whom would clearly rather be somewhere else. I got off to a great start, thinking I would try and energize them by challenging their intellects. I asked them, "What are the logical consequences of *tawhid* (the unity of God)?" and looked hopefully around the room. There was a stunned silence, squirming, and then one brave girl piped up, "What does 'consequences' mean?" Clearly, I had a lot of learning to do.

The opportunity to move upstairs came that Ramadan when the tenant, a party-hire place, decided to shut down. What a blessing that move has been, although it was strongly resisted by those who thought we wouldn't be able to cover the rent. The high monthly rent downstairs had always been a struggle; now it would be doubled. But Allah gave us the blessing, and the means to pay for it, *alhamdulillah*, and it has had a dramatic impact on the community.

I was elected to a new executive board for the *masjid*. That was a surprise for me, because I hadn't even planned to attend the elections. The community looked very much like a "men's-only" club, and as a newcomer, I didn't want to rock the boat by turning up at the election. But that day, one of my sixteen-year-old students asked me if we could go to the election that night. I thought if she asked, then it must be within the realm of possibility, and I wanted to encourage her in being involved. So we went to the election, and then one brother asked if we could nominate women. There was some discussion about the appropriateness of a woman attending meetings or not, but no one really objected, so he nominated me to the position of social activities coordinator, and I was elected! Actually, my husband was well respected by the brothers, and he had declined to be elected, and I think they elected me as a way of ensuring he would be at the meetings and involved. I heard someone say something to this effect afterward, and another brother commented "two for the price of one" or something; anyway, it didn't really matter.

So, once again, I was involved in building an organization from the ground up. My husband and I and the two other execs spent long hours drafting by-laws, getting the incorporation papers into order, and so on. We organized monthly social activities, picnics with quizzes for the kids, and slowly but surely a little community started growing up around the mosque. Attempts to get brothers' and sisters' *halaqas* (study circles) going largely failed. But we made significant changes to the school, and that started to flourish, *alhamdulillah*.

One thing that shocked me when I first started was the concern that children learn to read the Qur'an only, with no care whether or not they understood what they were learning. I was teaching the five- and six-year-olds, and they were reciting *al Fatiha* (the first chapter of the Qur'an) by memory. I asked them if they knew what the first sentence, *"Bismillah"* (in the name of God), meant. No one did. But it was obvious the children weren't really learning to read the Qur'an either. They'd sit with a teacher and read after him, being able to do so mostly by oral imitation. Point to the end of the page, out of the usual sequence, and they couldn't read anything. Once the whole Qur'an had been read like that, there'd be a party for the child having

Katherine with her husband and their older son, Zakaria, 'Eid, 2001.

Katherine Bullock

"finished reading the Qur'an" and everyone would relax, as if their job had finished. *Subhan'allah.* No wonder the Muslim world is in a mess: with Muslims learning to read the Qur'an but having no idea of its meaning, thence relying on elders who had been educated like them about what the religion entails. We instituted Arabic and Islamic studies. There was a bit of parental resistance to teaching anything other than reading the Qur'an (even, surprisingly, to learning Arabic; one parent also insisted we teach in Urdu), but most parents acquiesced and continued to bring their children. Many were happy with the changes, wishing they'd had that kind of education in religion as a youngster.

The following year a sister arrived and started a playgroup for preschoolers that I took over running when she moved to Seattle, and a *halaqa* that evolved into a youth group. The playgroup meets once a week at the *masjid,* and we have acquired a boxful of toys and books that stay in the *masjid* and are enjoyed by all the kids on our family nights. The youth *halaqa* meets at my house, so my little son doesn't deconstruct the mosque while we try to learn. These activities are exciting and also frustrating; it has been hard to get people to come regularly to mosque-based activities. Most people here are not activists; many are hard workers and eager to help out, but they want direction. For the few activists around, it is very easy to burn out.

Nevertheless, *alhamdulillah,* things are continuously, if slowly, improving, and a tight-knit community is forming. We were able to hire a full-time imam recently, and that has been of immense benefit to the community. The imam teaches Qur'an and Arabic four nights a week after school, and the weekend school continues. He also started weekly soccer for the brothers, and that has been a great success, drawing Muslims from towns as far away as forty miles north. Sometimes we sisters go and play soccer with the small kids. And an Arabic class for adults began on Tuesday nights.

I started a library at the mosque. This has been work that is a real pleasure for me, as I love books. We had a fund-raising bake sale after *jumu'a* (the Friday prayer) one Friday and raised some money to buy books and videos. I ordered the books, designed categories, and printed call numbers on labels. I commandeered a few of the young sisters to help me put the labels and due date pages on the books, and we had a grand opening where we handed out laminated library cards for anyone who filled in an application form. Even the five-year-olds got one, and everyone was quite happy. A new family arrived in 2002 and the brother was elected education officer. He plans a summer reading competition to encourage the children to use the library.

My biggest disappointment after we moved upstairs was the institution of the curtain. For nearly a year, we had a mosque the way mosques should be: no curtain, with the men praying at the front, and women at the back. At first I was the only woman at *'isha,* but soon we had a little community of five women and their families praying regularly. I looked forward to seeing them, even if briefly, every night. We read a *hadith* after prayers. And then, some of the imams who came from a town some miles south of us refused to come anymore, unless we put up a curtain. They were imams from an apolitical movement, based in the subcontinent, of Muslims dedicated to calling Muslims back to the practice of Islam (as they see it), and they were outraged that the women were not behind a curtain. *Subhan'allah.* I feel tired when I think of it now. It was a trying time. I tried to argue that the curtain is not *sunnah* (the Prophet's way *pbuh*), and at first they didn't believe me. I tried to get scholars and imams in Canada or the United States to speak up and say that the curtain was not *sunnah,* but it was hard to find anyone to come out formally and say so, even if they did privately.

We held a community meeting and the imams came to argue that we were setting a bad example for the rest of the Bay Area (imagine that, a mosque modeled after that of the Prophet, seen as setting a bad example...). Since most of the community are Afghan or Pakistani, and had grown up with a curtain, many of them also agreed that our *masjid* should have one. I tried to argue that the curtain cuts women off from the congregation, they need to see the imam while they pray, so they can know how to join prayer if they come late, if the imam makes a mistake, or does an extra *sajda* (prostration) during prayer. I argued that behind the curtain, women were cut off, and had no input in community decisions; that during *jumu'a,* or lectures, women just talked the whole time—because they felt they didn't belong to the congregation, they acted as if they didn't belong. Talking during *jumu'a* voids prayer, so it is a serious matter. But no one else saw the seriousness of this issue. One brother said having a curtain was easier: "out of sight, out of mind." Yes, easier than learning to lower the gaze and practice restraint. As for having sisters involved in community decision making, well, not many saw that as a priority, surprise! None of the sisters supported me, and one youth actually spoke out and asked for a curtain. Some brothers suggested a compromise—a curtain that the women could see through. At this time, a new imam from a neighboring *masjid* had started giving *khutbas,* and he commented privately to one of the elder brothers at the mosque that the women should be able to see the congregation during

Katherine Bullock

prayer. *Alhamdulillah,* thanks for him. This elder brother then brought the news as if he had never heard it before, and argued for a curtain we could see through. The community voted 9 to 7 to have a curtain, and then agreed on a compromise. Thank God for that. So one sister sewed the curtain with two lace panels, one at kneeling eye level, and the other at standing eye level.

The partially see-through curtain has been good as far as prayer goes, but it has had a bad impact, like it always does, on women's sense of belonging, with the men, to a community. They talk nonstop during *jumu'a* and during talks by invited speakers. At the election that followed the institution of the curtain, we couldn't hear the discussion, and the men nearly voted without asking us. If I hadn't spoken up in protest, that election would have set the precedent. Anyway, *alhamdulillah,* now the women are remembered, at least during elections, but there is no doubt the curtain, as good as a curtain can be, has had a detrimental impact on women's involvement. A woman can be the vice-chair of an American company, but when she comes to the mosque she is silenced behind the curtain. If she protests, many will accuse her of being a "feminist" or wanting to encourage loose morals, the way I was when I tried to defend our *masjid* against the imams. Many women see this state of affairs as normal, and either drop out of the practicing Muslim community or acquiesce in it—even perpetuate it to the next generation. But what a travesty and a derailment of women's role, as explained in the Qur'an: "The believers, men and women, are protectors one of another: they enjoin what is just, and forbid what is evil... " (9:71).

Fortunately our small and budding community was able to absorb this controversy without bitterness, and our monthly family nights are a great success. One sister has taken on organizing activities for the children. She comes early and sets up a mini "theater" with black silk covering the TV and wall behind, chairs arranged in rows, and popcorn and snacks. They watch a benign cartoon and love it.

Activism is a way of life, a way that is in tune with Islam, a religion that calls for justice, moderation, and compassion. While I am currently settled into the routine here, busy at home raising my young son, only God knows what the future will hold, and where the need for activist responses will arise. May God give me the strength and wisdom to know how to respond, and accept my good deeds, and forgive me my bad deeds.[2]

Notes

1 It has since been reinstated. FMW was invited to set up a booth at the 2004 event.

2 Just to remind us that we never know what is around the corner, after I finished writing my chapter but before the book was published, we moved back to Toronto. I was back on the board of FMW before I knew it! And I have also been blessed with another child, Tariq Muhammed.

5

My Life Journey

Muniza Farooqi

I am an eighteen-year-old girl who lives with her parents, three sisters, and a brother. I was born in Afghanistan and in search of happiness and security ended up in Livermore, California. I am currently attending Las Positas College in Livermore. The question, "How did you get to Livermore?" has a story attached to it. My life journey started in Kabul, Afghanistan, when I was about five years old. We wanted to find a way to reach my maternal grandparents in America. My mom had had this wish in her heart for many years and so it became one of our ultimate goals.

The story of the *mujahideen* (who are now called the Northern Alliance) taking over our beloved country had spread throughout Afghanistan. We saw the war start in front of our eyes. The fear of getting killed at any moment had taken over our hearts. Water, electricity, gas, or food, none had a sign of availability anywhere in Kabul. What we did encounter was staying up at nights in the corridor, hearing bombs drop, seeing people die, and blood shed on the streets. I can never forget one incident when a huge explosion took place beside our house. My older sister was in her bedroom studying, while the rest of our family was eating breakfast in the living room. All of a sudden, the house was shaken by a loud noise. We thought the bomb had hit our house and everyone started running for their lives. Glass was all over the floor and smoke filled the entire house. The doors were broken and in a matter of minutes our nine-year-old house was destroyed. As a result of this explosion, my dad and brother encountered minor injuries, my younger sister, out of fear, stopped talking, my mom and I had burst into tears, and my older sister lost her book under the rubble. It was horrifying. One can never imagine those scenes unless he/she has faced it. We could no longer bear the consequences. The only way of surviving this horrible war was to flee to the neighboring country, Pakistan.

We migrated to Pakistan and started a new life in 1991. For the first few days in Pakistan, we stayed at a relative's house but later we found a two-bedroom house for rent. When we settled in our new house completely, my parents took a visit to the U.S. embassy. This trip seemed to be very encouraging. The embassy had written our name on the list of immigrants and would keep us up to date as things progressed. Time seemed to be passing by very fast.

My siblings and I started school once again, while my parents found jobs. My mother, who is a teacher, started teaching. My dad, who had good experience in office work back home, accepted a job at a school office. Although both of my parents were working, we still were not financially stable. During this hardship, my grandparents from America had been contacting us and had decided to support us financially.

After many years of waiting, right when our feelings seemed to dissipate, the embassy started sending us information about immigration to America. After five years of waiting and seven years of living as immigrants in Pakistan, this time Allah (swt) heard our prayers and answered them. Now the time came to make another move which we hoped would be the last one. This one meant a lot to my mom. She had been away from her parents for more than eleven years. For myself, coming to America meant a better education and a better lifestyle. In 1999, we were in America, the so-called land of dreams and success.

America held great surprises for me. The life event that changed my life forever was the day I put on *hijab* (a headscarf). It might be astonishing to others to hear my story of wearing *hijab*. When I entered America, I was wearing a scarf though not the proper way. I was wearing a small, transparent scarf which was just barely fulfilling my duties as a traditional person but not as a Muslim. After some time educating myself about the meaning of *hijab* and the true way to wear it, I put it on right away, that first week of living in America. It was the best start one can ever imagine. My whole family was amazed by the step I took, but I knew that it was one of Allah's plans. I have learned so much about my loving religion in America that I never knew before, even living in Islamic countries. The thing I like the most about this country is the freedom of religion. We have the freedom that most people do not have in other countries of the world. To me, *hijab* means a part of my body and soul. It completes my life in many ways. The day I put it on, I found my faith, which was lost somewhere. I can never imagine turning my back on this wonderful religion. If a person becomes lost in this world, he/she should consider turning to faith, and he/she might be very much surprised.

When we came to America, my parents decided to live in Fremont, California, where my grandparents are also staying. I began school as a ninth grader in high school. A year passed by and we decided Livermore was a much better place to live. It has a calm and soothing environment as well as affordable housing. In Livermore, I was in tenth grade at the Livermore high school. I met many friendly Muslim sisters in school and at the Islamic center. I started getting acquainted with them and have several unforgettable and pleasant memories of those days.

One of the girls I met was Sana Abbasi. She is American born with Pakistani heritage. She started wearing her *hijab,* with the help of Allah (swt), in 2001. She and I always discussed topics like showing involvement in our community. It was the year 2001 when Sana came to me trying to find out if I was interested in helping her form a Muslim club. I liked her idea and accepted it. Summer passed by and school started again. It was my senior year and Sana was in eleventh grade and we were making plans about forming the club. That first week, Sana and I started our journey toward making the Muslim club. The first step that we took was to find the right person in charge at the school office. After filling out some papers in the office, we were ready to find an on-campus advisor. We wanted to grant this responsibility to a teacher who we had a solid relationship with, and one who we could trust. To our surprise, the first teacher we asked accepted our request. Before we knew it, we had our club formed. There were many experiences to overcome while organizing activities for the club.

In the first meeting we had an election; Sana was elected president and I was given the responsibility of vice-president. Our membership consisted of almost all of the Muslim brothers and sisters who were attending this school, about fifteen to twenty people. We were in the middle of planning some activities when the tragedy of September 11 took place. Being shocked and amazed at the same time, our club thought of leaving everything aside and doing something about countering misconceptions about Islam. We wanted to show what the true Islam is all about. Therefore, we invited a

Muniza and William A. Buchanan at the Las Positas Muslim Students' Association booth.

Photo courtesy of Muniza Farooqi

speaker, Kathy Bullock, to give a talk about Islam. She was an excellent speaker who has her PhD in political science. Her speech included a brief overview of Islam and its teachings, as well as a question-and-answer session. We had quite a number of concerned students and staff members show up for the event and received positive comments from them.

There were many other activities that took place within this one year, such as participating in community services, sale of traditional food on campus, *iftar* gatherings (a meal breaking the Ramadan fast), and educational Islamic displays during the cultural days in school. We also participated in the Livermore cultural display, where the community's religious and cultural groups had displays in certain booths at a park in the downtown area. At this one-day event, our theme was the beautiful architecture of Islamic countries. We also displayed Islamic books, pamphlets, clothing, and jewelry. Our teacher/advisor also sat at our booth. My various experiences at Livermore high taught me a lot.

After graduating high school in 2002, I decided to continue my education at Las Positas College (LPC). While attending this college, I realized the need for a Muslim club. I discussed this issue with my older sister, Muzhgan Farooqi, who is also going to LPC. She seemed very enthusiastic about the idea and so we attempted to form a club in our college as well. Since I had experience in starting one already at my high school, I thought it was not going to be hard. However, we had to put much more effort into it than we did at high school. Though the process of filling out paperwork and choosing our advisor was the same, there are a lot more rules and regulations to be followed. To me, since I had strong belief in Allah and also had the help of my sister, it did not seem impossible.

In a matter of a few months, the club was formed and was considered active. We started with a small number of members, and later, when more people became aware of it, more started joining the club. At our first meeting, we had an election for officers. Muzhgan got the position of president and I was elected as vice-president. As I write this essay, it has only been a few months since the forming of the club, so we have not done many activities yet. We have participated in the LPC college club fair and held an *iftar* gathering during the month of Ramadan.

For the club fair, all Las Positas clubs had booths for accepting new members. We had many items on our table. For instance, some brochures on the topic of Islam, a prayer mat, the holy book of Qur'an, along with other Islamic books, and, of course, some information about our club. We had very good results. We had about twenty people sign up for the club. We also had non-Muslims and Muslims who were just passing by pick up information about Islam.

The *iftar* was mostly for our Muslim youth in the community. We had around thirty people attend this on-campus event during the month of Ramadan. It was a joint event organized by the Muslim Club of Livermore High and the Muslim Student Association of Las Positas College. It was an educational get-together because we invited a knowledgeable speaker, Farhan Sayed, who belongs to the *daw'ah* group of Palo Alto, California. He spoke about fasting—history, benefits, and rationale. At the end, we were given some time to ask questions. It was a very successful event that lasted about five hours. We have many other plans for the future, such as organizing educational field trips, community service, fund-raising events, inviting speakers, and so on. I believe forming Muslim clubs is an excellent way to spread the message of Islam. Islam is a peaceful and great religion and to spread the word is our job. Such activity also brings Muslims in a community together to show support for each other.

My plan for the future, Allah (swt) willing, is to major in biology and attend a medical school. I am interested in becoming a pediatrician because I think children are the most innocent creatures of God and helping them is one of our duties on earth. My message to my fellow Muslim youth is that no matter where they are, what they are facing, and how busy they are, they must always remember Allah Almighty and His message. And our job as Muslims in this world is to reach everyone with this everlasting message and to be aware that Allah is watching us all. Life continues as usual but what we accomplish is what matters the most.

6

Rawahil

Khadija Haffajee

Rawahil is the plural of the Arabic word *"rahila,"* used by the Prophet Muhammad (pbuh) to describe Muslims who have the stamina to go the distance. *Insha'allah,* this is the motto by which I live.

September 1997: A standing-room-only auditorium in the Hilton Hotel, Chicago. The new members of the Majlis ash-Shura (Executive) of the Islamic Society of North America (ISNA) are being announced. I am sitting among strangers. I hear my name being called, but cannot get up from my seat, my heart pounds. I can feel and hear it. The moment passes and the first woman to be elected to this bastion of males remains in her seat. I have traveled many lonely miles to be where I am today. My life has always seemed to be full of events and occasions when I have pushed barriers for recognition of females.

It all started in a faraway land: South Africa, where I was born in the late 1930s. A small town, Pietermaritzburg, referred to as "Sleepy Hollow"—this was the birth of my activism, although it was an unknown word then, not part of the landscape, so to speak. The environment was a conservative Muslim one. Girls from "good" Muslim households did not attend regular schools; some were tutored in the 3Rs (reading, writing, and arithmetic) at home. I however was fortunate enough to attend school. Each year was a struggle, because of societal pressure. My older sisters, who did not have the same opportunities, were my stalwart supporters, convincing my widowed mother to let me continue. My mother, as any mother would be, was concerned about her daughter's reputation. Societal condemnation was not something she wanted to deal with. Being a widow was not easy. She finally succumbed to my sisters' pressure, because she knew my dad had wanted his daughters to be educated. My father had been a leader in the community. People looked up to him and he always treated everyone with equal respect, no matter what their social or economic status. My most vivid memory of my dad is the sound of his voice reverberating throughout our large house, reciting Qur'an after *salat al Fajr* (dawn prayer). He was *hafez al Qur'an,* he had memorized the Qur'an by age eight.

On my first return trip to South Africa I went to the local courthouse and read my father's last will and testament. Some of us were very young when he died in 1947, so his wishes were an inspiration. He had stated that all his children had to be educated, especially his daughters; this was surprising as both my older sisters had left school during his lifetime. I realized then that my desire for knowledge and learning came from my father. In fact I am very much his daughter—when I first participated in debates during high school and later in college, people told me that I was following in his footsteps.

At this time I had no Muslim friends as there were none in my classes at school. The girls were getting married and having babies. Deep within me I knew that denying someone an education was un-Islamic. How could getting an education be contrary to a religious teaching? Little did I know then the *hadith* (saying of the Prophet) that states, "Every Muslim, man or woman should acquire an education" or "Seek knowledge, even if you have to go to China."

A battle ensued about college attendance. My mother said she could not afford to send me to college—it was not just a matter of tuition, but of clothing (no more uniforms, as in high school). She was also concerned about my accommodation, as there were no dormitories for students. We had to board with families. All was resolved as I was the recipient of many scholarships and I completed my teaching diploma. At this time, two friends and I were the only Muslim females. The principal and staff were our "guardians." They wanted us to pave the way for other Muslim female students.

Finding a teaching position became a problem as we were told to teach in our hometown. The number of teaching positions was limited. My mother wanted me to teach at the local Catholic school, where generations of Haffajee children had been molded by the nuns, starting with my dad and his brother. Her wish was granted and I found a position at St. Anthony's School teaching Afrikaans (the second official language of South Africa).

A year later, when I had been transferred to the local Indian girls' high school, the situation worsened. Apartheid reared its ugly face at work. I was the youngest nonwhite member of the staff; the other two women were my dad's contemporaries. We were given a key to the outhouse as we could not use the "White Only" one in the main building. This was blatantly wrong, discriminatory, and humiliating as the student population was all Indian and the majority of the teachers were white females. We were straw role models for the girls.

Nonwhites in South Africa had to find ways to improve the condition of their people, so activism became a way of life. A group of young nonwhite women formed a club that focused on creating opportunities for our young women. We raised funds and awarded scholarships for them, and we provided facilities for extracurricular activities, such as monies for tennis courts. Social injustices were a way of life in apartheid South Africa.

In our household there was no discrimination regarding racial or social interaction. I had been used to seeing my mother having tea with her black friends in our large kitchen, which was the hub of our household. I appreciated this model only years later when interacting with Afro-Americans in the United States. I recalled carrying my sewing machine every Tuesday to the interracial sewing bee, where we made dresses for the African crèche (day care) from fabric donated to us by various businesses.

A few years later I decided to leave South Africa and went to the United Kingdom with a white friend. Ironically my white friend did not have a job and I did, teaching at a grammar school. All during this period in my life, I was a lax Muslim, and had no contact with Muslims. These were my *jahiliyah* days (days of ignorance). The only requirement that I fulfilled was fasting during the month of Ramadan. I was on my own and self-sufficient.

Restless, I left England for Canada in 1966. The first year was uneventful. I taught in a public school in Burlington, Ontario. In the summer I went to South Africa for a visit. The racial situation had not improved; it was even worse. My mother said that she was sorry that she had allowed me to get an education, because it had enabled me to leave home, and she missed me. A conversation I had with an "aunt"—my mother's friend—would turn out to be crucial in my later embrace of Islam. She told me that my mother would be happier if she knew that I had Muslim friends, suggesting that I locate some Muslims on my return to Canada. This was the beginning of the search that led to a new stage in activism—my Muslim activism.

Khadija Haffajee

I made contact with an organization in Hamilton and I attended a function or two. In May 1968, some friends asked me to attend a Muslim Student Association (MSA) conference being held at McMaster University. Wow! The images are still fresh thirty-six years later. For the first time in my life I heard individuals speak so eloquently about Islam, affirming its relevance in the twentieth century.

The next weekend, the earliest possible, I took the bus to Toronto and bought a copy of Yusuf Ali's English translation of the Qur'an. I still have that copy; it's been bound and rebound and is now falling apart again. Today, it is covered with notes and cross-references. *Alhamdulillah.*

The following year I decided to move to Ottawa. Prior to this I attended the MSA conference there to get to know some people in the Muslim community. *Alhamdulillah,* this was the most significant decision that I had made to date. Here the community was receptive and soon I was attending the mosque on a regular basis. No one prevented women's voices from being heard. There was a women's social group, the Ottawa Muslim Women's Auxiliary (OMWA). In the early 1970s it was the role model for other women's groups in Canada. It had progressed from a social group to one that reflected its Muslim roots. We organized a blood donor clinic and welcomed new immigrants at Citizenship Court. We were regular volunteers at the Snowsuit Drive (an annual fall activity when snowsuits are collected for later distribution to families who need winter clothing for their children). Imagine the surprised looks on the faces of the organizers when Muslim women from different parts of the world—Germany, England, Guyana, and so on— arrived to "man" the front desks. If this was not *da'wah,* then what is? These women were participating in the larger society that they lived in.

During Ramadan (the month of fasting) we held *iftar* gatherings every Saturday. I encouraged the women to give short talks after dinner before the evening prayer. It was training for them, as the community was small and they knew everyone. As a result of this activity, I was asked to head the women's committee of the Council of Muslim Communities in Canada (CMCC). As I traveled throughout Canada, I realized that Muslim women did not have a voice in any of the mosque/community activities. The task was to raise awareness and help them organize. The OMWA was used as a model. This was in the 1970s, during the first wave of feminism in the West. In 1976, I was asked to speak at the University of Toronto on this topic, "Feminism and Muslim Women's Perspective of Themselves."

A groundbreaking event in the Muslim community occurred in 1972.

The MSA (the precursor to ISNA) had its annual meeting in Toronto. I was asked to speak. I dared to set a condition: that I speak to a mixed audience. To my amazement the organizers agreed. When the time came for the session and I went up to speak, a whole group of brothers rose to their feet saying *"Haram, Haram"* (forbidden, forbidden) and left the auditorium at York University. Unfazed, I continued. Unbeknownst to me, I had an individual in the audience who championed the cause of Muslim women, none other than Dr. Hasan al Turabi, a young lawyer from Sudan who was an invited guest speaker. He spoke to me later, as did his wife; both encouraged me to continue and not be discouraged by what had happened.

Soon after this I left the women's committee and joined the Muslim Student Association officially. I was elected treasurer of the Ottawa Muslim Association, the first woman to be in this position. The mosque was being built and I was responsible for a million-dollar budget. Unfortunately today, the situation has changed again, since there are no more women active in the OMA. Our voices are sadly lacking. This grieves me; I know that as Muslim women, we have to be vigilant at all times, or our rights will be eroded. In any organization, if some members are not visible, they are forgotten, marginalized. This is not always intentionally. Where women are not present the same thing occurs; perhaps it's a human condition. But Muslim women must be at the forefront of events, especially as our presence is our God-given right. It is unfortunate that all our sisters are not aware of this. It is a new experience for both the men and women in Canada to be involved in the affairs of the mosque.

In the late 1970s, I taught English to French immersion students in a junior high school, and later I became a school librarian. At that time, it was unusual to see a *muhajjabah* (one who wears a *hijab*) teaching in the public school (I had started wearing *hijab* in 1979 when I went to Saudi Arabia for *'umra*, the lesser pilgrimage). When we had parent-teacher interviews, the parents would comment on my scarf, as they had heard about it from their children—all very positive! I was always open about my beliefs with my students. During Christmas season they bought me scarves, and the baked goodies had notes—no pork or alcohol. In the late 1980s and 1990s, as the Muslim student population grew, I organized lunchtime activities for them during Ramadan. We met in the library and read the Qur'an. This was only for those who were fasting.

Khadija Haffajee
Photo courtesy of Khadija Haffajee

Khadija with a group of young authors,
Carson Grove Public School, May 1993.
*Photo by Eleanor Pau,
courtesy of Khadija Haffajee*

Our experiences shape us: my lecture tour to Malawi and Zimbabwe in 1985 with Dr. Ilham Altalib brought home to me how this occurs without conscious thought. We were sent by IFSO (Islamic Federation of Students' Organization). I spent a week with young women to teach organizational skills, public speaking, and so forth. They were enthusiastic and gave me long lists of books they needed. This was interesting because it was the first time I was asked for reading materials. My friend and I had to lecture at various venues. Two stand out. The first was at a mosque in the African township outside Harare, Zimbabwe. We spoke in the main prayer hall of the mosque. At the end, a very old man who needed help to stand got up, tears stream-ing down his face, and told us he was so happy to see two women from so far away speak to a mixed gathering in the mosque! He thought he'd never see that day! The other was in the home where we were staying. One day, the lady of the house asked me if my friend and I lived in the same town and saw each other on a regular basis. She was surprised when I told her that we did not, and that we did not see each other for years. She looked puzzled. "But you are so attuned to each other, your thoughts and ideas are in sync," she said. *Alhamdulillah,* we had not realized this. It is a blessing from Allah (swt) that as Muslim sisters we are shaped by the Qur'an. This is similar to the relationship I had with Fatima Yassar in an Afghan refugee camp, as I recount below. It is this bond of sisterhood for the sake of Allah (swt) that drives us to continue our activism.

During the Soviet War in Afghanistan I was concerned that no mention was being made of the women, so I decided to go and see for myself. I spent the summer of 1987 in refugee camps and worked with the local Afghani women's organization. On my return, I did slide presentations about these, our sisters, titled "Afghan Women—Victims of War." Muslims, especially the women, were moved by my commentary and pictures. They had not been aware of the situation. All donated generously. I remember doing a presen-tation at a middle school assembly—four hundred young people who sat silently for the hour! They wanted to help the children. And they did. They organized activities to raise funds. This more recent war with the U.S. bomb-ing Afghanistan in 2002 is *déjà vu* for me. Since the young boys and men were at war, the camp population was women, children, and old men. Looking back, I realize that I probably met some of the future members of Taliban in 1987, when they were children in the schools in refugee camps.

Some of the Afghan women I worked with were an inspiration, especially Fatima Yassar, who was the head of the organization. She was an amazing woman—very focused. When we arrived at a camp, the old men would come out to meet her. She was gentle and caring, and she inspired everyone with her words of wisdom. Once I sat and heard her address a group of teachers. She used *ahadith* (sayings) and examples from the life of the Prophet (pbuh) and related the past to their present struggle. She has been a role model for me. I learned much from her about activism and being focused on goals.

During the late 1970s and early 1980s my vacations were spent at girls' camps. I enjoyed being with the young sisters. Today we still keep in touch. They are now mothers, and some are active in their communities, as principals in Islamic schools, counselors, physicians, and so on. I thank Allah (swt) for their contributions to my life. We learned together.

The Gulf War at the beginning of the 1990s caused me to expend more energy in a new area that I had not explored. I became involved by default. I had been on a radio show to discuss *hijab*. There was a dinner for all those who had been on that particular show. There I met a gentleman who invited me to an interfaith gathering. I went with a colleague of mine from work. We had been in the church for a while waiting for the service to begin, when one of the Muslim men came over and asked me to say a few words because there were women speakers from the other faith groups and he had not thought of having a Muslim woman. So I went up and did my impromptu speech. At the conclusion, during the social part, a priest came up and said, "I want you to be part of the Christian-Muslim dialogue." So I did— through the back door, so to speak (the Muslims had not asked me). We meet once a month and discuss a topic from both faith perspectives. Two people do a presentation, and then the dialogue follows. I have met many people and spoken at many gatherings. I have been asked to be on many steering committees related to interfaith locally, nationally, and internationally. In 1999 I was invited to Amman, Jordan, and attended the WCRP (World Conference on Religion and Peace) Assembly. (There are chapters of this organization in some cities here in Canada. I had been a member in the early 1970s, and now attend meetings only occasionally.) After September 11, 2001, I spoke at an event at City Hall in Ottawa, where all the leaders of the city—the mayor, police chief, and religious leaders—were present; I was the only female asked to do so. I was also the chair of the Christian-Muslim dialogue in 2001.

The mid-1990s were exciting. I was invited to be part of an International Muslim Women's NGO. There was a preparatory meeting in Amman, Jordan, followed by the Beijing Women's Conference. I attended both. As a result of this, I was asked to attend a major Muslim women's conference in Sudan in 1996. There were women from one hundred different countries. I was elected assistant secretary for international affairs for the International Muslim Women's Union. We met a year later in Turkey. Unfortunately I had to resign from this position for health reasons.

Occasionally I was asked to speak at the study circle held at Ottawa University. I enjoyed these sessions with the young sisters, and they did too. This is when I acquired the nickname "Sister K." When the group graduated, they kept in touch with me. Once in the workforce they felt isolated; they no longer belonged to an MSA, nor were they a part of the adult community. We discussed this, and so it was that the Book Club was initiated. We meet once a month to discuss a book. I facilitate the group. Initially I chose the book to give them a broader perspective on the world. Now they choose. It is from this pool of younger women that I draw to find speakers for elementary schools.

In addition, for the past twenty-five years I have held a study circle/support group for new Muslim sisters in my apartment. This is a mobile group, as individuals have moved to many different locales and new ones come. Just this week, as I write this essay (September 2002), three new sisters have started coming. Sometimes when the older ones are visiting Ottawa, we have reunions; it's wonderful to see their children grow over the years. I felt like a grandmother long before I officially became one!

In 2000, I was asked to be a contributor to a weekly column, "Ask the Religious Expert," in the local newspaper, the *Ottawa Citizen*. The column addresses questions of a religious nature in daily living. The answers are provided from different faith perspectives on the question being asked.

Throughout my life, marriage was never foremost in my mind, as I was too busy trying to do all I could to have a Muslim female presence at many levels of the community organizations. I did not have time to think about this aspect of my life; if Allah (swt) willed that it should happen, it would; and it did. I married in December 1989, to Dr. Mazhar Hasan, a physicist from Illinois. We were introduced by mutual friends. At first we had a commuter marriage, as we decided that we would both continue with our teaching positions. (My husband taught at the university.) We saw each other every two weeks, and during the vacations. I spent all my vacation time in Illinois. We did this for five years. *Alhamdulillah* we both now reside in Ottawa. He is supportive of my activity; we discussed this before our marriage. *Alhamdulillah* I have a ready-made family; I became a wife, stepmother, and grandmother all in one year!

Being an activist has not always been easy. I've had to deal with many trials over the years. Allah (swt) knows what is best for us. Being single in the early years of activism was a blessing. There were no family commitments to distract me from the task at hand, so I was focused on the work that had to be done. There were long meetings, all day long and into the evenings. It was lonely work because even my friends did not understand what I was trying to do. Locally there were obscene letters and telephone calls. Then some brothers set out to destroy the OMWA, and they succeeded. A few brothers who do not feel comfortable with assertive sisters did this. There were some sisters who assisted them as well. At the national level it was different. There was respect and I was always consulted on decisions. Occasionally a new brother would tell me that I was representing sisters, and so I should not express opinions on other matters!

Being on the Majlis ash Shura was a challenge; the brothers had to get used to having a sister at the meetings. At the very first meeting, some were hesitant to speak to me initially; they were hesitant, unsure about who would sit next to me at the meeting, during meals, and so on. Everyone adjusted, some faster than others. What is important is that the barrier has been crossed. *Alhamdulillah* at the subsequent election in 2001, we elected a sister as vice-president of the U.S. organization and another as a member at large. We still have a long way to go.

Unfortunately my mother did not live to know about all my activism—only that I was president of OMWA. Today, in Canada, young Muslim women are visible in ways they weren't when I first arrived some thirty years ago. They are in the streets, in *hijab*, participating in different ways. Unfortunately, affairs of the mosque are sometimes forbidden to them. In September 2002, at the ISNA convention, a session titled "Overcoming Obstacles to Women's Participation in Our Communities" was held. Why have a session on this topic? Because we know that Allah (swt), our Creator, sent His Prophet to put an end to female infanticide, and that within a century, in that same society, females were given positions of responsibility, and their opinions were highly respected. We have the example of A'isha (ra), the wife of the Prophet (pbuh) narrating *hadith* and being consulted by his companions. Our historic role models would be saddened by the situation of some of our sisters today. There are mosques in Canada that do not allow our sisters to enter; some imams do not recognize the presence of women in the mosques, and in others they are not welcome. Sometimes the sermons are very anti-women; they are told to stay at home and raise children, and it is forbidden to be involved in community life. Unfortunately there are some sisters who hold similar ideas. Despite all this, *alhamdulillah,* I take comfort that there are many out there still trying to practice *rawahil*—they go the distance.

7

Rocking the Boat and Stirring the Pot

Rose Hamid

> *God grant me the serenity to accept the things I cannot change,*
> *The courage to change the things I can,*
> *And the wisdom to know the difference.*

I'm not sure of the origins of this prayer, but it appeared in many places in my childhood home as it was one of my mother's favorites. This prayer could be the inspiration for all activists. My mother was raised Catholic in South America and my father is a Palestinian and is Muslim. After meeting in South America, they came to the United States in 1956 to seek their fortune. I grew up in Cleveland, Ohio, in the midst of an extended Palestinian family. What I learned about Islam was heavily mixed with cultural traditions. At the time, there wasn't a place to get a formal Islamic education. My father thought that learning about Catholicism was preferable to no religious education, so we attended the Catholic Church. Once the Islamic Center was established we went there as well.

My mother taught us to have faith in God and to stand up for what was right. She told of how, shortly after her arrival in the States, she had to obtain a Social Security card. Since she spoke no English, she went door to door in the neighborhood in search of a Spanish-speaking neighbor who could help her get the forms. This story is a small example of the bravery and tenacity that she has demonstrated throughout her life. I guess I get a lot of my "fight"

Rose Hamid with her husband, Imad Hamid, at a friend's wedding, July 2003.

Photo courtesy of Rose Hamid

from her. But then, I'm not sure if people would think of her as an activist or not; just what is an activist, anyway?

I balked the first time I was referred to as an activist. Activist? Me? When I heard the word it conjured up images of radical protest groups marching into the night with torches ablaze. Activists have political agendas and aim to topple governments. Don't they? An activist is someone who "stirs the pot" or "rocks the boat." These are negative things, aren't they? I'm not an activist. Or am I? I didn't consider myself to be an activist, but after hearing someone describe me as such, I began to reconsider.

I realized that I am someone who likes to get things done, to take action when necessary. One of my most challenging undertakings came as a result of a situation at my workplace.

I had wanted to be a flight attendant since I was a little girl. I achieved my goal in 1985 when I was hired as a flight attendant for a major airline. At the time I was hired I was not a practicing Muslim. Although I had attended the Catholic Church, I was disillusioned by the many things that to me seemed illogical and that were to be accepted "on faith." My father had tried to teach us about Islam, but as a teenager I was not interested in learning about religion. It was not until my husband, a Palestinian, and I began our family that I began earnestly to study Islam. I realized that Islam answered the questions about faith I'd been asking all my life.

After working happily as a flight attendant for ten years, I suffered injuries in an auto accident and had to be out of work for two years. As Allah would have it, there was a new imam in my city (Charlotte, North Carolina) who inspired and motivated me. During that time I had the opportunity to study even more about Islam. I started wearing *hijab* in late 1995. The doctors telling me that my foot was damaged, to the degree that I might never be able to return to my position as a flight attendant, was one of the factors that helped me decide to start wearing *hijab.*

Eventually I underwent a surgical procedure that allowed me to return to work in 1997. By then I'd been wearing *hijab* for almost two years. I was familiar with the work being done by the Council on American Islamic Relations (CAIR) to help Muslim women keep their jobs while wearing *hijab,* and their work inspired me. I felt certain that once my company understood the rationale behind *hijab,* I would be allowed to return to my position as a flight attendant.

Unfortunately, my company did not understand. CAIR gave them literature and tried to educate them, to no avail. I was told that the *hijab* violated company uniform policy. I had some choices: I could leave the company and give up a job I'd enjoyed for twelve years, or I could find a different position that did not require the wearing of a uniform. In doing so I would lose my pay scale and seniority (both valuable commodities in the airline industry). I was aware that if I challenged the company I could lose my job altogether, but I was not concerned about that at the time. For me, removing my *hijab* was never an option, and being forced to leave a position that I so enjoyed was an injustice. I had faith that if I lost this job Allah would provide me with something better. It might not be in this life, but Allah willing, in the next.

I contacted the Equal Employment Opportunity Commission. They found that my company was in violation of the law, which required them to provide "reasonable accommodation" for my "sincerely held religious belief." In the end their "reasonable accommodation" was to allow me to keep my position, seniority, and pay scale, but I would work in the flight attendant training center, where a uniform is not necessary. I accepted the offer.

Working as an instructor is not something I would have chosen for myself. I did not have the training, and I did not think I had the skills necessary to be an instructor. I ultimately developed the skills that have made me a good instructor, and I have found that I have a knack for and enjoy it immensely. Although I miss flying as a flight attendant, I consider my position in the training center to be a blessing from Allah. It is an example of how putting your faith in Allah to guide your life can bring rewards that you might not have ever thought of.

While growing up I would not have considered practicing Islam to the degree that I do today. It seemed to me that being a Muslim meant a lot of things were *haram* (forbidden). As I learned more about Islam, I realized this was simply not true. I want my children to know that being a Muslim doesn't mean you can't have fun. I want them to build friendships with other Muslim children so when they become adolescents they will have a network of friends to support them when they are faced with the challenges of living in a non-Islamic environment (i.e., dating, alcohol, etc.). I had been taking my children to Islamic study classes on

Rose explaining the operation of the emergency exit on a mock-up in the training facility.
Photo courtesy of Rose Hamid

Rose Hamid

Sundays, but they were not enjoying it because the classes were disorganized, and also because it took up their Sunday. I helped restructure the school and update the syllabus, so now my children enjoy school more, but like any other kids, they still don't like giving up their Sunday.

In order to help our children realize that being Muslim doesn't mean you can't have fun, I contacted the local Boy and Girl Scout organizations and discovered that the scouting programs stress service to community, leadership, and reverence to God (to name a few of their ideals). These are ideals that mesh with the principles of Islam, and I set about starting a Boy and Girl Scout troop in our *masjid*. The scouting organizations welcomed us enthusiastically. On a national level, the Girl Scouts takes pride in its diverse population and works hard to encourage girls of all backgrounds to join. Locally our troop has been asked to put on presentations to other Girl Scouts about our holidays, our diverse cultures, and our faith. My Girl Scouts have learned a lot from this because they have come to realize that people want to know more about Muslims, and they have learned how to explain their faith to others. Participating in these activities has strengthened their faith. I believe that being involved in the Girl Scout program helped my daughter make the decision to start wearing *hijab* when she started middle school in sixth grade. *Alhamdulillah* (thank God) she has not had any problems from any students or teachers about her *hijab*.

I also believe that our presence has benefited the scouting program as well. Our district has a yearly event where girls from local troops (ours is the only Muslim troop) spend the night at the YMCA swimming. The first year we attended, one of the lifeguards was a man. I let the organizers of the program know that my girls would not be able to swim because there was a man present. Since there were enough female lifeguards for the girls that were there, they sent him home so my girls could swim. Last year I let the organizers of the overnight know that my girls would not be attending the program due to another commitment, so they would not have to worry about hiring exclusively female lifeguards (which they had been doing every year we were there). The organizer told me that she realized it was in the best interest of all the girls not to have a male lifeguard, so their policy from then on had been to hire female lifeguards for that event. Our involvement in scouting has served the dual purpose of helping the Muslim troops maintain their Islamic identity while being involved in a larger, non-Islamic environment, and has also served to educate the scouting community about Islam.

I have found it necessary to become active in my Islamic community in many instances, especially related to erroneous beliefs regarding women's roles in Islam. Once, a learned brother was reprimanding children because they had been very noisy as they gathered for prayer after weekend school at the *masjid*. He said they had caused the principal, a woman, to commit a small sin by making her raise her voice in the *masjid* to get them to settle down. When he was later asked to clarify that statement he said, "As you know, a woman's voice is her *'awra*." (The *'awra* is that part of the woman that should be covered in front of unrelated men.) A sister asked him to present proof of that statement. He said he would present his evidence to her husband. Several sisters set about gathering evidence in the Qur'an and Sunnah that the voice of a woman is not part of her *'awra*. The husband of the sister presented the information to the brother, who by way of explanation said he had been misunderstood. The following week we distributed the proof to the students and were surprised at the number of adults and students who erroneously thought that a woman's voice was not to be heard. At the prayer that week, a clarification was made to all present. Several weeks later a guest speaker came to the *masjid*. As he started his presentation he asked people to stop talking, especially the sisters, because "a woman's voice is her *'awra*." To the delight of those of us who had challenged the brother who had made that same statement earlier, he and several other brothers corrected the guest speaker. *Allahu Akbar!* (God is Great!).

This anecdote shows that a lot of misinformation about Islam is spread in our communities based on the cultural habits of people's homelands. This is a problem of which all right-minded Muslims must be cognizant. As North Americans, we have an opportunity to study Islam free from the cultural baggage that so often gets intermingled with Islam. We all must take an active stance in not allowing misinformation to spread to future generations.

I became active in my children's public schools in Charlotte, North Carolina, because I wanted their classmates to see a Muslim woman in a positive role. I became the "Room Mother," the one who organized class parties and brought the goodies to class, the "fun" mom. I volunteer at the school carnivals and at the office. I also teach Junior Achievement classes, a program that provides volunteers with all of the tools and lesson plans to teach children about business. It is a supplemental program that does not require any special training; I only have to go into the class for five sessions of forty-five minutes each. Students love it when the Junior Achievement person comes because it's a break from class, and since they see a Muslim woman leading the program, it puts a positive light on Muslims.

Rose Hamid

I have also been active in my children's schools during Muslim religious festivals. The teachers and administrators recognized Christmas, Chanukah, and Kwanzaa as cultural traditions, but they did not recognize any Islamic traditions. My children were thus bombarded about holidays from other major traditions, but not from their own. My response was to offer my services to teach the students in my children's classes about our "cultural" traditions of Ramadan, 'Eid Al Fitr, and 'Eid Al Adha. As Allah would have it, Ramadan fell around the Christmas holidays during the years that my children were in elementary school, so the program I developed fit in well with the "Holidays around the World" topics that were being promoted. Of course this convenience will not last, since our holidays are not tied to a particular month on the Gregorian calendar. Still, that should not prevent us from going to our children's schools to explain about our Islamic holidays. I urge all Muslim parents to do this at every available opportunity. For the most part, school administrators welcome these presentations as long as they are promoted as a part of our culture and traditions, as opposed to presenting the religion.

Now that my children are attending middle and high school, I have made my services available to the social studies teachers because Islam is part of the required curriculum in seventh and tenth grades. I provided the teachers with up-to-date literature, and I have made presentations about the basics and history of Islam. I have also taken artifacts to show them. One of the things the students like most is the ornate clothing that I've collected over the years. Outlines for presentations in public school are available from a variety of sources and can be found by contacting national Islamic organizations.

One of the challenges every non-Christian parent faces in public schools is the annual Christmas concert. Although there has been a marked improvement over the years to characterize the concerts and parties as "Winter" themed, it may be a long time before individual teachers and administrators realize that they will have to adjust to an increasingly diverse community. One year, my eighth-grade son found himself taking chorus because he had taken all the other electives available. I told his teacher that my son would not be able to participate in any practice or concert that had religiously themed songs. I suggested that if the teacher had to use holiday songs that they be secular in nature. I was therefore shocked to learn that the songs he had chosen were "Silent Night" and "Salsa Noel." I sent a letter to the teacher and the principal protesting this choice of songs. I pointed out the religious connotations of these songs which non-Christians would have trouble with: some of the words in the song "Silent Night" are "Virgin Mother," "Holy infant," "Christ the Savior is born," "Son of God," and "Jesus, Lord at thy birth." The song "Salsa Noel" has the following words: "Born is the King of Israel" and "Born is the King of Kings." These words represent some of the foundations of the Christian faith, but not of other faiths. It also seems to me that Christians would object to non-Christians saying these words as it trivializes and devalues the significance of the words. I expressed my disappointment that my son would have to be excluded from class because of the unfortunate selection of songs.

When the principal received this letter she called to tell me that the song "Silent Night" would be removed from the program. The move pleasantly surprised me, but since the other song was left in, he was exempt from the concert and from the class when they were practicing. If parents continue to point out how inappropriate it is for such obviously religious songs to be sung in school, things will change. However, this change will not happen if people do not speak up.

Activism is born of a need: the need for justice, the need to right a wrong, the need to change behavior, or the need to educate. Activism is closely linked to volunteerism, and to the ideal that each of us is a part of a larger *ummah* (community). We cannot exist in the vacuum of our home or our workplace. It is necessary for all human beings to realize that they play an important role as part of the society they live in. It is through volunteerism that a society becomes truly functional.

Activism and volunteerism are not things that need to consume one's life. Activism can take many forms: following the laws of the land; voting; attending PTA meetings; attending parent/teacher conferences; going to lunch with your child; or writing a letter, making a phone call, sending a fax, or sending an e-mail to elected officials, educators, businesses, or employers.

Statements like, "That's the way it's always been done" are the antithesis of activism. It is a line used by people who are afraid of change, who are afraid to go against the tide, even though the tide may be going in the wrong direction. What must be cautioned against is the complacency that allows those with the loudest voice to dictate matters. When there is a wrong that needs to be righted, one's voice does not have to be loud, but it must be heard.

The Qur'an dictates: "Let there be a community among you who call to the good, and enjoin the right, and forbid the wrong. They are the ones who have success" (3:104). With that, I realize that activism is an element of my faith. "Activism" should not be associated with negative connotations.

I thank Allah for giving me the serenity, courage, wisdom, and stamina to accomplish the things I have been able to do. In looking back, I realize that when I see a need, Allah gives me the courage to "rock the boat" and "stir the pot." *Alhamdulillah* (thank God), I am an activist.

8

Struggling with Words, Striving through Words

My Odyssey in Activism

Gul Joya Jafri

"Activist Muslim woman?" The truth is, I have been a scaredy-cat most of my life. I did not start out as an activist, and I definitely didn't start out as a "Muslim" activist, at least not in a conscious sense. Sure, I learned early on that life was neither just nor fair—whether from mean schoolmates' taunting, teasing, and racial slurs, or by the smirks of those privileged with trendier clothes and fancier toys. However, I rarely had the confidence, in those days, to fight back—and maybe that's part of the reason that so much of my time, now, is spent doing just that. Nonetheless, I have one early memory of speaking out, and fighting back—literally:

I was in fourth grade when "Brian Madison" (not his real name) somehow got into our backyard. I was perched high on our swings when Brian appeared from behind a hill located next to our house, and spotted me. He picked his way over toward our lawn.

Brian and I hated each other, because my best friend had a crush on him and insisted that we follow him around at recess every day.

We sneered at one another. "This is my house. Get lost." I spat out with hostility.

He was not deterred. "I can do what I want." He stalked defiantly into our backyard. I remained on my perch above him.

The sliding door opened, and my grandmother, dressed in her usual *shal-*

war kameez, peered out with curiosity. No doubt our loud voices had alerted her that something was going on. "Who is this boy?" she asked me, in Urdu.

Brian looked over at her. "That's your grandmother?" he smirked.

"Yeah, so what?"

"She's ugly! And she's dressed weird too!" he laughed. His statement angered me to no end. Even if I secretly thought part of it was true, he had no right to say it. The adrenaline began to pump furiously through me, and I jumped—catlike, for once—and marched over to where Brian was standing. He had stopped laughing.

I had never, ever, fought with anyone. Not even with another girl. In fact, it was not uncommon for someone to threaten to beat me up, at which point I would cower in fear and run to friends for protection.

But this time was different. I was so mad, I didn't care. Having no clue how to punch, I balled up my fists and waved them madly toward his own raised ones. After a couple of minutes of our flailing arms brushing past each other, Brian turned and fled.

I had rarely felt such triumph. I, the cowering chicken, had beaten up a boy!

Head held high, I marched back toward the house. My grandmother, whose cries of alarm I had ignored during the fight, now attacked me with questions. "Who was that boy?" she asked again. "Why were you fighting him?"

I shrugged and walked past her into the house. "He was trying to make fun of you," I said. "It made me mad."

She could not hide her pleasure at being the center of attention, even if it was due to a fight. "Really?"

I nodded, high on the adrenaline and euphoric with victory. The rest of that day I remained extremely proud of myself for having stood up for my grandmother; even today, the incident brings a smile to my face.

Nonetheless, that was, thankfully, the first and last time I resorted to a physical struggle.

Instead, I learned that though fists had their place, words were the true source of power. By high school, my friend and I had adopted the motto, "the pen is our sword" as we glided confidently through the halls in our senior years. Having discovered the UN *Universal Declaration on Human Rights* in our law class, we resolved to fight for our rights through our careers, which at that point were narrowed down to journalist, lawyer, writer, or teacher. I had memorized with relish articles of both the *Universal Declaration* and the *Canadian Charter of Rights and Freedoms,* and dreamily quoted them at opportune times: "Everyone has the right to life, liberty and security of the person…"

Unfortunately, our "word power" did not manage to go beyond our roles as editors of the school yearbook, for which the theme was "Welcome to the Jungle." With most students more interested in the "wild" side of school, it was difficult to insert UN declarations and similar sentiments into the yearbook text and copy.

Years passed. The phrases of the UN declaration began to fade from my mind, and instead I was deluged with the winding sentences and seductive concepts that run rampant on university campuses, such as "performing identity," the "sublime Other," and "Jungian interpretations of Islam." Beginning to feel buried under these languages, my vision about the world, what it represented, and who I was within it began to blur.

This was when the true battles began. More threatening than any Brian Madison, the struggles over Language, Truth, and Representation became more momentous. Basic—and yet terrifyingly complex—questions about God, about nature, and about humanity had to be asked. It meant not only questions about the world "out there," but very personal questions about myself. What was faith all about, and how did I practice it? As I began to explore these questions, the distortions and misrepresentations of Islam, both outside our religious traditions and within them—began to gnaw at me.

As these questions grew in my mind, I found myself, after graduation, working at the office of the Afghan Women's Organization (AWO) in Toronto, as coordinator of a project addressing representations of Muslim women in Canadian media. It was in this context that, on a personal and professional level, I found myself buried even more deeply in questions of identity and faith; and it was only through the exposure to dialogue, debate, and analysis that I began to be able to articulate my identity as a woman, as a Muslim, as an activist—as all three.

The primary purpose of the project itself was to assess the portrayals of Muslim women in print media in Canada specifically, but also to help increase media literacy and build the capacity of Muslim Canadian women to advocate for more fair media representation. For the most part this involved collection and analysis of news articles on Muslim women, and organization of focus groups and workshops with women in the community. However, in the process of coordinating the project I was thrust into debates at two ends—with journalists at one, and diverse sections of the Muslim community in Toronto on the other. The discussions with Muslim community leaders opened my eyes to the diverse ways in which faith was understood in regard to achieving social justice. It also made me realize how "new" Muslim

Gul Joya Jafri

activists were, for the most part, to dealing with the media as an industry. Meanwhile, dialogue with journalists revealed to me the frenetic, "bottom-line" atmosphere that drove the pace and the products of mainstream media.

One dark evening, I was stuck in the office with a determined and opinionated reporter. The Taliban had been busy invading villages and towns in Afghanistan and had recently taken control of the country. Journalists were scrambling to cover the "story," and in particular the situation of women, which in their view was now newsworthy due to the Taliban's rulings on women's dress, behavior, and employment. Yet violations of human rights, most particularly for women, had been rampant in over two decades of conflict in Afghanistan. The Taliban was simply the latest version. However, their rulings on issues such as purdah were now garnering much more attention from Western media.

The reporter who had come to visit our office was greedily photocopying our stash of articles on Afghanistan, desirous of material so that she could write her own piece on the crisis. Ready to go home, I walked over to where she stood photocopying a pile of articles (at our expense). A picture of a row of women clad in colorful *burqas* diverted my attention. A predictable title (as usual, with a play on the word "veil" inserted somewhere in the sentence)—summarized the situation with sufficient sensationalism. I was irritated and decided that I needed to engage this reporter in some dialogue about media representations.

"Why are these stories always so stereotypical and sensational? And why are they so focused on the Taliban? What about all the other things that have happened in Afghanistan over the past twenty years?" I demanded, trying to be as inquisitive as any hard-nosed reporter.

I was subjected to the stare journalists normally reserve for politicians.

"Do you have any idea what this reporter had to go through to get his story?" she asked me, offended, as she pointed to the article in question. "Reporters risk their lives to communicate these stories. They don't have time to worry about what's stereotypical or not. They just report what they see. Isn't it true, what the Taliban's doing? Isn't it true, that women are punished if they don't dress in these things?"

I opened my mouth to reply, knowing that I had a legitimate point to make—but was at a loss as how to express it. "Yes, that's true, but it doesn't need to be reported in this way," I added lamely. Why, oh why, could I not be more articulate! My indignation sank into hopelessness as the journalist, articulately and precisely, challenged my arguments.

As it turned out, this tense tête-à-tête was only the beginning. A few months later, a friend and I wrote to the *Globe and Mail,* a national Canadian newspaper, critiquing the essentialist representations of Islam in a news article discussing the "Islamic" cohorts of Osama bin Laden. Our letters were buried in the letters to the editor page, and a few days later we were rewarded with a large, accusatory headline in the Saturday editorial page labeling us "Islam's Disingenuous Defenders," thanks to a self-righteous *Globe and Mail* reader. Along with the headline this fellow's reply had merited, there was a large graphic depicting stylized daggers to represent Islam. This incident led the Canadian Islamic Congress to file a complaint with the Ontario Press Council, noting that the headline and graphic accompanying the responses to our letters "constituted a dangerous generalization which propagated hate against Muslims in Canada."

Hence began my mission against the anti-Islam forces—at least, within my enclosed circle of academia, politics, and activist discussion groups. In courses, and in activist circles, secularist viewpoints at times bordered on the "fundamentalist" in the sense of intolerance for alternate worldviews. It was difficult to find equal respect for a faith-centered vision. Thus compromises were often grudging, although most colleagues and professors were cognizant, at least in principle, of the "freedom of religion."

It was another year before I found a more accepting "mainstream" space to express my views in a more articulate manner. I had been working on the AWO Muslim women and media project for over two years. Although the project lasted only a year and a half, the work continued—whether it followed me, or I followed it along, is now hard to say.

Thus, I found myself—first in graduate school and then during a summer stint at the UN in New York, editing, yet again, a revised version of the final report of the AWO project, incorporating comments and suggestions sent to me by a devoted former advisory committee member—Katherine Bullock—who even from the distance of thousands of miles remained committed to the project from her new home in California. We were hoping to refine the document in order to get it posted on several websites.

Gul Joya Jafri

Photo courtesy of and © Navdeep Dulay

Having come this far, and toiled many hours on the document, we then decided to write a paper based on the research done during the project, for the journal *Canadian Woman Studies.*

Many more long-distance e-mails were sent as Kathy and I co-wrote our article. Our final version was submitted to the journal's office precisely a half-hour after I had handed in my 160-page MA thesis and barely two hours before I was due to catch a flight to Islamabad to attend my cousin's wedding.

Today, our article is on the reading lists of several university courses and is being cited in federal policy research papers, journals, and textbooks. For me, this serves as a source of encouragement to continue with my efforts—both the publication and the citations of the article serve as a legitimization of our perspective and an acknowledgment of its validity to the "mainstream."

Looking back on the past few years, I will be the first to point out that these are very modest accomplishments. I have not single-handedly brought transformative change in my community, or even in my neighborhood. I cannot claim accomplishments that would merit high-profile recognition. And, having worked with, and learned so much from, inspiring women such as Adeena Niazi (director of the AWO), I am reminded of how much harder I need to work. At the same time, I would like to think that I am just one example of the idea that *any* individual can make her or his "ounce" of difference toward a larger, collective contribution to societal transformation and global justice.

Having recently attended the ninth International Forum of the Association of Women's Rights in Development—a global gathering of twelve hundred individuals where inspiring Muslim women spoke of justice and women's rights from a faith-centered perspective—I feel greater hope that our voices are being heard and that there is a gradual movement toward recognizing the strength of spirituality and the empowering potential of faith in the lives of women and men around the world.

9

Working to Help All the World's Children

Laila Al-Marayati

"**W**hat page are we on in *Treasure Island?*"

"I wrote a speech for running for treasurer for school council, do you want to hear it?"

"Mama, can you come over now?"

The above quotes from my three children seem standard enough for any mother whose kids are clamoring for attention. The only difference here is that they were asking these questions from the comfort of home in L.A., talking to me on my cell phone while I was on my way to the Egyptian border at Rafah to enter Palestine. I kept my voice as normal as possible, so as not to reflect my anxiety, considering that my family's town (our destination) in the Gaza Strip had sustained major casualties from an Israeli attack the day before.

"Well, I'm pretty sure we were on Chapter 4, Zayd, just after the inn is burned," I told my eight-year-old, who then handed the phone to his ten-year-old brother. "Yes, Malek, I'd love to hear your speech." He then read what he'd written, sounding like he was on his way to becoming a pretty smooth politician. Finally, Jinan, two and a half, comes on the line. "OK, baby, I will come home soon. I love you."

Of course, I hated to get off the line, but as soon as I did I redirected my energy to the task before me: getting into Palestine. I was on my way

Laila Al-Marayati with her children (l-r), Malek (eleven), Jinan (four), and Zayd (nine).
Photo courtesy of Laila Al Marayati

to the area on behalf of KinderUSA, a newly formed American Muslim charity that was organized in response to the closures of several charities in the aftermath of 9/11. As a Palestinian American, I felt that the Bush administration was sending us a message that any groups who attempt to help Palestinians would be scrutinized and impeded. I was incensed when it became clear that my president targeted the Holy Land Foundation, more at the request of Ariel Sharon than anything else. We had to show that it is our right as Americans and as Muslims to help the needy wherever they may be.

I joined with Dalell Mohmed and Drs. Riad and Basel Abdelkarim to demonstrate to our community that we would not be intimidated, even if the government ultimately works against us. We suffered a major setback early on when Dalell and Riad were detained by the Israeli authorities, put in solitary confinement, subjected to prolonged interrogation, and then finally released without ever being charged with any crime. They were subsequently deported and barred from reentry for ten years. That's when I knew I had no choice but to go, since we had already established an office in Gaza. As an obligation to our donors, we all agreed that we would conduct oversight of the operations in the field, not just from our phones and computer terminals in the United States.

How can I describe the way that Allah (swt) protected us and made our journey smooth? I was traveling with my sister, Lamis, who had never been to Palestine. My last trip had been to Jerusalem as part of the U.S. Commission on International Religious Freedom the year before (more on that later). During the entire trip, I thought about Riad and Dalell's ordeal, knowing I couldn't be sure we were safe from Israeli arrests until we left through Jordan two weeks later. *Alhamdulillah,* we returned safely, having accomplished our goals of meeting with the staff and representatives from other NGOs and visiting the project sites for KinderUSA (full report on the website at www.kinderusa.org).

The day I left L.A. for Palestine, my ever patient and tolerant husband, Salam, drove me to the airport, helped me check my bags, and kissed me good-bye as I entered the secure area at LAX. Before he left he said, "I hope you have a good trip… because you're never doing this again." Both of us knew that was wishful thinking on his part.

Who can blame him when the mother of his three young children goes off to what many consider one of the most dangerous places on earth? Was I crazy? No: but I was determined, as I had been planning the trip for some time and could not imagine not going. As I prayed *istikhara* the days before I actually bought my ticket, I asked God for guidance, allowing myself to submit to whatever His response would be. The next day, I awoke in peace, knowing that it was right and that we would all survive. After all, I would only be gone for two weeks. While we were in Cairo, my husband called, his voice tense, "Did you hear about the attack in Khan Yunis?"

"No."

"Turn on the TV." We watched the images of the injured being taken to the hospital (that we later visited) in a bit of shock. "Well," he says, "Are you still going?"

"I'll call you back."

Then I called my aunt in Khan Yunis, who reassured me that all was still well. Our director in Gaza, Abu Amjad, said the same and mentioned that a physician we were supposed to meet was afraid we wouldn't come. I thought of them there, living through this hell every day, eagerly awaiting our visit to them in their prison that is the Gaza Strip and thought, how could I turn back now? Again, I prayed that night, and God bestowed calm on us the next morning when we left at 4 A.M. for the border.

I kept in touch with home on a daily basis, talking about how "normal" everything was. We were busy visiting relatives who delighted in providing us with some of the best tasting food we have ever had, in typical Palestinian fashion. Of course, I left out much about the demolished homes, the gunshot holes in the hospital window, the Israeli military presence everywhere, the fear in everyone's eyes, and the sadness in their voices. There would be time enough to tell the stories when I came back home. At the moment, the only thing I wanted was to help my husband relax.

Interestingly, my mother, Jane El Farra, who has been living with us and helping look after the children, was never worried. She is a person of great faith who longed to be with us in my late father's homeland, visiting our beloved family. She sent tons of gifts with us that we packed in an entirely separate suitcase, making sure we

Laila Al-Marayati in Palestine.

gave each gift to the right person. Leaving home with Salam and Mom in charge gave me the peace I needed to be able really to focus on what was before me.

As someone who can't resist the call to activism, whether on behalf of Muslim women, religious freedom, or Palestinian children, I would be paralyzed if I didn't have the support system that I do. It isn't possible to do this sort of thing without a family who can not only fill in the gaps when you're gone, but who truly believes in the mission of what you care so deeply about. Since I work full-time as a gynecologist, I face the difficulty of the choice of not staying home with my children. I have chosen a path with my career that is much less ambitious than many of my colleagues so that I could be home more. The only problem is that I find that I am also more involved with Islamic activist work. Achieving the balance isn't easy and requires a lot of prayer and consultation with God as I embark on what I believe are all such important parts of fulfilling my mandate as His vicegerent on earth.

Two years earlier, I received a phone call from President Clinton's office, an administrative assistant asking me if I would be willing to serve on the newly formed U.S. Commission on International Religious Freedom. I dreaded that call, but I knew it was coming as I had just finished serving on the commission's precursor, the State Department's Advisory Committee on Religious Freedom Abroad. During that time, I had testified before Congress and, at the request of the State Department, at the OSCE (Organization for Security and Cooperation in Europe) meeting in Poland regarding religious intolerance against Muslims in Europe. I asked myself, What in the world am I doing talking about religious freedom? My area of interest and expertise is in women's rights and medicine, especially reproductive health.

To tell the story is to comment on the issue of Muslim access to Washington… or lack thereof. When Clinton was elected, a friend of our family's here in Los Angeles was asked to work as a political appointee at the State Department. When the State Department was organizing the official U.S. delegation to the UN Fourth World Conference on Women in Beijing in 1995, she recommended me, as the president of the Muslim Women's League (MWL), to join as a private sector advisor to the delegation headed by First Lady Hillary Clinton. That meant I would pay my own way, but I would be able to "participate" in all U.S. delegation activities, including negotiations with other governments regarding the Platform for Action to be published at the end of the event. Of course, the MWL jumped at the opportunity, and so I went as part of the U.S. delegation, and several other

MWL members joined the thousands of other women who attended the parallel NGO Forum, held near Beijing. (A full report is on the website www.mwlusa.org.)

This was my first real introduction to the Washington environment. At the time, the Clinton administration was keen to promote relations with the American Muslim community, perhaps more for public relations and promoting a positive image in the outside Muslim world than anything else. But, we thought, it's still worthwhile to participate as it gives us access and helps us network with people in government that we may need to turn to in the future.

Later, when the State Department was considering appointments to the Religious Freedom Advisory Committee, my name came up as a possible Muslim participant, and because I had already been vetted by the UN Conference on Women, I was eligible. It didn't matter that I was beyond my ken with respect to religious freedom issues. I was safe, somebody known. No loose cannon. Little did they know...

For my testimonies, I would download information from Amnesty International, Human Rights Watch, and the UN on religious intolerance against Muslims in Europe, e-mail and call people in the know... anything so that I would sound like I had some knowledge about the subject at hand. I did all this in between seeing patients at my office, their patience often running very thin at the delays in my schedule. I did try to suggest other people who would be more suitable for the task, but I was gently rebuked by the contacts at the State Department, who left me with the feeling that if I didn't participate and attempt to represent Muslim interests, it's possible that no one would.

So, when the call came for the Commission on International Religious Freedom, I felt that I had no choice but to accept, that it was a religious obligation that I could not turn away from. In retrospect, I can't say if my participation made any difference on behalf of Muslims in America or elsewhere. It did have a profound effect on my understanding of Washington politics, confirming my general impression that there are serious forces of differing ideologies working against Muslim interests in Washington, whether emanating from hard-line extremists from the Christian Right or from extremist Zionist elements, with the two groups working very much in concert. Both factions are important components of the cadre of neo-conservatives advising President George Bush Jr. During my time on the commission, I gave birth to my third child and, a few months later, I lost my father very unexpectedly. Surely, God was putting me to the test.

At every meeting, statements against Islam and Muslims were the norm, ranging from criticism of *shari'ah,* wherever it exists, to denial of Muslim suffering at the hands of both non-Muslim and Muslim despots. The commission made no attempt to advance or promote reconciliation and understanding, but I diligently worked to make sure Muslim issues of concern remained on the table, while not shying away from legitimate accusations of human rights abuses committed by Muslims themselves.

The entire process came to a head when the commission decided to send a delegation to the Middle East. After much deliberation (basically because of my stubborn insistence bordering on obnoxiousness), the group agreed to add Israel to the itinerary, which already included Egypt and Saudi Arabia. So, once again, I left my family to pursue something that I thought was in the cause of God, again believing that I was obliged to go. The trip was fraught with frustration and internal conflict, but in the end, when I ended up in Jerusalem, praying and crying at the Dome of the Rock, I knew why I had suffered through the previous two years.

For some time, although I'm Palestinian, I kept a distance from Palestine, only showing a passing interest in the efforts of my father to help rebuild his homeland after the Oslo agreements. I thought that if he was involved then I didn't have to be. Then he passed away suddenly, after a trip to the Middle East. Not long after that the Al-Aqsa intifada began and I started paying attention to the region. I was grateful he didn't live to see the destruction of everything he had worked so hard to build in Gaza, and I realized that I couldn't possibly let his dream of Palestine die with him. A year to the day after his death, I grieved anew, praying under the great slab of granite in the Jerusalem mosque. I knew that God's will had been to bring me back to Palestine, remove the psychological barrier, and guide me to a new path of activism, this time on behalf of oppressed Palestinian children.

In the end, the commission failed to agree on a statement regarding religious freedom in Israel, although we did comment publicly on the issue in Egypt and Saudi Arabia. At the eleventh hour, I drafted my own statement on the situation in Israel and the Occupied Territories, which had to be published as a dissent and therefore was made part of the commission's official report of 2001 and is available on the commission website at www.uscirf.gov. Needless to say, I didn't make a very good impression on certain members of the commission, who now occupy important positions at the State Department and in the administration, so, for now, my Washington days are over.

That's OK, because I think that others should step in. In the post-9/11 world that is not an easy task as the bias against us is at an all-time high. Yet, younger generations of Muslim professionals, attorneys, and others have a chance to play a role, to show that American Muslims are capable of participating not only on behalf of the interests of our communities, but on behalf of American interests in general.

Now, I'm focused in the work of KinderUSA, currently helping Palestinian children in need, planning, as we grow, *insha'allah,* to assist needy children anywhere. And, I continue to do my part advocating for the rights of Muslim women as the spokesperson for the Muslim Women's League in Los Angeles. While I continue to participate in other adventures, I realize that I never stop caring about what happens to Muslim women, here and abroad. Many of us are fighting the same battles and sadly, my most difficult moments have come from dealing with hostile Muslims who see any attempt at advocating for women as a desire to turn God's order of the world upside down. On the one hand, I'm busy talking to non-Muslims about misinformation about Islam and women, while at the same time I'm banging my head against a wall as I listen to Muslims (men or women) justify physical abuse of wives as sanctioned by the Qur'an or female genital cutting as part of the Sunnah. To be sure, more and more voices are emerging to call for the bridging of the gap between the ideal of women's elevated status in Islam and the reality of the subjugation and oppression of women in the Muslim world.

The MWL is a small group, organized by a few women struggling to balance work, family, and activism. Our website gives an idea of some of the issues we have tackled, from violence against women to women's participation in the political system to an analysis of recent cases involving adultery allegations against Muslim women in Nigeria. In addition, we sponsor a yearly sports camp for Muslim girls that also provides opportunities for leadership training. When others approach us about Muslim organizations for women in the United States, we are struck by the fact that there isn't a single group, ours included, which can honestly claim to be a national grass-roots organization for American Muslim women. Perhaps it's because of lack of interest in the community to finance such a group, or because women are too busy being responsible for too many other people to dedicate themselves to such a group. Perhaps we don't need it because so many Muslim women are represented in other, heretofore male-dominated organizations. OK, I admit, the last comment is just a fantasy of mine. Nevertheless, the time has come for such a group, as our needs are increasing and it is vitally important that Muslim women speak on our own behalf regarding all issues that affect us. Second- and third-generation Muslims are entering all fields of expertise, which means that we should be able to tackle the challenges before us.

God has put before us a very full plate, requiring our attention. Every issue I've mentioned so far is something I can't walk away from. All are important, all are part of *sabeelillah,* the cause of God. I trust that He will never put before me a burden greater than I can bear, but sometimes I feel as if I am choosing between Islamic activism and raising my children.

Have I done the right thing? Or have I made too many sacrifices? How will my children feel about Islam, activism, Palestine? Will they feel that those things have taken their place, competing for my love and devotion? Will that make them bitter? Or will they be inspired to be active and committed them-selves to the cause of God, the cause of helping their fellow human beings?

I do not know the answers to these questions and I continuously pray for guidance from God. My story, our story unfolds in a different direction each day, especially now that the future is so uncertain in the post-9/11 world. But today, I'll just pick my kids up from school after I finish an afternoon vol-unteering at the Muslim-run Umma Free Clinic in South Central L.A. Maybe we'll go for pizza, play video games, or just hang out as I try to make them feel like I have all the time in the world only for them.

10

Building a Community for the Next Generation

Olivia Monem

I am a Muslim Canadian-born woman of Egyptian heritage. I studied education to become a public school teacher, but eventually found myself too busy to teach. Besides being a wife and mother, I became the author of a teacher's manual about Islam, a Muslim Ladies Committee chairperson, the principal of the local weekend Islamic school, and even sometimes an interior decorator at the local *masjid*. I have been invited to over a dozen public schools (and a few churches) to talk about Islam, and have been a speaker at our local college's "Islam Awareness Week" more than once. I thank Allah and my parents for all that I've been able to do so far, and I'd like to share with you my personal story.

Growing up in a non-Muslim society was a challenge, but my parents and my local Muslim community (the Islamic Society of Kingston) were always there to provide support. For example, during public school, when peer pressure was at its worst for me, my parents made me feel like I could discuss anything with them without guilt. Whenever they couldn't answer my questions, they referred me to a trusted member of our community or to a written resource. My parents understood that if I were to explain my beliefs to my friends and/or classmates, I had to be solidly convinced myself about the reasons behind our practices and rituals. My mother never answered a question with "Just because," but tried her best to provide me with as many details as possible. For example during Ramadan we, as Muslim students, had the responsibility of explaining to our teachers and peers why we didn't eat during lunch, and why water and even chewing gum were not allowed. Everyone around us seemed to focus on the food, when we wanted to focus on the spiritual and social aspect. We were excited about attending the *taraweeh* prayers in the evenings (special prayers during Ramadan), the *iftars* (dinners) at each other's house or at the *masjid,* and of course the 'Eid-Al-Fitr at the end of the month! While we were excited at home and at the *masjid,* we couldn't share our excitement at school. Only our close friends empathized with us and supported us while it seemed the rest of the world didn't care. At times we found ourselves repeating the same thing to people: we don't actually stop eating and drinking for the whole month, but just between dawn and sunset daily during that month! The other activities we did, like works of charity, the extra praying, and the 'Eid celebration, didn't seem to matter to them. Again, Mom was the one who made Ramadan special by decorating the house, making special food, taking me to the *masjid* for *iftar,* and shopping for new clothes. Sometimes it felt like we Muslims were living in two separate worlds.

On weekends I attended the weekend Islamic school, and all of the teachers were parents of Muslim friends I had grown up with. Our community was like an extended family to me, and it was there that I learned some of the skills I use today. For example, before and during high school I had to learn how to talk about Islam to non-Muslim audiences because of the constant stereotypes in the media about Muslims regarding women and the concept of *jihad.* Fortunately some of those parents believed in us and took the time to train us how to present Islam to non-Muslims. We were given many opportunities to practice public speaking, and they helped us to prepare for the future. For example, going to local schools to talk about Islam, taking turns presenting topics to parents after the *dhuhr* (noon) prayer at the weekend Islamic school, and presenting plays and recitations to community members at the *masjid.* Our community also had a youth group, which consisted mostly of second-generation Canadian Muslims, like myself. During those years of being a member of the youth group, we planned and organized many activities, including social events, speakers, fund-raisers, and even sports events. When we met bi-weekly it was a chance for us to discuss issues like living in a non-Muslim society, our parents' expectations, and our personal academic goals. Even though all of us from the youth group have moved away from Kingston (or even Canada), we still keep in touch with each other.

In university I was actively involved with the Queen's University Muslim Students' Association in Kingston. As a group we organized social and religious events, public talks by Muslim speakers, political rallies (e.g., Palestine, Bosnia), weeklong events (Islam Awareness Week), and fund-raisers. My favorite was Islam Awareness Week, during which we'd organize three to five days of activities and talks. We used to book an open area on campus (downstairs or upstairs of the John Deutsch University Center) and fill the area with information booths and displays. With music or a video playing, we had food for sale and of course volunteers to answer questions. We took great pride in our posters and displays, and all the volunteers took great care in preparing themselves for questions from the public. Muslim community members helped with the event, and especially with the food, making individually wrapped falafel sandwiches and delicious samosas!

After university, I spent a few years working on a teacher's manual on Islam with the coordinator of the Islamic School of Ottawa. The project involved preparing complete lesson plans for public schools, grade one to grade nine, following the Ontario Ministry of Education and Training's guidelines. Each grade included twelve thirty-minute lesson plans covering the following topics: Relationships, Occasions, Beginnings and Endings, Signs and Symbols, Rituals and Customs, Journeys, Harmony with Nature, Leadership, Sacred Books and Places, Contribution to Human Civilization, Social Justice, Knowledge, and Peace. For example, under the topic of Social Justice, the lesson plan for grade two was called "Helping the Needy," while the lesson plan for grade seven was "Equality of Males and Females." The project is yet to be published, but the website for it is http://www.geocities.com/o_monem/islamforpublicschools.html.

The weekend Islamic school became my favorite place, and I taught Islamic Heritage there for three years before becoming the principal (as part of my duties as education coordinator in 1996–1997). As a weekend Islamic school graduate myself, I tried to help children make the link between public school and Islamic school by incorporating activities that the children would do during regular public school. For example, one activity was the "Islam Fair," in which each student was asked to make a display about any Prophet, which would be judged by a panel of neutral judges (i.e., not teachers), similar to the "Science Fair" at public schools. There were prizes for the first-, second-, and third-place winners, and each display was put up in the *masjid* during the next community event for everyone to see. After I'd worked for one year as principal, and while I was still working on the

Olivia Monem

teacher's manual, my husband, children, and I moved to a small town in Virginia, in the United States, in 1997.

Blacksburg was the name of the small town, and we spent the first year trying to balance our involvement in two Muslim groups that had just separated a few months before. We missed the warmth and unity of the Islamic Society of Kingston; we tried to create the same atmosphere, but at first it seemed impossible. One evening, I tried to hold an English Ladies Halaqa at one of the *masjids*. There had been no ladies activities at all, so I decided to start a "Peace Net" *halaqa*, like the one I'd attended in Kingston. Even though I hardly knew anyone, I spent a week sending e-mails to the general listserve and posting posters in the *masjid* to advertise a "new" Ladies Halaqa. When the evening finally came, I went to the *masjid* with my heart thumping and a topic prepared. After the *maghrib* (sunset) prayer, I told my husband to go back home, and that I would join him after the *halaqa*. I made myself comfortable in the sisters section of the *masjid*, and waited and waited and waited. No one came to the *masjid* that night until the *'isha* prayer, when a couple of gentlemen came to pray and then left. The door closed and the room was silent again. With tears in my eyes, I went home and called my parents. How I missed my old community! But my parents and my husband encouraged me not to give up, so the following week I tried again. Eventually a couple of ladies began to attend, and now after five years we have a weekly minimum of twelve attendees! I started a Ladies Committee ("Islamic Society of the New River Valley Ladies Committee"), which has its own website (http://www.geocities.com/o_monem/isnrvladies. html) and listserv, and we began regular activities like the English Halaqa, monthly swimming, an 'Eid Gift Exchange after each 'Eid celebration, potluck desserts, and decorating the *masjid*. A few of us even took it upon ourselves to help renovate the basement of the *masjid* by painting the walls and shopping for new kitchen cabinets (which were installed in 2002). More and more people (men *and* women) began to use the *masjid* for weddings, personal dinner invitations, other *halaqas*, Arabic and English lessons, and especially during the last ten days of Ramadan for *etikaaf* (staying at the mosque for extended period of worship, usually over several days). The doors are open for the five prayers, and there are quite a few people who pray there on a regular basis every day. It was only when *both* the women and men got more involved that the *masjid* became a warmer place and the community became friendlier. As a matter of fact, this year (2002) when a group of gentlemen came from *jama'at al tableegh* to our *masjid*, they asked some of us what we did to keep our community so active, and they said that we were a good example to others!

There had also been a weekend Islamic school when we moved to Blacksburg, and it was held for a few hours every week. There were less than twenty students at that time, and most of the teachers were parents of attending students. I taught there for three years and then became the principal in 2002. Now we have almost fifty students, and again I'm trying to bridge the gap between Islamic school and public school. For example, providing new textbooks, supplies, and school desks for the students and classrooms, having regular tests and exams, and organizing extracurricular activities like a "Qur'an memorization competition" and "'Eid Presentation." The parents are also involved this year by taking turns providing snacks for all students and staff once during the year, and volunteering as supply teachers or teaching assistants. The most difficult challenge is choosing a curriculum for Arabic, because we have students from different cultural backgrounds. Some students are from Arabic backgrounds and already speak Arabic at home, while others are from non-Arabic backgrounds. Choosing books to accommodate both types of students is difficult. Also, the classes are all held at the *masjid*, so we can only hold five classrooms for students aged three to sixteen. Hopefully in the future a separate Islamic school can be built.

The MSA on campus (Virginia Tech) also gave me the opportunity to become involved with their activities. For example, "Islam Awareness Week" has become an annual event since 2001, and I have been asked to be one of the speakers more than once. Since 2001 I have spoken on "Family Life in Islam," "Jesus in Islam," "Social Life in Islam," and "Social Life and Family Life."

My husband and I initiated the first "Palestine Awareness Week" on campus, during which we organized the setup of a display and the presentation of national foods. This three-day annual event first took place in November 2000, and both the MSA and the community members took part. Another "Palestine Awareness Week" was organized in 2002, which included speakers and a public rally.

After the tragedy of September 11, I felt vulnerable and a sense of global shame for all Muslims. The media was aggressive in its attacks on Islam and Muslims, and Islam hate crimes were happening all over the world. However, I believed that improving the situation was in our hands alone, so I decided to do my part. I wrote a letter to all of our local public schools offering help.

Olivia Monem

The response was enormous, and more than ten local schools and churches contacted our community asking for a speaker. After talking with the students and members of the various churches, I realized that the best solution to the negative portrayal of Muslims was education. We have the responsibility as Muslims to educate the people around us and to set good examples. After every talk I remembered my parents and community in Kingston and wished that they could have attended my talks also. They used to involve us as youth in their public talks, and later I wished that I had brought along a few youth with me too.

From my personal experience of thirty-three years, growing up in North America as a Muslim was a challenge but also a blessing. In dealing with the problems of living as a minority, I've also been given the opportunity to start building an Islamic community for the next generation. Our parents, who immigrated here, were the best teachers, and I hope that I can eventually become one too.

11

In Pursuit of Peace and Justice

Nadira Mustapha

The quest to achieve peace and justice remains the heartbeat of every activist. The ardent desire to pursue a promising global agenda constantly and vigorously runs through the activist's blood every second of his/her life. The overwhelming yearning and willingness to make a significant, worthwhile, influential, and long-lasting change is viewed as a grave and imperative matter. The matter is neither a hoax nor a game. It is a matter of turning dreams into living realities. Furthermore, it is crucial to experience at least the budding phases of these dreams in the activist's life span, God willing. The activist's life knows not the meaning of free time, and sleep knows no friend for the task. The task is accomplished with sheer pleasure, utmost gratification, precision, and finesse. The world's injustices, whether political, economical, psychological, or socioreligious, must come to an end.

It is the goal of every activist to attempt to implement and achieve the preceding elements in order to make a substantial change. Whether or not one is viewed as influential is not a concern; to alleviate crises in the world remains an imperative matter. We refuse to remain stagnant, and through writing, speaking, teaching, and lobbying, we will continue to offer unwavering support for the cause until justice is served.

Roots of Religious Activism

The Ikhwan al-Muslimoon, the Muslim Brotherhood, was established in Egypt in 1928 after the collapse of the Khilaafa (universal Muslim political system) in 1924. Its founder and leader was Hasan al-Banna, who was executed by the Egyptian government in 1949 because his philosophy and the formidable success of his movement were interpreted as a threat to the government. He formulated the Ikhwan al-Muslimoon as an organization with well-established and intricate rules so that the movement would continue long after his death. Today, the organization functions in over seventy countries around the world. The Ikhwan al-Muslimoon works to establish worldwide peace by first establishing peace within the individual. Thereafter, this internal peace, sincerity, love, and compassion should follow to the development of the family, the community, the "state," and eventually throughout the world.

Hasan al-Banna and aspects of his inspiring, prestigious, and sincere movement prompted my religious activism from an early age. Central to my activism is an appreciation of the benefits that an Islamic "state" can bring forth. The purpose of a "state" in Islam is to provide a unification mechanism for the community or the *ummah,* to make available a governing forum for Islamic laws, and to establish peace and justice in the community.

Hasan al-Banna's spiritual philosophy is one of the major factors that led me to a spiritual awakening. This philosophy remains the backbone of my religious-related activism, and is one of the key elements that channeled me to select my first career as a teacher at the secondary level in order to work with the next generation.

Another factor catalyzing one's religious growth and life paradigm is one's family background. Born in Canada and of Caribbean descent, and thus raised in a Western cultural environment, I grew up within a family embracing strong Islamic morals that engraved in me the true meaning of the oneness of God, the logic of religion, the dynamics of spirituality, the meaning of this temporary life, the importance of humility, the significance of ethical and physical purity, the value of organizational and leadership skills, and the permissibility of enjoying this temporary life within God's guidelines.

Each member of one's family plays a different role in developing, shaping, and crystallizing one's personality. My parents, activists within the Muslim community, hold notable leadership roles as well as formidable organizational qualities. While the implementation of the five pillars of Islam, especially the five daily prayers, is of grave importance for my parents and their household, my father's implementation of the religion is scientifically based while my mother's implementation of the religion is spiritually based. My father maintains a substantial Islamic library for research and increasing understanding of the faith, whereas my mother propagates the fundamental faith-bound principles of the religion such as the oneness of God and absolute trust in God.

The exposure to spirituality at an early age assists in acquiring characteristics such as God-consciousness and accountability. My three older brothers all played meaningful roles in the development of my understanding of Islam and religious activism. My eldest brother, who is ten years my senior, was an especially influential spiritual figure; he was exposed to Islamic jurisprudence, *usul-al-fiqh,* when he was twenty. Thus I was enlightened about the intricacies and essence of the four schools of *fiqh* (Islamic law) at the tender age of ten. In addition, I was amiably taken along to youth group meetings that my brother attended. The importance of the *hijab* was delicately introduced to me by my brother, and this teaching culminated in my wearing the *hijab* at the age of twelve, although my mother was wearing the *hijab* only outside the workplace at the time. My brother also resolutely conveyed to me the potential dangers and controversies behind pop culture. All these *fiqh*-related issues, introduced to me at an early age and in a nonconfrontational manner, molded my personality and facilitated the development of essential Islamic values.

The prolific and fruitful environment nurtured by the youth group of Winnipeg, Manitoba, was inspirational and morally nourishing. The members of the youth group were highly motivated and the quality of the programming was of an extraordinary and elevated level. The encouragements to read extensively about the religion as well as to be spiritually tuned produced individuals who today exhibit fervent religious characteristics and unique leadership qualities. My own personal friendship circle during this period of my life, praise be to God, mirrored similar characteristics.

Religious Activism, 1986–1998

The exposure to Hasan al-Banna's spiritual teachings, my family, and the environment cultivated by my youth group all contributed to my religious activism. The dream to establish an Islamic niche for the Muslims in our community was instilled in the youths' minds from an early age. The youth organization, the Muslim Youth Council (MYC) of Winnipeg, Manitoba, encompassed various elements of an independent, self-governed as well as coexisting Islamic niche within the larger environment. Thus the projects that were implemented tended to be in the following spheres: spiritual, educational (secular and religious), political, economical, and recreational.

Equal rights and opportunity for both genders in sociocultural and religious life was a very strong focus of the youth group. The experience of gender equality was so phenomenal that I personally did not realize, while in junior and senior high school, that in certain pockets of the Muslim world inequalities existed between men and women. My involvement in the Muslim Youth Council dominated every spare moment of my life throughout junior and senior high school, primarily to assist in developing and achieving the kind of peaceful environment that Hasan al-Banna envisaged. I received my first MYC project at the age of twelve. Other projects followed, such as organizing study circles, both basic and advanced, for non-Muslims and Muslims; participating as a summer camp counselor from 1987 to 1997 in several cities across Western Canada; organizing and directing camps and conferences; organizing numerous sporting events; and organizing fund-raisers for both the local youth group and Muslims abroad, such as the orphans of Afghanistan during the ten-year Soviet-Afghan war.

The right to education was also a matter of absolute equality for both genders. From attending basic or intensive study circles to praying night prayers at the mosque during the month of Ramadan, from attending Friday prayer to attending month-long educational retreats, both males and females experienced equal opportunity. As a result of the religious environment cultivated for both genders, in addition to the religiously oriented work I was involved in, I entered into a period of high spirituality with Muhammad Al-Ghazali (a famous Muslim scholar and mystic, d. 1111 AC) as my mentor and guide commencing at the age of fifteen. Engaging in acts of worship on an increasingly higher level, followed by an appreciation for the seriousness of this life and our duty as God's servants within the world, became the cornerstones of my life. When I was in grade ten, I altered my style of dress from wearing baggy pants to wearing long skirts; in grade eleven, I wholeheartedly wore the *jilbab,* a long-flowing outer garment. Al-Ghazali states that modesty remains the infrastructure of Islam and reflects the internal condition of the heart.

The youth group stressed the profound value of physical health and sports for both genders, which was implemented within segregated settings. Although I enjoyed playing most sports from an early age, in elementary school I engaged in figure skating at a competitive level and continued training throughout junior high school; in senior high school I swam to the Bronze Medallion Level, and I earned my black belt in Tae Kwon Do. I completed Royal Conservatory Piano in junior high school but refrained from playing the piano in senior high school in the midst of my religious awakening phase. This decision was made since certain musical instruments are questionable in Islam.

The importance of grasping the fundamentals of the Arabic language in order to comprehend and appreciate the beauty of the Qur'an was also engraved in my mind by the youth group. For this reason, I completed my high school in two years and utilized the third year of my senior high school in 1993 to travel with an older friend to the language institute in Islamabad, Pakistan, the International Institute of Islamic Studies. Although the trip did not serve my intended purpose of learning Arabic, it did serve a secondary purpose—travel experience and knowledge of Muslims in other parts of the world.

While pursuing my first degree in 1994, a bachelor's of education, I continued in my inclination to transform my aspirations into living realities. I had the opportunity to be president of the Muslim Youth Council from 1995 to 1996, where I was in charge of chairing meetings and supervising over twenty youth group projects. In 1996–1997 I was vice-president of the Muslim Students' Association, where I took part in advising as well as organizing various projects for university students at the University of Manitoba. I also served as supervisor of the Summer ISNA Internship Program at the ISNA headquarters in Indianapolis, Indiana, for college students preparing for the Thirty-Third Annual Islamic Society of North America Convention in 1996.

Public speaking and teaching, for the sake of furthering my dream of establishing universal peace and justice, were always of great interest to me and were encouraged by both my family and the leaders in the Muslim community of Winnipeg. For example, in 1995, when I was codirector of an Islamic youth camp in Alberta, I delivered several motivational speeches on the struggles of the first pioneers of Islam, men and women.

In 1998, working as a medical receptionist, an employment administrator, and a teacher in the weekend Islamic school, in addition to student-teaching, reduced my ability to assist in the programs of MYC and MSA. I graduated in 1998 with a bachelor's of education, majoring in the field of Canadian and European history and minoring in biology.

Nadira Mustapha, 2003.
Photo courtesy of
Nadira Mustapha

Amalgamation of Politics and Religion, 1998–2000

Islam calls for the amalgamation of religion and politics, and thus if one is attempting to adhere to his/her faith in a holistic and sincere manner, a Muslim activist should strive to unify these two spheres. Balancing these spheres simultaneously in one's own life, in relationship to understanding the theory behind its nature within Islam, is quite a challenging process. Consequently, this is one of the reasons that the marriage of these spheres at the state level in the contemporary Islamic world has not yet been an area of considerable success. Therefore if one is able to adequately perceive and implement this unification within one's own life, one should be able to make a proper and significant contribution to our contemporary world, beyond the individual level, and become successful in the political arena in the true sense of the word—through honesty, sincerity, wholesomeness, and integrity. It is a challenge that Muslims wish to achieve within themselves, the *ummah,* and subsequently, worldwide.

During the years 1998–2000, while studying in Montreal, Quebec, for my master's degree in the field of Islamic Studies at McGill University, I began to understand as well as initiate the implementation of amalgamating politics and religion in my own personal life. This stage of life eventually altered my focus for activism. While I was always aware of the political sphere within Islam, due to various external circumstances in Montreal, I began to discover the dynamics of political/Islamic activism—that is to say the incorporation of politics in my dealings and life's objectives on a more meaningful and substantial level.

While I was continuing my religious activism in Montreal and assuming the responsibility of organizing educational study circles and social gatherings for an average of forty young Muslim women at McGill University on a bimonthly basis, several major events sparked a political change that altered my personal life, the focus of my activism, and my perspective on my practice of the religion.

First, while I was pursuing my Islamic studies degree, specifically in Islamic law, it became apparent through certain courses offered by my faculty, such as "State and Government in Islam" and "Islamic Jurisprudence," that the implementation of religion at the state level in our contemporary Muslim countries required and still requires extensive analysis and development. While religious activism remained my emphasis prior to 1998, it became ever more apparent that in order to implement Islam—a sociopolitical religion—a comprehensive understanding of politics is required. Ideas such as these were already present in my mind, but my master's degree and, especially, knowledge of the current superficial implementation of Islamic law in the various so-called Islamic states motivated me to undertake a critical, intricate, and comprehensive study of the Islamic political situation—past, present, and future.

Nadira preparing for a demonstration.
Photo courtesy of Nadira Mustapha

In addition to my studies, the environment at the university proved to be quite politically challenging. Coming from a fairly small Muslim community in Winnipeg, with a little more than five thousand Muslims, to a larger Muslim community in Montreal, with over one hundred thousand Muslims, I had to make numerous adjustments, such as forming a circle of friends with similar interests and educating myself about the unfamiliar environment. Whereas the Muslim community I had been accustomed to in Winnipeg is relatively religiously oriented, the Muslims at McGill University seemed relatively secular.

The university itself, considered the "Harvard" of Canada, hosts and attracts famous professors, politicians, and scholars from around the world. Simultaneously, famous speakers such as Robert Fisk and Noam Chomsky, by invitation from politically oriented student groups and the student union, lecture at McGill University and the immediate environment on a regular basis. This atmosphere increases the level of political activism and awareness of this large student population and the surrounding environment.

Student group activism is inspiring in a variety of ways. For example, various Palestinian organizations in Montreal allowed me to gain a proper understanding of the situation in Palestine, an issue that was always dear to my heart from a young age due to the third holy site in Islam, Al-Aqsa, in Jerusalem. While attending most of their politically inspiring lectures, I also made it a priority to attend their demonstrations, their open houses, and weeklong documentary movie marathons in order to support and better understand the Palestinian cause.

Political Activism 2000–2002

Palestine is suffering enormously from the United States' hypocritical and imperialistic Middle East policies, a specific area where I focused much of my activism during the years of 2000–2002, both before and after the tragedy of 9/11/2001.

In the year 2000, although I was only able to reach the Palestine/Jordan border and observe Israeli military camps scattered across the mountains of Palestine—from Salah al-Din's Fort in Ajlun, Jordan, where he fought the Crusaders in the twelfth century—I observed the plight of the Palestinian people in refugee camps both in Syria and in Lebanon. Two of the refugee camps in Syria, Mukhayyamat Filistin and Yarmouk, which are two of the better refugee camps, resemble the poorer areas within Syria. The situation is strikingly different in the Sabra and Shatila refugee camps in Beirut, Lebanon, sites of the 1982 four-day Sharon-led and Israeli-sponsored rampage that brutally massacred over 2,750 innocent Palestinian refugees. The aftermath was appalling. As I can recall from visiting the refugee camps in the year 2001, many houses and buildings that were hit by Israeli missiles in 1982 remain in their original demolished state. The center of the camp holds a garbage dump the size of an average American football field with everything from garbage bags to demolished cars. The mass grave of those who died in the massacre is located in the main market area and the residents of the camps must walk past the grave daily. Covered in thick, green moss, the mass grave is used occasionally as a playing field, especially by young children who know no better, since there are no open areas to play in the camp.

After analyzing the plight of the Palestinian people, observing the political and economical situation in the Middle East, and surveying numerous breathtaking historical sites in Syria, Lebanon, Jordan, and Saudi Arabia, I understood the world we live in much more fully, both politically and religiously. With the events and aftermath of 9/11, and my previous travel experience, my involvement in politics increased significantly. My knowledge of the ubiquity of heinous attacks against Muslims pushed my political awareness to its limit: the attacks on innocent civilians in Afghanistan; the United States' unwavering support of Israel's annihilation of the Palestinians, especially in the case of the Jenin massacre of 2002; and the ten years of American sanctions on Iraq, causing between 1 and 1.5 million Iraqis to die, one-third of them children. At this point in life I developed concrete and well-defined goals for myself. While I wished to pursue a PhD in the field of Islamic studies, specifically in Islamic law, my focus simultaneously was to be, and forever to be, what I designate as "Ummah Relief."

Through Internet communication, I networked with various groups such as American Muslims for Jerusalem (AMJ) in order to investigate how to make a substantial change. As a result, I attended AMJ's Advocacy Training and Capitol Hill Lobby Day Training Program, followed by lobbying on Capitol Hill with staff of congresspeople and senators in Washington, D.C., April 19–22, 2002. I wished personally to investigate why the American government dedicates unwavering support to Israel in the spheres of foreign policy and economic aid. Furthermore, while in Washington, I attended a conference titled "Globalization, U.S. Militarism and the Struggle for Justice in Palestine," a demonstration for Palestine on Capitol Hill consisting of seventy-five to a hundred thousand people, and a rally against the American-Israeli Public Affairs Council (AIPAC) Conference 2002 in front of the Washington Hilton. The weekend was very productive as well as inspiring.

Prior to that weekend I had visited the president and founder of Students for International Peace and Justice (SIPJ) in Orlando, Florida, and shortly thereafter I became the vice-president of SIPJ. I also visited the mentor of SIPJ's president, in addition to a well-respected relative, Muhammad Hamidullah (d. 2002), on whom I wrote my master's thesis, "Muhammad Hamidullah and Islamic Constitutional Law" (McGill University, Montreal, 2002).

Upon my return home to Winnipeg, Canadian Muslims for Peace and Justice (CMPJ) was formed by numerous concerned individuals across Canada. The network was established in the spring of 2002 for organizations throughout Canada to combat universal injustice. It originated as a result of the silent uprooting of Jenin but is currently serving both a political as well as an apolitical agenda. I was asked to be chairperson of the national network through which various projects are implemented on a national level by the umbrella emergency outlook project section, Justice Now. One of these projects, the CanWest Protest Campaign 2002, is a campaign to terminate financial support to CanWest-sponsored newspapers for their unprofessional conduct in addition to numerous biased and distorted reports dealing with issues such as the Palestinian conflict. Other projects include the September National Demonstration 2002 for the Sabra and Shatila Massacre of September 1982, and national monthly letter-writing campaigns to members of Parliament concerning a variety of causes such as the massacre of two thousand Muslims in Gujarat, the deportation to Syria of the Syrian-born Canadian Maher Arar while he was in transit in the United States on his way back to Canada from Tunisia, and the occupation in Palestine. The national network hopes to widen its horizons and outlook in the near future in order to better address injustices occurring worldwide, including at home in Canada.

During this period of political enlightenment, 2000–2002, I strongly adhered to my religious activism. For instance, in the summer of 2000, I was asked to be the codirector of an educational retreat titled ALIM (one who possesses knowledge and perpetually continues in the pursuit of higher knowledge) in Ann Arbor, Michigan. The one-month program attracted approximately fifty university students from across North America. Furthermore, in the year 2000, when I attempted to visit Palestine and to observe the Palestinian refugee camps, my original purpose of travel to the Middle East had been to grasp the basics of the Qur'anic language by studying classical Arabic in Syria. Other equally important objectives for traveling to the Middle East were to become familiar with the region through visiting various countries and religio-historical sites in Syria, Jordan, and Lebanon. In addition, through visiting Mecca, Medina, and Jeddah with thirty of my colleagues from Europe, the United States, and Canada who were studying Arabic in Damascus, at Abu Noor Institute, I wished to become familiar with religio-historical sites as described in the Qur'an and Sunnah, such as the Cave of Hira (where the Prophet, peace be upon him, received his first revelation), Quba Mosque (the first mosque in Islam), Qiblatain Mosque (where the revelation to change the direction of prayers from Jerusalem to Mecca was received), and historic battle sites, such as the Battles of Badr, Uhud, and the Battle of the Trench (Khandaq). The climax of the journey, which occurred during the last ten days of Ramadan 1420/2000, was performing *umrah* (the lesser pilgrimage).

Conclusion

The role of the Muslim woman in Islam is one of grave importance to which we, Muslims, seem to be oblivious at times. The Muslim woman wearing the *hijab* remains a symbol that portrays, for Islam, educational advancement and moral liberation. By her own conduct and her activism, the Muslim woman can demonstrate to the world the reality and dynamics of the gender equity within Islam. This in turn reflects the beauty of Islam at all levels of society: individual, family, and the community.

Unfortunately, in many parts of the Islamic world today, the treatment of Muslim women is one of culture and/or personal, selfish and wanton desires, and not of faith as taught and implemented by the last Prophet of God, Muhammad, may peace and blessings be upon him. Thus the obligation and responsibility of both Muslim men and women in order to change this state of affairs is to return back to the pristine teachings of the Qur'an and Sunnah. One of the chief problems in the Islamic world today is the lack of Muslim women assisting in the implementation of the *shari'ah*. Thus at times the rulings given in the Islamic court of law, in areas of personal opinion, are frequently imbalanced or misapplied. It is for the foregoing reasons that Muslim men and women must continue educating the Islamic world as to the rights and obligations of both Muslim men and women as dictated by the *shari'ah*. Currently, fulfilling the role of a daughter, sister, and aunt of eight nephews and two nieces, this is one of the reasons that I wish to continue to pursue my PhD degree at McGill University in the field of Islamic law, or *shari'ah*.

All Muslims must struggle to elevate the sociopolitical status of Islam and thus its citizens worldwide. The plight of our brothers and sisters at this moment is one of neither safety nor stability. Muslims are being annihilated in all walks of life and in all spheres of the globe, such as in Afghanistan, Chechnya, India, Iraq, Kashmir, Palestine, and the Philippines, to name a few. For this reason, I continue to assist with *ummah* relief initiatives such as CMPJ on a national level. In addition, I currently participate in various activities of the Muslim community on a local level such as writing, editing, and/or publishing thought-provoking truths and realities, for example, co-editing *Unveiling the Real Terrorist Mind,* by Nadia Batool et al. (Xlibris, Philadelphia, 2002) and participating in the July 2003 anti-war demonstration in Winnipeg, Manitoba, as one of the spokespeople, to publicize the unjust war waged by the United States on March 30, 2003, against Iraq.

The quest to achieve peace and justice at a worldwide level both politically and religiously is not a simple endeavor. It commences with one's own personal and pure understanding of his/her religion and the implementation of amalgamating politics and religion within one's own life. When we have true and sincere leaders of this disposition and spirit, we will be in a better position to make substantial and permanent changes throughout the world, by the will of God.

Nadira Mustapha

12

Activism
A Passion for Justice

Samadah Raquibah Amatul Nur

It is said that "good character is not formed in a week or a month. It is created little by little, day by day." My faith in Allah, my desire for a just society and a peaceful world, have framed my life and strengthened my character for the past forty years. I was born in Erie, Pennsylvania, and raised in Buffalo, New York. I am the only child born to Raymond Johnson and Willie Mae Johnson. However, like so many of us, I have an extended family. My extended family includes thirteen siblings with whom I have a supportive, loving, and caring relationship. Twenty-seven years ago my *umie* (mother) took her *shahadah* (declaration of faith to Islam) and is now Khadijah Nur. Currently, my home is metro Atlanta in Georgia.

While I had a glimpse of my passion for justice as a child, it was during the late sixties that my activism found fertile ground. I participated in marching for civil rights and seeking the end to segregation, actively registered voters, confronted police brutality, and worked with the group that evolved into the National Organization for Women to protest and to redress the inequity in wages between men and women. Additionally, I was an active member of the Young Black Leadership Caucus. These days, my activism has been transformed into motivating and teaching our youth to respect themselves, improving their communities, creating products to uplift humanity, and espousing the need to have unified families. "Activism" is a part of my persona, and while I haven't marched in a few years, should there be a need to march, trust that I will be on the forefront. Currently, I am actively involved in a number of organizations that serve as agents for social change and cultural awareness. They include the National Black Herstory Task Force; Baitul Salaam Network, Inc.; Sisters United in Human Services, Inc.; the African American Female Business Owners of the Atlanta Business League; Atlanta Business League; Metro Atlanta Kwanzaa Association; Buffalo Kwanzaa Committee; National Black Child Development Institute; Muslim Chamber of Commerce; the Islamic Crisis Emergency Response System; the Amana Academy, and the Muslimah Consultation Group. Despite being afflicted with a debilitating lung disease, I have no intentions of retiring. In fact, I view my illness as the catalyst that caused me to listen to the higher force and as the source for me motivating those who are ill or disabled to follow their dreams.

I have a strong sense of responsibility to make our world a better place for all humanity. My work with the Civil Rights Movement in the 1970s instilled in me the belief that my work is not just for African Americans but for all people and especially the youth, the leaders of tomorrow. I envision a multicultural/multiracial one-world where citizens would have access to adequate health care; communities would be rid of drugs, homelessness, and underemployment/unemployment; hunger would be eliminated; wars would cease; education would be valued and available; families would be strong; and we would respect each other. With this vision it is evident why I am motivated to work to build such a society. During the late seventies I established a Saturday school program—the Young Afrikan Sisters Club—in Buffalo for young girls ages five to thirteen to prepare them for their future. The only requirement for admission was that they would agree to completing homework assignments. In addition to completing the assignments, the young sisters learned about voting rights, the importance of succeeding in school, their African heritage, proper grooming, and healthy diet, as well as how to wrap their hair. Some of these young girls are now adults who have graduated from college or university and who, in their own way, are helping to build the world of which I dream.

I also co-created another Saturday school called the Afrikan Studies Workshop (ASW) with Sharon Holley and Karima Amin for both boys and girls ages five and older. ASW used creative teaching methods to aid in the participants' total education by helping them to become aware of Afrikan and Afrikan American history and identity. As creators we felt that the instruc-

Samadah Raquibah Amatul Nur at the 2003 ASM
Islamic Convention in Chicago, in the exhibit room
where her Allahu Akbar puzzle was on display.
Photo courtesy of
Samadah Raquibah Amatul Nur

tions, activities, and presentations by members of
the participants' community would help to motivate
the children to develop a sense of purpose. This
innovative program was featured in the fall 1980
issue of *Black Child Journal.* Also, during my studies at San Jose State
University, I conducted several educational workshops for the Black Studies
Department for Student Teachers on Educating the Black Child and
Curriculum Development. Upon my graduation I was instrumental in establishing the first Afro-American graduation for the Black Studies Department.
Minister Farrakhan was the keynote speaker at that event.

I am faithful that a just, peaceful society is attainable. As a Muslim
woman, I feel that Allah has blessed me with this vision and I am confident
that this is my life's purpose. While there are some who believe that a woman's
place is in the house, I respectfully believe my place is wherever I am. In the
home, I have been married twice and have raised three sons, Edward Welch,
Jr., Abdul Zahir Nur, and Tauhid Nur, who are my most ardent supporters.
The encouragement from my *umie* (mother), my *abu* (father), my brother
Randy, Uncle Johnny D, and Sheikh Mubarrak Abdul Hasson has been
unfailing; they are always inspiring me to keep up the good work. Of course,
my siblings and other family members are supportive of my work, and many
have paid me the ultimate compliment by following my lead. They are
inspired to make a difference in the lives of their human family and are
doing so by working or volunteering with organizations with similar goals.
Some of them are starting their own businesses. I am also the proud *grandumie* of six grandchildren: Edward Welch III, Whitney Noble, and Savon,
Khalil, Isaiah, and Tauhid Nur.

I attained an AA in early childhood education and a BA in social science,
as well as certification as a technical writer/engineer and beginners sign language teacher. During my early journey, I served my communities as educator, community and political activist, and technical engineer. I also created
the first *Commonly Asked Questions* manual for the Telebit Corporation Tech
Support Department of Sunnyvale, California. I credit this initial phase of
my life for preparing me for my current roles as a businesswoman, inventor,
motivational speaker, educational consultant, and workshop presenter. My

workshops cover topics such as stress management, cultural awareness, entre-preneurship, employee and teacher training, and product knowledge. My audiences have been mainly educators, community leaders, parents, children, employees, and corporate executives throughout the United States. As an extension of my workshop presentations, which are mainly geared toward education, family, women, and youth and are presented with a strong empha-sis on cultural awareness, I founded my company, AN-NUR Creations, in the late 1970s.

However, it wasn't until 1998, after I was diagnosed with the lung con-dition, that I began to concentrate on the company's growth. Through AN-NUR Creations I am now offering products like the innovative Islamic/Kwanzaa stickers, which include sign language, colorable mouse pads, and the Allahu Akbar puzzles, which introduce Salah. I strongly believe that these products will help Muslims as well as helping Muslim children feel good about themselves and their religion. In addition, the products are extremely useful education tools in the non-Muslim community because they are used to teach tolerance and respect. The comments from both commu-nities, so far, have supported my views. The International Museum of Muslim Cultures, located in Jackson, Mississippi (the only Muslim museum in the United States), is now exhibiting my puzzles and stickers. I am honored that my Allahu Akbar framed puzzles now beautify the office walls of Imam W. Deen Mohammed and the Honorable Minister Louis Farrakhan.

I have also released my *Calling All Women* CD, which inspires listeners "to go into your community and make the necessary changes." Additionally, I continue to be a creative and motivating force in introducing Kwanzaa—the cultural celebration that occurs December 26 thru January 1—to new audiences in more communities; this includes an annual presentation at the governor's mansion in Atlanta, Georgia. I have also authored two books: *All about Ramadan* and *The Seven Powerful Words*. Both books include sign lan-guage. In addition to incorporating sign language in my works, some of the Kwanzaa products are also available in Braille. I have remained true to the AN-NUR Creation's motto: "Educational Products Designed with You in Mind." I have been praised for my foresight and sensitivity by both my visual and hearing impaired clients because they are pleased that I thought of them in designing the products. I have also been recognized for some of my works and have received numerous awards and honors, including Outstanding Teachers Award, Educational Department, Erie Community College; and the Apple Pie Award, Atlanta Artists against Gun Violence, and

Million Mom March Chapter, Atlanta, Georgia. In addition, my *Calling All Women* CD has been honored by the National Black Herstory Task Force. I have been given the honor of being one of the many Uncrowned Queens for our work in the development of our communities by the African American Women Community Builders of Western New York.

In all my works, I show humility and credit Allah for what I have achieved and what I envision to come. I give thanks for my being used as the vessel to accomplish the tasks. It is this confidence in my calling from Allah that allowed me to refuse swearing on the Bible when I was ordered to do so by the court. It is this assurance that strengthened me when I refused to uncover my head for interviews or when it was suggested that I do so in the workplace. Such faith and assurance that Allah is guiding me must have been a part of my foundation. Perhaps they were there all along and were coaxed into my consciousness by my *grandumie*. It is the memory of this wise woman that causes me to smile and brings a certain sense of peace over me. Sometimes I reminisce about my *grandumie* teaching me to pray with my hands apart and by putting my forehead to the floor, thus going to God as low as my body allows. I also remember my *umie* leading the family in fasting and praying whenever divine guidance was needed to solve problems. She was there to encourage all of us. However, it was the lesson that I could communicate directly with God that I found most liberating and one of the main reasons my transition to the Muslim faith felt so natural. Worshiping God as a Muslim woman felt like a homecoming. I knew I was in the presence of Allah.

The decision, however, has at times strengthened my character while in other instances it has caused me to draw from the depths of my character. Facing intolerance and other challenges outside of my Muslim community have caused me to show a boldness and fortitude which belie my petite stature, gentle demeanor, and soft spoken words. I have fought for my right to be respected in the workplace and my right to wear my hair covered. In the late 1960s through the early 1980s, a period in the United States when many employers found hairstyles like afros and braids unacceptable in the workplace, wrapping one's hair with an Islamic headdress or African-inspired material was definitely frowned upon. Unfortunately, I also experienced these attitudes in the early 1990s. I have, however, stood my ground, ignored both overt and more subtle disapprobation, exercised my rights, and won the approval to practice what I knew was right all along. I also educated employers and employees on the importance of fasting during Ramadan, observing the 'Eid celebration, and observing Dr. Martin Luther King's birthday (before it became a national holiday), as well as celebrating Kwanzaa.

Our society usually paints a picture of a leader as male, tall, and sometimes having a deep baritone voice. Usually the leader is not described as an activist. But being in my presence and watching my eyes as they twinkle when I share my vision of a just world, you will leave with the knowledge that you have been in the presence of a true warrior leader. And while I may not have the baritone voice, I certainly have much more. I have the strength and wisdom of my sisters/friends, mother/mentors. Women like Mary McLeod Bethune, the great educator and visionary, as well as Ida B. Wells and Harriett Tubman, two fearless warriors, guide and sustain me. I also draw from the timeless lessons and grace of my *grandumie,* Corean Clanton Henry; my *umie,* Khadijah Nur; and the Prophet Mohammed's (pbuh) wife, Khadijah, a strong businesswoman. As if I still need to fortify this cadre of guides, I call upon the greatness of the queen, Sister Cleopatra. Keeping company with such powerful women and knowing that Allah directs each step I take, it is easy to understand how I am a woman of character. I will continue to work to create a society that is just, a world that knows peace and where people are respectful of each other. I will do so little by little and day by day. Activism is my mission. It is my life. Allah has chosen this path for me and I give thanks to Allah for sending me Angels to help me through the trying times. I believe that my *grandabu* (grandfather) Henry Clanton, my great aunts and uncles, siblings, friends, and other family members who have passed on are smiling.

13

Activism
A Part of Life

Mona Rahman

The term "activist," to me, describes someone who goes beyond the call of duty to work for changes in society. As such, it is not a term I would use to describe myself. The "extracurricular" activities which I have taken part in throughout my life are not things that I consider as activism but, rather, as part of one's duty as a Muslim.

One of my favorite *surahs* (verses) in the Qur'an is *Surah al-'Asr* as, to me, it defines, very concisely, how one is to conduct one's life:

> By (the Token of) time (through the Ages), Verily Man is in loss,
> Except such as have Faith, and do righteous deeds, and (join
> together) in the mutual teaching of Truth, and of Patience and
> Constancy. (*Surah al-'Asr* 103:1–3)

Indeed, the linkage of faith with doing righteous deeds is a recurring theme within the Qur'an; in fact, to my understanding, references to "those who believe" in the Qur'an are often (if not always) followed by the phrase "and do righteous deeds." In other words, it is not enough to just "have faith." Everything in Islam is about balance—between the spiritual world and the *dunya* (material world). So, it is not enough to say "I believe," but this faith must be translated into action by the performance of righteous deeds, that is, doing things *fisabeelillah* (for the sake of God).

For me, there are several spheres in which it is important for an individual to be actively involved. First and foremost is education of oneself. We cannot expect to be able to represent Islam to others, know of our rights and duties as Muslims, and so on, if we do not know our own *deen* (way of life). We also each have duties toward our families and the Muslim community. A community or association cannot function without the contribution of its individual members. As Muslims we have a responsibility to do *da'wah*, that is, educate others about Islam. More often than not, especially in times such as this post-9/11 era or, previously, during the Gulf War, we find ourselves in a "reactive" stance, defending Islam and clarifying misrepresentations thereof. However, I think it is equally or even more important to be proactive through our behavior, and also through presentations and displays at schools and universities and the like. Furthermore, as Canadians, we have a responsibility to contribute to the society in which we live. And, of course, we need to remember those who are suffering around the world and help them in any way we can.

A companion of the Prophet *(pbuh),* Abu Sa'id al-Khudri, narrated that he heard the Prophet *(pbuh)* saying:

> He who amongst you sees something abominable should modify it with the help of his hand; and if he has not strength enough to do it, then he should do it with his tongue; and if he has not strength enough to do it, (even) then he should (abhor it) from his heart and that is the least of faith. [Sahih Muslim]

Obviously, we cannot all deal with every aspect of Islamic work at each level. However, we each have our "expertise" and our scope. For example, as youth, we would do presentations on Islam within our high schools and contribute to the community as a group through various activities of the youth group. As students at university, we focused our efforts on campus, providing guidance to the youth, and so on. As such, much of my activities have been focused on campus, as I was a member of the Queen's University Muslim Students' Association (QUMSA) for eleven and a half years, during my undergraduate and graduate studies at Queen's University. This led to some involvement at various levels of the MSA of the United States and Canada. As we grow, we also have a responsibility to pass along what we have learned to those of the younger generation. Otherwise, a community will only be active as long as the older generation is active. Thus, one of my priorities is to work with the Muslim youth in our community, especially since I grew up in the same environment as they.

Another aspect of what one is able to do depends upon the amount of time one has and, more importantly, support from others. As a student, attending university in my hometown and living with my family, my time was relatively flexible. Part of student life is structured around extracurricular activities such as participation in various clubs. For me, and many of my friends, extracurricular activities were centred around QUMSA. In graduate school, my schedule became more flexible as there were not as many rigid time deadlines to work around. I recall that one QUMSA alumnus advised me to take advantage of the time I had in school, since once I was in the "real world" it would become difficult to find more time. However, I know of several Muslim women who are raising families, some while going to school, and also those who have entered the workforce, who are very active in Islamic work. I believe that it is possible to find the time to do something if one has the will to do so. This may require some time-management skills, as well as the support and encouragement of one's family/parents/spouse, but Allah (swt) will make it possible, *insha'allah.*

My Environment

I was born and raised in Kingston, Ontario, Canada, a relatively small community and one that is dominated by institutions, with two universities, a community college, and about ten penitentiaries within the area. Indeed, when my father arrived at Queen's University as a graduate student in 1968, followed by my mother in 1970, there were a mere handful of Muslims who resided in Kingston, including students and some families, mainly professors at Queen's University and their families. Like many communities of that era, in time, the Queen's Islamic Society evolved into the Islamic Society of Kingston as many of the early students put down roots and the community expanded. *Masha'allah,* there are now over two hundred Muslim families in the Kingston area.

Alhamdulillah, growing up in Kingston taught my generation the importance of brotherhood/sisterhood in Islam. Because we were such a small community, the members of the community became like one extended family. Those of the parental generation were all our uncles and aunties, tants and *'amus,* no matter what their background. Thus, my generation was literally raised by the entire community which, *masha'allah,* made great efforts to raise us with Canadian Muslim identities but also to be proud of our respective and each other's cultural heritages. I think my "activism," if you wish to call it that, comes from my exposure to the initiatives of my parents' generation. When we were young, they saw the need for Islamic education, and so they started the weekend Islamic school, where the parents were volunteer teachers for the children. They even held adult classes for those who wished to learn Qur'anic Arabic. This, as well as the presence of regular *halaqas* (study circles) showed us, as children, that acquiring knowledge is something one does throughout one's lifetime. Moreover, being a small community was not seen as a limitation for resources; the campus environment was taken advantage of in order to bring speakers from outside the community like Imam Siraj Wahaj, Dr. Jamal Badawi, and Sr. Khadija Haffajee, both to benefit the Muslim community and to provide an opportunity for *da'wah.* As the children of the founding families grew and became older, the youth decided there was a need to form a youth group (the Kingston Muslim Youth) to allow them to organize Islamic activities for themselves. In the 1980s, when this first generation of youth entered university, they, along with Muslim students who had come to study, reestablished the Muslim Students' Association, renamed as QUMSA (Queen's University Muslim Students' Association).

Since we were a small community, if something needed to be done, it was up to those of the community to make it a reality. There was no option to leave it to "someone else," nor should there be. Prophet Muhammad (pbuh) stated that "Believers are like the parts of a building to one another—each part supporting the others" (related in Bukhari). A wall cannot serve its function to its full capacity without the contribution of each of its component bricks. Moreover, like the bricks in a wall, believers surround, support, and strengthen each other to create a strong unified barrier to external forces. While a "weak" brick is strengthened by its adjacent neighbors, its loss creates a gap that ultimately weakens the overall structure. I think this experience is something that was shared by my generation in communities across North America, resulting in the formation of MYNA (Muslim Youth of North America) in the 1980s and the subsequent revival of the MSA of the United States and Canada in the 1990s.

Kingston is unique in that there are ten penitentiaries located in the surrounding area. The presence of Muslims in the prison system, many of whom came to Islam during incarceration, resulted in the early establishment of a prisoner visitation program and, most recently, the appointment of a Muslim chaplain. The fact that many of our parents would visit brothers and sisters in the prison system, teach them about Islam, provide educational materials, establish *jumu'ah* prayers, and so on, further emphasized to us the importance of helping one's brothers and sisters in Islam no matter what their situation, as taught to us by the Prophet Muhammad (pbuh). Moreover, on special occasions such as Salat-ul-Jumu'ah and 'Eid, those in minimum security would be permitted to attend prayers and functions with the community. I think our exposure to these brothers showed us that we all have the capacity to change, and taught us the importance of not judging people by their circumstances.

The members of the Kingston Muslim community were very active in the community at large by participating in efforts such as the Multicultural Breakfast Forum of the Board of Education, the Kingston Police Advisory Committee on Race Relations, the establishment of the Human Rights Office at Queen's University, and various interfaith groups in the community and on campus, as well as organizations providing services such as the Kingston District Immigration Services and the United Way. They instilled within my generation the identity of Canadian Muslims and the importance of being involved in the community in which you live and working together to educate the larger community about Islam, our beliefs and practices, as well as to work within the various systems to accommodate both Islamic practices and those of other faiths. Since we were always taught in school that Canada is described as a multicultural mosaic or "salad bowl," to work toward understanding and accommodation is simply a "Canadian thing." But more importantly, it is an "Islamic thing," as the Qur'an says:

> O mankind! We created you from a single [pair] of a male and a female, and made you into nations and tribes, that ye may know each other. Verily the most honoured of you in the sight of Allah is [he who is] the most righteous of you. And Allah has full knowledge and is well-acquainted [with all things]. (*Surah al-Hujurat* 49:13)

There was also a very close association formed between the Muslim community and Queen's University. Since we were not able to build a mosque until the mid-1990s, many of our events, such as *jumu'ah,* 'Eid prayers, and social events, were usually held on campus, primarily at the International Centre at Queen's University. Thus, the staff of the

Mona Rahman

International Centre and those involved in the administrative services in general were very familiar with the needs of Muslims, to the extent that I was once reminded by the university administrative staff that we had not yet made the bookings for *jumu'ah* (Friday) prayers for the term. Indeed, there are members of the International Centre staff who have known me since childhood. This familiarity and good relationship with those in the administration has facilitated the work of Muslims on campus and, at times, also helped to alleviate problems stemming from misunderstandings between groups as well as blatant actions against Muslims. On a closer note, the head of the Department of Biochemistry at one point noticed that my colleague and I would disappear for *jumu'ah* prayers in the middle of departmental seminars; this was one of the factors behind a decision to change their timing to accommodate us, *alhamdulillah.*

This proactive approach of the community in *da'wah*—getting involved with and being familiar with the community at large—has been of great benefit to the Muslim community during difficult times such as post Sept. 11, 2001. At the time of the Gulf War in 1991, unfortunately, there were several instances of threats against Muslims on campus. Several of my friends, being highly visible in *hijab,* were verbally assaulted, and one friend was even attacked by a drunken man on probation. The situation during this time resulted in the formation of interfaith groups both in the community and on campus. As a result of these and other relationships, after the tragic events of September 11, 2001, there was an immediate response by the non-Muslim community, especially throughout the school board and Queen's University, to be aware of any potential incidents against Muslims. Moreover, there was an overwhelming show of support for the Muslim community from various religious leaders but also, to our surprise, from the general population. One woman, after seeing how Muslim women were being treated in larger cities in the United States, even offered to do groceries for Muslim women in Kingston, assuming we were living under similarly threatening conditions. *Alhamdulillah,* the overall environment in Kingston was very supportive of the Muslims. This was exemplified by the open house held at the mosque soon after the tragedy, which was attended by almost a thousand people, mostly because of the publicity put out by various religious groups to their respective communities.

This is the environment in which I was raised. *Masha'allah,* my parents have been active in the community since their arrival to Kingston. My father served as president of the Islamic Society of Kingston (as well as the Queen's

Islamic Society) for a total of about eighteen years, the majority of my formative years. Thus, I recall many evenings when my sister and I were recruited to stuff envelopes for the community newsletter. As a student, he was also involved in MSA activities at the continental level. In fact, he was part of the organizing committee for an MSA national conference held at Queen's University in 1970. Twenty-five years later, Queen's University was again host to the East-Zone Canada MSA Conference, in which we both had the opportunity to welcome participants on behalf of the ISK and QUMSA, respectively. Both he and my mother have always been very active in activities involving the community, whether organizing events and activities, attending *halaqas*, or providing support to the youth and children. They, like the other parents, were also very aware of nurturing an Islamic identity in their children. They sent us to Islamic summer camps, took us to conferences, even put us on a bus with youth from Ottawa to attend MYNA conferences in Indiana, *masha'allah*. This allowed us to make connections with Muslim youth from other, usually much larger, communities... many connections which, *alhamdulillah*, are still intact today.

I consider myself blessed, as I am at the younger end of this first generation of children of founding families; many things were already established for me to participate in as I reached each phase of my life. When we were young, I recall looking forward to when I would be old enough to go to "youth group" like my older brothers and sisters. I think they also wanted to encourage our involvement as younger brothers and sisters. I recall being secretary/treasurer of the Kingston Muslim Youth at the age of twelve. However, I am sure the only responsibility given to me by the president at the time, Eanass Fahmy, was to phone people about meetings, if that. She took care of the finances and some of my other responsibilities, given my young age. In time, as we grew, we each took our turn as president. As members of the youth group, we were encouraged to be actively involved in the affairs of the community, specifically that of fund-raising for the building of the *masjid*, a project that took a decade to fulfill. The projects of the KMY were also encouraged and supported by our parents, including sponsorship of a child in Iraq and fund-raising (sweatshirts, 'Eid cards). One year, we organized a variety show for the residents of a residential cancer center.

The high school I attended was one that Muslims had attended for several years and that had hosted many Malaysian students sent here for OAC (Ontario Academic Credit, i.e., grade thirteen) before entering university. *Masha'allah*, the Malaysian brothers and sisters made a positive impression on the schools they attended, especially their commitment to the *deen*. Thus, the teachers and students at the school were already familiar with Muslims, and those who had attended prior to us had already made arrangements for prayer facilities. In fact, our history teachers used to approach us to make presentations on Islam to their classes. I recall one teacher, Mr. MacLaughlin, bringing up points which he knew were misrepresentations of Islam to allow us to clarify them. Our high school presentations grew into a youth group project in which we researched and produced a standard presentation dealing with various aspects of Islam and common misconceptions, which individuals could then use to give presentations in their respective schools. Later on, even as university students, we would return to the same classes to make similar presentations.

When in the youth group, while our "elders" were attending university, I looked forward to the day I would be part of QUMSA, which was very active when I was in high school, with many activities such as *halaqas*, public lectures, and so on. There was a very close relationship between QUMSA and the ISK, especially given the fact that there was no *masjid* at the time, and we as youth looked to them as our older brothers and sisters. They included us in some of their activities and we, as the Kingston Muslim Youth, would also host events for them, such as the KMY Annual Tea on the last day of QUMSA's alternate Frosh Week each September. Thus, I see my involvement in the various levels of the community as following in the footsteps of my older brothers and sisters, an inheritance which was passed down to us.

Alhamdulillah, one of the indicators of community growth is the establishment of a cycle. The Queen's Islamic Society evolved into the Islamic Society of Kingston, the children of which reestablished the Queen's University Muslim Students' Association. A similar cycle resulted in the formation of the Muslim Kids' Club. *Alhamdulillah,* my sister and I were blessed with a younger brother after fifteen and a half years of being a duo, clearly a member of a new generation. He was only seven years old when the Islamic Centre of Kingston was built, and thus he had the blessing of growing up with a *masjid,* something that my generation lacked. *Masha'allah,* the community had also increased in numbers, with a significant portion made up of children. With the establishment of the *masjid,* it was clear that our community was lacking in programs (outside of the Islamic school) which were aimed specifically at children. During dinners and other functions at the Islamic Centre, the children were relegated to the playroom. In fact, aside from the programs during the 'Eids, there was nothing which would encourage them to come to the Islamic Centre. This was a shame, as it is really this portion of the community for whom the *masjid* was built. In order to alleviate this problem and encourage children to come and be familiar with the Islamic Centre, my father suggested that a program be established aimed at children under the age of twelve and, thus, the Muslim Kids' Club (MKC) was formed in July of 1996.

Alhamdulillah, we had the example of the Ottawa community, which had established both a Muslim Girls Club and a Muslim Boys Club at the time, and were looking into establishing Muslim Scouts. The MKC started off as monthly meetings, which soon became biweekly. We try to tap into the talents of those within the community; volunteers come in to do a variety of activities with the children including arts and crafts, baking, learning stories, scavenger hunts, learning songs, games, and sports. After three years as MKC coordinator, I passed on the responsibility to Tant Fatma Fahmy, one of my "moms." *Alhamdulillah,* a core committee was also established. *Masha'allah,* over the past two to three years, she and the rest of the core committee have established the MKC into an organized weekly activity for children with activities at the *masjid,* as well as field trips around Kingston (e.g., the fire station, the food bank, the police station). *Insha'allah,* it is hoped that through this program, children will feel a connection with the Islamic Centre of Kingston and, more importantly, this will provide the children of this generation the opportunity to spend more time and build friendships with other Muslim children. *Alhamdulillah,* the first generation of the MKC has already graduated into the youth group and, *insha'allah,* the cycle will continue.

Sisters Activism

> The believers men and women are protectors one of another: they enjoin what is just, and forbid what is evil: they observe regular prayers, practice regular charity, and obey Allah and His apostle. On them will Allah pour His mercy: for Allah is Exalted in power, Wise. (*Surah at-Tawbah* 9:71)

"Sisters' activism" is not a phrase that I used until after my undergraduate days, mainly because the phrase implies that, in general, there is little or no participation of women. *Masha'allah,* while I was growing up, my family and my community never differentiated between brothers' and sisters' activism, just as the *ayah* (verse) in the Qur'an states. Both men and women are equally accountable for their deeds and for the building of a community, by enjoining good and forbidding evil and observing the fundamental duties of Islam; gender is not a factor. Moreover, there was always support and encouragement to be active. Our "parental generation" strove to ensure that we were educated in both our duties and our rights in Islam as Muslims and females in particular, and that our opinions were to be voiced and considered. I recall, as a youth, during one presentation to a high school class in which we talked about the rights and duties within a family, one girl raised her hand and commented that it seemed that the men were at a disadvantage. Perhaps we went a bit overboard in trying to dispel the myths about Muslim women! Like many executive councils, our community has a "women's representative" to ensure that the perspectives of the sisters are taken into account. However, the sisters of the community have always been actively involved in community affairs, beyond participation in the "sisters' group." To this day, there has always been at least one sister holding an executive position in addition to that of women's representative.

During my undergraduate days in QUMSA, and even before, sisters played an active and integral role in the organization's affairs on campus. During that time, the demographics on campus were such that the majority of the sisters were undergraduate students who had grown up in Canada and who had been actively involved in their own respective communities. The majority of the brothers were international students in graduate school. There were also several active Muslim women, from Canada and abroad, who were pursuing graduate studies, either master's or doctoral degrees, some single and some married with children. Each brought his/her own perspective and experiences as a Canadian, Egyptian, Pakistani, Sudanese, Indonesian, and so on, to the group. There was also a sense of respect for each other, both brothers and sisters, which led to strong bonds of brotherhood and sisterhood. As a teenager just entering first-year university, I was amazed that the older graduate students referred to me as "Sister Mona," especially since, just the year before, I had called some of these brothers "Uncle." I also remember there not being any feeling of judgment; we may have been at different levels of faith, knowledge, and understanding, but I never felt that anyone was looked down upon by others. We were all there for the sake of Allah (swt) and, as such, worked together to educate ourselves about the *deen,* teach those

around us about Islam, and also work toward raising awareness of injustices occurring around the
world. Indeed, I think this is the underlying reason
why the group was so active at that time. While
the sisters and brothers had separate *halaqas,* sports
events, and so on, we also met together for biweekly
meetings, "QUMSA Nights," when we discussed issues. This allowed us to
learn from each other, from each other's experiences and knowledge bases
within the guidelines of Islamic *adab* (etiquette). Those of us who were
raised in Canada brought to the group our experiences of living as Muslims
in a non-Muslim society. *Masha'allah,* through the years we also had the
privilege of learning from our brothers and sisters who had the opportunity
to have a more Islamically based education than we. For example, there was
Br. Sherif Abdul Azeem, who, *masha'allah,* is Hafiz-al-Qur'an (has memorized the Qur'an in its entirety), and whose book *Women in Islam versus
Women in the Judaeo-Christian Traditions: The Myth and the Reality* started
as a *jumu'ah khutbah* (Friday sermon) on campus. It was also this group at
QUMSA, initiated by Sr. Jennifer Rahman, who started the revival of the
MSA of the United States and Canada in the early 1990s.

Moreover, within QUMSA at the time, the integral role of both brothers and sisters in Islamic work was recognized. One of the earliest projects I
was involved in during my first year was "Islam Days." This was a regular
event undertaken by QUMSA akin to the Islam Awareness Weeks coordinated by MSA of the United States and Canada today. For this particular
event, the coordinators had decided upon topics such as Islam's view on the
environment, Islam's view on alcohol, on racism and, of course, Islam's view
on women. Each topic was researched and a display put together by a subcommittee. The subcommittee I was on was "Islam's view on women," and
it consisted of both brothers and sisters. This, of course, was the largest part
of the display as there were so many rights to describe and myths to dispel!
At our Islam Days, we always made sure to have both brothers and sisters
present since, as one person put it, no matter how knowledgeable a brother
may be about women's rights in Islam (e.g., the right to an education, that
the *hijab* is not a means of oppression, etc.), unfortunately, his view is not

as credible as if it were being stated and demonstrated by a woman. And what better place to demonstrate the rights of a woman to pursue an education than at a university campus where Muslim women were visible, pursuing bachelor's, master's, and doctoral degrees.

Sisters also played an integral role in the executive committee of QUMSA. Interestingly, during that time, although sisters were a minority in numbers, *masha'allah,* the percentage of sisters involved was significant. Often sisters made up at least half of the executive committee. One year, there was only one brother on the committee (and he was not the president) whom I suspect felt rather outnumbered at times! Moreover, to have a sister as chairperson was a regular occurrence that seemed to happen at least every other year, until I held this position in my first year of graduate school. Indeed, during my term, I recall getting an e-mail from another MSA to get advice about having sisters as leaders of an MSA. This came as a surprise to me since this had never been an issue for us. In fact, prior to my term, several sisters had held this position (e.g., Hoda Fahmy, Jennifer Rahman, Sabreena Haque). There were many more who served on the executive committee throughout the years. The year I served as president was actually a new experience for me as, for the first time, I was the only woman on the committee. *Subhan'allah.*

I also found support to be active at Queen's University from outside the Muslim community. One of the positions that I inherited from Br. Aalim

Zakee Fevens, who had served as president before me, was a position on the Interfaith Council on campus. I think the chairperson, Reverend Brian Yealland, also wanted to demonstrate to the larger community that Muslim women were not "oppressed" by the veil, that they could pursue an education, and have a voice. During one of my first years on the council, he asked me to speak on behalf of the Interfaith Council at the memorial for the "Montréal Massacre," the tragedy that had occurred during my first year at Queen's University at École Polytechnique in Montréal, resulting in the shooting deaths of fourteen women.

Mona Rahman's PhD Convocation,
Queen's University, May 2001.
*Photo courtesy of
M. Hafizur Rahman*

Alhamdulillah, I have had many role models of active women in my community as well as in my years at Queen's University. There have also been other women whom I look up to as role models and who taught me the importance of Muslim women being involved in community affairs, as was done by the women at the time of the Prophet (pbuh) and the early Muslims. Sr. Khadija Haffajee, Sr. Aminah Assilmi, and Sr. Ekram Beshir are, *masha'allah,* three role models who have shown my generation, by their example, the importance of sisters' activism within the community, in doing *da'wah,* and, most especially, for standing firm to the principles of Islam as outlined in the Qur'an and Sunnah in our non-Muslim society. Furthermore, it is the consistent and persistent work of sisters such as these, *masha'allah,* that has resulted in the removal of many of the barriers for Muslim women of my generation—things we take for granted today.

Unfortunately, there are many misconceptions regarding women in Islam, their rights, their duties, and indeed even their position, among non-Muslims and even among Muslims themselves. This is why it seems that, throughout the years, no matter what the forum, we always come back to discussing the rights of women in Islam, the myths and misconceptions regarding women in Islam. As high school students, we tried to dispel the myths and educate our classes. In university, every few years, we would invite someone to speak on this topic. Also, it is always dealt with at the various Islamic conferences we attend in North America. This is not surprising, however, as it seems that we are constantly bombarded with these negative stereotypes through the media and, sadly, by the inferior treatment of women in some predominantly Muslim lands in which cultural practices have become intertwined with Islam.

As Muslim women, our *hijab* is like a flag for Islam. Thus, just by being active in the community, in whatever aspect, it implicitly makes people question the stereotypes they may have. For example, I once worked with a summer student in our laboratory who asked me whether women were allowed to have an education in Islam, a question she asked me since she was confused as to how I, who was obviously Muslim and practicing, wearing *hijab,* could be doing my PhD. Thus, I find *hijab* in itself is also an open door for *da'wah,* as it immediately identifies you as a Muslim.

Masha'allah, for the most part, I have not encountered any negative attitudes toward me because of my *hijab.* I once had an elderly person approach me to inquire about the significance of the color of my pink scarf, as he had only ever seen women wear white or black. I responded that the color matched my outfit; this could easily lead to a discussion on the reasoning behind the *hijab.* The visibility of the *hijab* is also a blessing as it serves as a reminder to

Mona Rahman

us, as individuals, of our own behavior. As one of my friends put it, it is like "the weight of the Ummah is on your shoulders," since no matter where we go, people will associate Islam and Muslims with how you behave.

Through the years I have been fortunate to have developed strong bonds of sisterhood with many sisters whom I have met on campus, at conferences, and through work with various organizations. This has also been a source of strength, encouragement, and support as I have been able to share and learn from their experiences. Indeed, as Muslim women, we face unique yet common obstacles which our male counterparts are not exposed to. I have found that having a "sisters space" to retreat to, be it sisters' *halaqas,* social get-togethers, circle of good friends, or a virtual space such as Sisters Net, allows us as Muslim women to nurture these bonds of sisterhood and develop a support structure for each other. Indeed, this is one of the reasons underlying the creation of "Sisters Net" by Sr. Hoda Fahmy in 1992.

Sisters Net is an e-mail network exclusively for Muslim women (although non-Muslim women interested in Islam are also welcome). The main purpose for its creation was to form a support group for Muslim sisters around the world. Indeed, Sr. Hoda formed the network in response to discussions with other women on MSA Net who felt a need for a sisters-only forum to discuss issues they may not feel comfortable discussing on a mixed-gender net. Sisters Net has four goals: (1) to increase our Islamic knowledge, (2) to allow sisters to discuss tribulations, aspirations, and triumphs in an informal manner, (3) to encourage each other to stand up and work for the sake of Allah (swt), and (4) to have fun networking with our fellow sisters. Although Sisters Net was a student-based network at its inception, as e-mail became more popular outside the campus environment, the demographics changed, and the network came to be made up predominantly of non-students. In fact, the first "surge" in membership occurred when its existence was announced by Sr. Sheema Khan during one of her lectures at an ISNA convention in 1994. My experience as Sisters Net administrator, another position I inherited, has enabled me to meet remarkable Muslim women all over the world and I have benefited immensely from their experiences and knowledge.

Alhamdulillah, I feel blessed for the experiences I have had as well as the environments I have been exposed to. My life has been filled, not with obstacles, but doors of opportunity which those around me have opened in my path. Indeed we, as Muslims in North America, are not here by accident; Allah (swt) has a plan. This is something I recently heard at a conference but is also something my father has always said. *Alhamdulillah,* we in North

America have the benefit of living with Muslims who originate from all parts of the world. I have always felt that this has enabled us to more easily separate cultural practices from what is in the Qur'an and Sunnah. Moreover, we often have more freedom to practice our *deen* more completely than in some predominantly Muslim countries. *Subhan'allah,* this is a stark contrast to places like Turkey, where women in *hijab* have been prevented from obtaining a university education and barred from public office, or other places around the world where the rights of women, as decreed by Islam, are ignored. Granted, we must also constantly deal with the ignorance of those within this society about Islam and Muslims, but *insha'allah,* with time and patience, this will change.

I beg Allah's forgiveness if I have erred or misled anyone in any way. Anything good in this essay is from Allah (swt); all mistakes are due to my own weaknesses.

Subhanaka Allahomma wa bihamdik.
Ash-hado an la ilaha illah Ant
Astaghfiroka wa atoobo ilayk.

(Glory and praise be to You, O Allah.
I declare that there is no god but You.
I seek Your forgiveness and repent unto You.)

Mona Rahman

14

Life of a Muslim Woman Activist

Margaret Sabir–Gillette

It is not righteousness That ye turn your faces Towards East or West;
But it is righteousness—To believe in God And the Last Day, And
the Angels And the Book, And the Messengers; To spend of your
substance, Out of love for Him, For your kin, For orphans, For the
needy, For the wayfarer, For those who ask, And for the ransom of
slaves; To be steadfast in prayer, And practice regular charity; To ful-
fil the contracts Which ye have made; And to be firm and patient,
In pain (or suffering) And adversity, And throughout All periods of
panic, Such are the people Of truth, the God-fearing.

(Qur'an 2:177)

I was born to Ethel (Keener) McNair and Daniel McNair March 31, 1934,
in Clayton, Alabama. When I was three, my father decided he had had
enough of sharecropping and moved my mother, my three brothers, and me
to Johnstown, Pennsylvania, where he had previously lived with his first wife
and baby daughter, working for Bethlehem Steel Corporation. (His first
wife later became ill and died, and my half-sister was raised in Youngstown,
Ohio, by her foster mother.) I graduated from Johnstown High School in
1952, married Donald Gillette in 1953, and subsequently moved to Buffalo,
New York, in 1955, where my husband had family.

The members of my family were very devout Christians and we grew up
regularly attending Sunday school and church services at Mount Sinai Baptist

church in Johnstown, where my father served as a deacon and my mother was involved in missionary work and taught Sunday school. From the time we were very young, my mother strongly encouraged us to work in the church and in the community, and to assist others less fortunate than ourselves. She baked, cooked, and canned, and we fed people in the community regularly. We learned to be especially kind to the elderly and to respect and revere them. My brothers and I would run errands, wash dishes, and do whatever chores we could to assist the seniors. Our mother also taught us to study hard, read, and to do our best at whatever we became involved in. As a child, I was very involved in church, school, and community programs. My activities included singing in the church choir and in an interdenominational choir, serving as an usher, and speaking at church and community programs on requested topics, as well as singing and participating in school, where many times I was the only minority present.

My father, as a young man, had been a follower of the Marcus Garvey movement and was keenly interested in African culture and history. He read every black newspaper he could get his hands on, and had a volume of books by J. A. Rogers that he taught us from. My sister and her husband joined the Ahmadeya movement of Islam in the early fifties in Youngstown, where they resided. My father was very intrigued, and he and his son-in-law had many conversations about the religion. I think this was a conduit for my father's later interest in learning more about the late Elijah Muhammad from a column that he wrote in the *Pittsburgh Courier* in the mid-1950s. My father wrote to him to ask if there was a place of worship nearby; the answer was no. When a temple finally opened in Pittsburgh in 1957, under the leadership of Minister Robert X (now Imam Mustafa Hussein), my father and brother attended, and they accepted the religion of Islam as taught by Elijah Muhammad (leader of the Nation of Islam, who claimed to be a Messenger of Allah).

Shortly after this, my father began attending the temple in Pittsburgh. He visited my family in Buffalo and invited us to attend Temple No. 23 there to listen to this "new religion." My husband embraced the teaching immediately. It took me another six months of attending the services and listening to the lectures to make up my mind to leave Saint John Baptist church that I had attended since arriving in Buffalo. I was reluctant to leave, since I had made friends and sang in two choirs and was very active in the church. I think one of the persuasive factors for me was the fact that Malcolm X visited Buffalo regularly at that time to lecture at the temple, and his presentations helped me to make up my mind to embrace the religion as practiced by the Nation of Islam.

I became very involved, serving for a time as Lieutenant of the MGT-GCC (Muslim Girl's Training and General Civilization Class). I had the honor of meeting with Elijah Muhammad on a Savior's Day trip to Chicago and discussing the role of leadership in the women's class. The meeting with Elijah Muhammad remains a very memorable event in my life, and I left Chicago very impressed with this great man. When I was introduced to him, I was fumbling for words to express myself; he looked at me, smiled, and said, "Sister, I am your humble servant." Today when I listen to his son, Imam W. Deen Mohammed, who is so wise and so adept at teaching the religion of Al-Islam, I feel the same humbleness.

In 1975, when Elijah Muhammad died, his son, Minister Wallace D. Muhammad, became the leader of the organization. He changed the direction of the movement to coincide with the universal teachings of Islam followed by Muslims all around the world. We had been taught, in the Nation of Islam, that God was a man and that the black race was superior. There was no life after death and we didn't observe *jumu'ah* prayer on Friday. The universal way of Islam teaches us that God cannot be a man, that the Holy Qur'an is our daily guide to live by, and that the Prophet Mohammed (pbuh) is the last (or seal) of the prophets, the one whose example we should follow. My entire family, with the exception of my oldest brother, John, who had left the temple, made the transition. My brothers chose a new family name for the Muslim members to reflect this transition. They chose "Sabir" because our father was a very patient, peaceful man.

My father died on January 1, 1962, and my mother moved to Buffalo that year. My brother Eaustria Sabir and his family moved to Youngstown from Johnstown in March 1967. My sister's husband died in 1960, and before my father died, he instructed Eaustria to help my sister and her seven children. Although my sister, Selmeyyah Muwallif, never embraced the Nation of Islam (she and her late husband had embraced Islam in the early 1950s, becoming inactive after some years but remaining true to the teachings of the religion), her twin sons, Ali and Akmal, had embraced it and worked very closely with their uncle. After the transition in 1975, my sister also worked diligently in the Muslim community in Youngstown. My youngest brother, Wali, who had lived in Buffalo for many years, moved to Youngstown and later became the first family member to start a "migration to the South," when he moved to Atlanta, Georgia, in 1976.

My husband and I had two sons, Donald and Harry, and two daughters, Donalyn and Kristal. Harry died in 1975 at age fourteen from very severe asthma. (Donalyn was born when my older son, Donald, was a senior in high school in May 1974 and Kristal came four years later. They all live and work now in Atlanta.) When the boys were young, I spent most of my time working in the temple and caring for them as they both had serious problems with asthma. I participated in an educational group for asthma and served as president for several years. We promoted educational programs, lobbied the county legislature to pass a bill that would allow state aid for children with severe asthma, obtained discounts at local drug stores, and loaned various machines to families for use at home when their children had problems. This group operated under the Allergy Foundation of America. In 1973, just before the American Lung Association opened an office in Buffalo, the new director visited me and asked me if I would work with them. I was active for many years working with the Family Asthma Program and serving on the Education and Diversity Committee, helping to promote appropriate asthma educational programs in the inner city. I made several appearances on local television shows about asthma and spoke to community groups on the topic.

After working various jobs, I attended Bryant and Stratton Business School and became employed at the State University of New York at Buffalo (UB) in September 1970. In August 1970 our younger son was sent to Denver, Colorado, to live in a special rehabilitation center for severe asthmatic children (CARIH, or the Children's Asthma Research Institute and Hospital). A group of Jewish women involved in fund-raising for CARIH enlisted my assistance to help their members as well as the local public understand the importance of their donating to this world-renowned institute.

At the university, I acted as a liaison between the Black Studies (later changed to African American Studies) Department and the wider community. I organized university-community programs that involved working with the Black Student Union, the Muslim Student Association, and the Minority Faculty and Staff Association. I always feel wonderfully blessed to have been able to work with so many young people, some of whom I work with in the community as program directors and elected officials. I also organized a number of women on campus to work with minority student affairs as well as with the community. This group, consisting of faculty, staff, and administrators, was known as UB Black Women and was later changed to African American Women at UB. I also served as president of the STEP (Science, Technology Enrichment Program) Parent Association for

Margaret Sabir-Gillette and Oswaldo Mestre Jr.,
director of Buffalo Weed and Seed, outside the
front door of the ILMW Community Center.
Photo courtesy of Margaret Sabir-Gillette

five years. STEP is an afterschool enrichment
program at the university. I retired from the
university in June 1994 after my younger daughter, who was diagnosed
with lupus in 1993, became very ill and needed my full attention.

In 1991, I began volunteering at VIVE LaCasa, which is a temporary
shelter for refugees and immigrants who are waiting to migrate to Canada.
My involvement included taking people to the *masjid* for services, providing adequate clothing to the women when needed, taking them shopping,
providing social outlets, and bringing other Muslims to visit them. For
several years, there were many Somali families at VIVE waiting for their
paperwork to be processed for entry into Canada. Sometimes I would take
the women and children to visit Somali families living in Buffalo or take
Somali families to visit VIVE. If there were problems, I would be called to
help solve them. Immediately after September 11, 2001, VIVE was full
beyond capacity because people were being detained much longer at the
Canadian border. Our organization sent volunteers to help out with paperwork, doing crafts with the children and donating needed supplies. I still
work with this facility and recently met with the new director to discuss ways
we could be more helpful to their staff—helping to attend to the needs of
the Muslim refugees who are temporarily housed there.

In April 1993, I initiated the organization of the Buffalo chapter of the
International League of Muslim Women (ILMW). This organization was
started by seven Muslim women in Detroit, Michigan, in 1981, who felt a
need to assist needy individuals and families. It was a single unit for many
years. Currently there are four chapter affiliates in Africa and twenty-five in
the United States. The Buffalo chapter hosted a very successful annual conference in June 2001.

A house was donated to the organization by a local citizen in 1997 that
is currently being used as office space and as storage space for clothing, furniture, and household items for donations, as well as meeting space for
community meetings and tutoring for youth on the street. The sisters in the
league are thankful for the blessing of this house. We have become an integral part of the neighborhood and the wider community that we serve.

On a typical day I might get a call from Khadija, who has been in Buffalo longer than the other families, to tell me that a woman whose husband was killed in the war and her seven children can't drink milk because their refrigerator is broken. I will then make an appointment to have a service man (one authorized by social services) to go to the home and look at the refrigerator. If it can't be repaired, she will get the proper documentation. I will then get the paperwork to her social worker, who will issue a voucher to have the refrigerator replaced. I will take her to a few places on the list supplied by the social worker to choose another refrigerator and arrange to have it delivered. A fax might come in from the United Way listing furniture, household, or clothing donations. I will call to say I am interested. The United Way will supply the name and telephone number of the donor and I will call to set up a time to pick up the donations. Sometimes I can get the items in my car, or a volunteer will provide a pickup truck; other times we will have to rent a U-Haul truck, get a volunteer to drive it, and get others to help lift the furniture and deliver it to the families in need. There have been times when one of our members has even driven the truck.

I might get a call that there are problems in school; I will go to the school to meet with teachers, principals, and parents to try to solve the problems. A big problem is people not being able to read correspondence that is received, which sometimes results in welfare benefits being temporarily suspended because the person did not come to an appointment or respond to information that needed to be sent to a social worker. The neighbors will call to enlist assistance in obtaining help for their children in school, a obtaining a recommendation letter for a job, requesting the councilman's office to put up a "no loitering" sign on the street (this was recently done), or to have a letter typed or a fax sent out.

A call from the Western New York Peace Center came requesting assistance in obtaining information about celebrations for Martin Luther King Day and how they could become involved. After a few telephone calls, arrangements were made with the program director at the Martin Luther King Urban Life Center to forward an announcement to the appropriate person. I also suggested that some collaboration between the two entities would probably be beneficial to both groups.

Some days volunteers will come in to sort donations from local colleges or help in the office, and often people will bring donations of food, clothing, and sometimes money because they have heard that we help the needy. A telephone call might come from the nursing home to request assistance for the Muslim senior sister who has no family in Buffalo. The president of the New York City chapter calls to say she is having problems obtaining their "articles of incorporation" and it has been returned from Albany. The information is faxed to the office in Buffalo. Upon discussing the issue with a representative in Albany, I am told that things have changed a lot since the Buffalo chapter obtained their articles of incorporation in 1994. She is very helpful and the necessary adjustments are made to the document submitted by the New York chapter.

A very recent call came from a woman who has a television program; she asked me to bring another Muslim woman to tape a show on Islam. She is particularly interested in hearing about Muslim women, because she says she always sees the men in the newspaper and the television and wonders what the women do and think. An appointment has been made to do the taping. The show was aired on public television and received favorable comments.

The ILMW has formed an association with Neighborhood Legal Services, who have been wonderful about representing Muslim clients. In addition, some of the local elected officials and personnel who work with youth have assisted in helping to obtain jobs for Muslim youth in the summer. We have taught them about getting physical exams, taken them to City Hall to get working papers, driven them to offices for interviews, coached them on what to say and what not to say, and sometimes driven them to the work site the day before and checked bus schedules so they will get to work on time.

Transportation is always a big problem, and it would help if we had a van. We are trying to find a way to involve some of the refugee youth in a tutoring program that we currently have for youth on the street. We are also setting up some meetings with some of the teenage male youth to meet with men in the community who can serve as mentors, as many of these youth have lost their fathers in the war and we hope that positive interaction with Muslim men in the community will help to keep them on the right path. We have had several workshops for the girls and even for the women, but we have never focused on the teen males.

The International League of Muslim Women was approved as a welfare-to-work training site, and I have worked with several young women for three years, including one refugee woman whom they were not able to place anywhere else. Buffalo Weed and Seed collaborates with the organization and helps with the programs and functions that serve the youth in the community. Last summer we had a community garden, and flowers and vegetables were planted by youth volunteers. This summer, *insha'allah,* we hope to

expand this effort. A food pantry has been talked about for some time and we hope this can become a reality this year.

The ILMW collaborates with the United Way of Buffalo and Erie County, United Neighborhoods, local elected officials, and community groups. As president of the ILMW, I have been invited to meet with elected representatives from Washington, D.C., as well as the FBI, when they meet with Muslim leaders in the community to discuss issues of concern that have arisen since September 11, 2001.

A large part of my time is spent in refugee resettlement assistance for primarily Somali families who don't receive services from the organizations that brought them here. This involves taking them to social services, helping with problems that arise in school, unraveling complex medical problems because of misunderstanding on the part of the clients, and so forth. I also get involved with landlords that sometimes take advantage of families, and work with city and county health inspectors because families are often moved into substandard housing. We provide furniture and household items through in-kind donations received through the United Way. We provide new and used clothing to refugees as well as to groups such as Hispanics United, Everywoman's Opportunity Center, and other clients as recommended to us from time to time.

The refugee assistance work has become very demanding, and my telephone rings even on weekends because people are seeking assistance with various problems. Sometimes letters and other documents need to be read because even if there are young people in the house who can read English, they still might not understand what a letter means. I have utilized the services of Neighborhood Legal Services to help refugee families with various problems they face from time to time. We have organized workshops and seminars on health issues and criteria for becoming a citizen, and we have obtained working papers and summer jobs for the past five years for numerous Somali youth.

I have organized picnics, skating parties, trips to the science museum, and other social activities for the youth. I have recently been asked to serve on a newly formed committee for refugees and immigrants for the Buffalo

Prenatal/Perinatal Task Force. This is an organization that tries to ensure that all women (particularly the underserved population) receive adequate prenatal care.

Our international president of ILMW, Sahirah Muhammad, became a court-appointed special advocate for children in Detroit several years ago. She has strongly encouraged all chapters who have the organization CASA (Court Appointed Special Advocate-Voices for Children) in their cities to become trained also. I completed training to become a CASA volunteer in May 2002. As trained advocates, volunteers are appointed by family court judges to be a voice for children whose parents are involved in neglect and/or abuse cases. Volunteers work with attorneys and social workers. They review records and research information, talk to everyone involved—parents, teachers, family members, and of course the child. From this information, the CASA coordinators present a recommendation to the judge as to what is best for the child. With this information, judges are able to make informed decisions on foster care, reunification with families, or adoption. As most of the focus is put on getting the parents back on the right track, it is all too easy for children to become lost in an overburdened child welfare system in which no one has sufficient time to devote to their best interest. So the job of CASA volunteers is to make sure that the needs of the children are met and that they are getting the best care possible.

In addition to serving as president of the Buffalo chapter of ILMW, I am a special assistant to the international president, Sahirah Muhammad. My role involves setting up new chapters in the Northeast region, monitoring these and existing chapters, and helping in any other area the president feels that I need to be involved. I organized a chapter of ILMW in Syracuse, New York, in February 2002, which is a very active chapter. I am in constant communication with the president of the New York City chapter, which is less than one year old. One special assistant has been appointed for the Southern region, Deborah Abdur-Rahim, and we collaborate often with the president and each other.

I also serve on the boards and committees of many organizations: the Weed and Seed Steering Committee; the Citizen's Advisory Committee to the Police Commissioner; the Toxic Waste/Lupus Committee; the Policy Committee for Hunger; and the Faith-Based Committee on Domestic Violence. In addition, I have been a volunteer for the Lupus Alliance for several years, which involves talking to groups about lupus and participating in health fairs at churches, schools, and community buildings. I am serving a second two-year term as first vice-president of the western New York chapter of the American Muslim Council. As a member of the American Society of Muslims (ASM) under the leadership of Imam W. Deen Mohammad, I serve on the Family Life Committee of the monitoring team. We participate in the annual convention held each Labor Day weekend in Chicago. At Masjid Nu'Man, where I currently attend religious services, I served for several years as coordinator of sisters' programs and as secretary of the board of directors, as well as working closely with the imam.

In 1999 I was selected as the outstanding adult volunteer for the city of Buffalo; $1,000 was donated to ILMW in my name, and I received a crystal sculpture and a gold-plated plaque. J. C. Penney sponsored this Golden Rule Award. I have also received awards from the African American Studies Department at the State University of New York at Buffalo, Masjid Nu'Man, the Common Council of Buffalo, the American Lung Association, the Lupus Foundation of American, the Minority Students' Association of the State University of New York at Buffalo, the Western New York Peace Center, Buffalo Weed and Seed, and STEP at the State University of New York at Buffalo, as well as proclamations from the Buffalo Common Council and the American Cancer Society. On April 30, 2004, I was keynote speaker for Daemen College's Service Learning Department's award ceremony and was presented with an award for working with some of their students. Two of the students wrote papers on Islam and the roles of Muslim women.

Since September 11, 2001, I have been asked to speak at local churches and other groups about Islam and particularly the role of women in Islam. I recently participated in a program at a local church given by Church Women United. The title was "Daughters of Abraham Called to Peace." I was pleasantly surprised afterward when several women approached me and thanked me for enlightening them about the role of women in Islam and made comments such as, "We didn't know women in Islam were held in such high esteem."

Although I sometimes get tired when I am involved in many of the projects I do, it is always a wonderful feeling to know that you have helped someone in your endeavors. I recently organized a local effort called "Thanksgiving Action against Hunger" as a part of an initiative of New York Action against Hunger. This effort was to raise the awareness that hunger exists in New York State for many people and that some changes need to be made to address this issue. I enlisted the aid of Somali youth to come to the league house and pack 130 bag lunches, which another member, Judarah Hassan, and I carried to a soup kitchen the following day and passed out to the people who came to eat their lunch as they left. In addition, we helped prepare food to be used for Thanksgiving dinner. I feel very strongly that, as Muslims, we should be involved in these kinds of efforts at times other than Ramadan. The need is there all year long.

People sometimes ask me where I get all of the energy to do the things that I do, and often they don't understand why I do these things. I just know that when I see people suffering, it bothers me. Even when I read stories in the paper about a young mother who can't manage to take care of her children, or a senior citizen who has been abused or neglected, I just want to do something about it, even though I don't know them. It is very hard to explain, but sometimes I wake up in the middle of the night and lie in bed just thinking about how things could be better and what we might do to make things easier in the lives of people who can't help themselves. I believe that Allah gives me strength to do the things that I do, and it is my way of thanking Allah for blessing me and my family. I also feel it helps to "pay the debt" for all of the people in my life who helped me when my children were ill and when my son passed away.

I sat in the hospital room a week before I wrote this essay with a Somali woman and her children, and I wanted to burst into tears when I saw that her children were not adequately dressed for the cold weather. I knew it was not because she was a bad mother, but because she didn't know that heavier clothing was needed for a cold day. I spent the next few days working on a way to get underwear and stockings for these children. This same woman is living in a house with a kitchen window that doesn't close and the landlord has been promising to fix it. So I know that, as I have done many times before, I will need to take my camera and photograph it and report it to the proper authorities in order to get him to fix it.

People say to me, "What would they do if you were not here?" My reply is, "But I am here, and when I know about a problem, I am going to try to do something about it. My conscience won't let me rest if I don't." Sometimes I can't get to everyone who needs my help right away, and there are others I can call on to help, such as league member Leta Mussa and her children Kai and Timothy, who I rely on to assist with refugee problems. I find that there are people in the community who sometimes don't do things because they are not aware of the conditions of the refugee population. I have learned to rely on collaboration with groups such as Urban Christian Ministries, AmeriCorp volunteers, the United Way, the Western New York Peace Center, and several local Muslim organizations, as well as people that I work with on various boards and committees, such as Oswaldo Mestre, Jr., director of Buffalo Weed and Seed, and individual Muslims and non-Muslims. I am very blessed to have a few very dedicated and talented Muslim and Christian friends who have worked closely with me for many years and whose support I can always depend on. I also appreciate the support and assistance of my husband and children. My two grandchildren, Terrian Gillette (age twenty-five, living in Charlotte, North Carolina) and Darius Gillette (age thirteen, living in Atlanta), have also added to the richness and fullness of my life.

I truly thank Allah for allowing me to do this work in the community. I also thank my mother for teaching me the importance of serving others. I believe that we are obligated to do more than just attend the *masjid* for service on Friday and read the Qur'an and pray. I know that all of these things are important and necessary, but as a Muslim I feel the need to do more. I do look forward to reading the Qur'an and to attending a Sunday morning Arabic class at the *masjid*. Studying the life of Prophet Mohammed (pbuh) only reinforces my belief that we should strive every day of our life to do some kind of good deed. It never ceases to amaze me how good it makes you feel to see a child's eyes light up for even a small kindness or the very humble feeling that you get when you walk into the house of a woman who has no one else to turn to, hugs you sincerely, and says "thank you Ma Margaret." Often just by making a few telephone calls, you can make a difference in her life. It truly makes you appreciate the fact that even though you have had trials and tribulations in your life, your children and your grandson have all graduated from college and are working, and doing well, and they all are volunteers in their respective communities. Allah has blessed your mother to live to the age of ninety-eight years old and still be able to function normally until three months before her death on January 15, 2004. You are thankful that your siblings are all living and that your youngest brother is now a "senior citizen." I am also thankful to Allah for a family that keeps growing (I had six great-great nieces and nephews born in 2002). Our family has traveled, prayed, worshiped, and worked together. We can count five generations of Muslims among the family members, many who are active in their respective communities. In 2003, my brother Eaustria completed a successful pilgrimage to Mecca—the first one in our family to do so.

Working in the community has afforded me the opportunity to participate many times as the only Muslim, the only Muslim woman, and sometimes the only African American Muslim woman in many activities that I get involved in. Imam W. Deen Mohammed teaches us that this is a wonderful time to be Muslim and that America is a good place for us. There is an increasing effort for Muslim men, as well as women, to be involved in the uplifting of humanity and in trying to make our communities a better place to live in for all humankind. I know that you can work in the community and preserve your dignity as a Muslim woman. I believe one of the best ways we can promote our religion is to live our life as righteous Muslims by sincerely practicing what our Prophet Muhammad *(pbuh)* said—of "wanting for our brothers and sisters what we want for ourselves."

Margaret Sabir-Gillette

15

Muslim Activist
Mother and Educator

Freda Shamma

I was a typical white, Anglo-Saxon Protestant (WASP), born and raised in a small town in northern California. My ancestors fought in the American Revolution and the Civil War. They traveled to Missouri in a covered wagon and settled there as farmers, storekeepers, teachers, and upright churchgoing members of their communities. Their children, me included, assumed they should be moral, active citizens as well.

By the time I was five I knew that I wanted to be a teacher. When I declared my Islamic identity some twenty years later, I still wanted to be active in education, but now my focus was Islamic education. Religion had been our favorite topic of discussion, so once I declared my Islam (in 1969, after two years of marriage), my husband encouraged me to continue my education, focusing on the needs of Muslim children. I am very blessed in my husband. He himself has always been willing to help in furthering Islamic endeavors, and he expected me to also be active in Islamic activities once I became Muslim. He has always been supportive of me when I wanted to be active, and has spent additional time with the children when that was needed.

It is one thing to read about Islam and how a Muslim should act. It is difficult to translate that brain work into physical reality. My husband showed me how to integrate Islam into one's family life, but it took a move to Indianapolis in the mid-1970s for me to understand how a Muslim society should be. We moved there so my husband could work full time for the Muslim Students' Association (MSA). The ethnic mix of the MSA was diverse, with no nationality predominating. If anyone was sick, everyone soon knew about it, and food was provided, child care was made available, rides to the doctor were given, and other needs were met. It was there that I learned about Muslim sisterhood. I needed someone to babysit my children while I studied. An Iraqi sister that I hardly knew offered to take care of my baby because she already had two small daughters at home. At the end of the first month when I tried to pay her, she got *very* upset with me. Wasn't I her Muslim sister? Then why was I insulting her by trying to pay! Then I blundered on to my Egyptian friend's house to pick up my other children. I knew better than to offer to pay her for her help, but to my amazement she invited us for dinner. "How can you feed three or four extra people without notice?" I asked. "Come see," she smiled. "I've got two pots of food on the stove. There's plenty for everyone who comes." At first I took, took, and took from this community. Then I discovered that I had something to give as well. I had a station wagon and knew how to entertain children, so I picked up all the children that could fit and we went wherever the children would have fun. It was in this community that I discovered that the Islamic social system works perfectly for everyone's benefit, as long as each person does whatever he/she can, for the sake of Allah, without regard to social standing, ethnic background, or personal gain.

A Sudanese sister was an activist in that community who always remained behind the scenes. I don't believe she was ever "in charge" of any activity, never a speaker or chair of any committee. Her husband was working full time for the MSA/Islamic Society of North America (ISNA), and because of his generosity and the constant flow of visitors to the ISNA offices, he was always bringing home unexpected guests for lunch and/or dinner. This meant that with half an hour's notice (at most), she was expected to prepare a full lunch and/or dinner for as many as a dozen extra people, and she still had to clean house and care for five children at the same time. I was commiserating with her one time, since I couldn't imagine being able to do this on a regular basis. Her response? She regularly gave thanks to Allah that she was able to contribute to *fisabeelillah* (for the sake of Allah) in this way. Every meal she prepared was done with the same spirit of generosity and dedication to Allah. This was her contribution to Islamic work. Many wives of active Islamic workers prepare meals for unexpected guests, but how many do it with the right intention? She never expected any recognition for her service; it was done to please Allah. Later, necessity forced her to seek employment outside her home. She began working as a secretary for a Muslim organization, and until today she is still involved in this capacity. She is indispensable for the organization because she is the recorder and memory of the organization. Others come and go, but she is the backbone, the one who brings order and smooth transition from one phase to another. And yet, if you visit the office, you will not be aware of her work or her importance because she demonstrates no attitude of superiority, no unwillingness to do even the lowliest task. She is "simply" a Muslim doing her best. She and the late Joyce Partomah, may Allah bless her soul, were silent activists, doing whatever needed doing that was in their power to do, without expectation of earthly recognition or reward. I am so grateful to Allah, and so appreciative of them for what they taught me about living as part of the Muslim *ummah*.

Joyce Partomah was a white American Muslim. She was so quiet and unassuming that it took me a number of years to get to know her well. We attended the same Arab Muslim camp one summer. There were three or four of us who didn't know Arabic so we weren't attending any sessions. Joyce spent this free time teaching some of the sisters how to drive. It hadn't even occurred to me to spend this time wisely, much less use it to help someone. When I mentioned it to her, she told me that she felt that she wasn't contributing in any other way, and so thought that she could help in this way. This made me laugh because to me it was obvious that she had been contributing significantly for years, but this modesty was part of her character. Several years earlier her husband had been president of the Muslim Students' Association. I didn't know them at the time, but was very impressed by the activities of this president. There was regular correspondence between him and the MSA members. Conferences and meetings were well planned and well announced. I wondered why he was so much better at the job than others before and after him. Joyce was a contributing factor. She was the one who did most of the typing and organizing. She never claimed any credit, and she never received any, but she was the first female Muslim activist that I knew. May Allah bless her soul. She and the sisters in Indianapolis clearly demonstrated to me how many ways it is possible to be active in Islamic work.

It is not always easy to become active in the Muslim community. Before we moved to Indianapolis I had offered to teach in our weekend school in Cincinnati. The community declined my offer because they felt that I, as a new Muslim, didn't know enough. I was upset at the time, but later realized

Freda Shamma

that they were quite correct. When my husband agreed to be in charge of the MSA annual convention (1970, I think), to be held in a Green Lake, Wisconsin, campground, I volunteered to do the children's program. I knew about children and about teaching, but I didn't know much about Islam as I was still rather new to the religion, and I had no idea what these children would already know. To be safe, we focused on the five pillars. Due to simplistic, repetitive programs like this over time, the youth soon complained that they could make a better program for themselves, and the idea of MYNA (Muslim Youth of North America) was advanced. Although my attempts to plan for the youth were inadequate, I did contribute to the success of MYNA in that my children all became active in it. My second child, Noura, fought her way into the original group of fifteen- to eighteen-year-olds (she was thirteen) with the argument that she was a future MYNA member and thus she should be able to give input even if she was underage! My oldest child, Riyad, waited a year to join—until he found out that MYNA activities included lots of recreation and sports. He has since "redeemed" himself by serving as their adult national advisor.

My next attempt to be active in the field of Islamic education was to agree to be the chairwoman of the MSA Education Committee. When I joined the Muslim Students' Association in 1967, almost everyone was a university student with few or no children. Even so, as early as 1970, education of children became a stated priority, although for years it was all talk and no action. With limited financial resources, the MSA focused its energies on campus MSA organizations, internal administration, and Islamic education of its members, rather than their children.

When I called for a meeting of the MSA Education Committee at the annual convention in the early 1970s, about eight people attended, and all agreed that they would be active on the committee. I spent the entire year writing letters to these people without any success. There was no one else in my local community who was interested in helping, and I didn't know enough about Islamic education, nor did I know any other people who could help. I was most probably the least effective chairperson that committee has ever had. I had good intentions but was "clueless" as to how to proceed.

So I'd been rejected as a teacher, and I'd failed as a children's program organizer and as an education committee chairperson. Did I quit? I remembered that Allah says we are held responsible for our intentions, for our trying. We are not held accountable for our successes or failures. So I continued.

At my husband's suggestion I went back to the university to work on my doctorate in education, one or two courses at a time, because I was now the mother of two and later three children. As a fairly new convert (or "revert") to Islam, I was aware of my lack of knowledge and wanted to attend classes to learn more about Islam. I talked to others new to Islam and we started a study group. I remember asking the Muslim-born women of the community to join us. All refused, but one sister's response has stuck in my mind. "Oh, I know all about my religion," she explained to me. "I don't need to come to a study group."

"You are exactly the person we need," I exclaimed enthusiastically. "None of the rest of us know much about our religion, so we need you to come teach us!"

"Oh, no!" she protested. "I don't know enough about my religion to teach!" Remembering this scene always makes me laugh at its inherent contradiction, but it is unfortunately an all too common feeling among both immigrant and local Muslims that a basic knowledge of the required rituals is all that is necessary.

I also bought every Islamic book written in English that came my way. At first it was difficult to find books as there was no Islamic publishing company in the English-speaking world, and no American publishing company would publish books written by Muslims. The MSA quickly realized the serious lack of available Islamic literature in English and started its own printing press, International Graphics. One of its first scholarly printings was of the late Dr. Isma'il al Faruqi's (may Allah bless his soul) translation of *The Life of Muhammad,* by Muhammad Husayn Haykal, in 1976. I was honored to be one of the proofreaders for this book.

At the MSA convention in 1970, an announcement was made that a new group was being formed, the Association of Muslim Social Scientists (AMSS), and they would be having their first meeting that afternoon. I attended along with perhaps fifteen others, all male. The low attendance by sisters proved to be a pattern; I was one of only a few sisters who began attending their annual conferences. I was asked to present a paper in 1974 on Islamic education at the AMSS conference in Indianapolis. Since there was no babysitting, I left my two young children with friends in Cincinnati, where we were living, and planned to drive the two hours there, present my paper in the afternoon, and drive back that evening. The program was suddenly changed so that I was to present in the evening, and I was unable to return home until the next morning. It bothered me a great deal that I was leaving my children for over twenty-four hours, because they were my priority, not

Freda Shamma, May 2003.
*Photo courtesy of
Freda Shamma*

delivering this paper. I asked the president of the AMSS why they didn't provide babysitting, and he replied that this was a scholarly gathering and no place for children. Since most MSA/AMSS women were also mothers of young children, that explained why there were so few women attending the conferences. One brother asked me what they could do to encourage more women to take an active part in the AMSS programs. Guess what I suggested!

A year or so later the AMSS announced that they were having a meeting to discuss education, to be held in Philadelphia. The word "education" of course caught my attention, so my husband agreed to take care of our children while I attended the meeting. Not only was I the only woman present, but I was the only one there who wanted to discuss elementary and secondary education. Everyone else was focused on the idea of establishing an Islamic university. When I voiced the opinion that our focus really should be on the education of younger students, the chairman of the meeting, the late Dr. Isma'il al Faruqi, may Allah bless his soul, responded with, "That's fine. You be in charge of establishing an Islamic elementary school, and we'll focus on the university." Well, they did focus, and the International Islamic Universities in Malaysia and Pakistan are a direct result of their focus. I went home and raised my five children.

Raising children is a full-time job. When I had one child, I worked at it full time. When the next four children came along, it continued to be a full-time-plus job. As I look back on the 1970s and 1980s, I see that certain aspects of child raising were especially important to my husband and me. One of the most important jobs of Muslim parents is to immerse their children in an Islamic environment. We tried to implement Islam in every aspect of their lives. We made a point of referring to Allah and Islam throughout the day. When my children watched television I watched it with them, making casual comments on the Islamic perspective toward the incidents portrayed. When the children were old enough to watch undesirable shows, their father and I offered videotapes that we considered more along Islamic principles. We did whatever was necessary to make sure our children had good Muslim friends. That meant going outside of our own ethnicity. We made friends with people because they had children who practiced

Islamic behavior, not on the basis of whether they were Egyptian, like my husband, or American, like me. Many times our children struggled and suffered as ethnically oriented parents would invite only children of their own ethnicity. Sometimes our children rebelled. "I'm not going to invite those kids [a particular ethnicity] because they never invite me to their house!" (Our response was, if you don't invite all the Muslim children your age, then you don't have the party.) Due to the lack of Muslim friends in town for our children, we tried to attend every MSA/ISNA convention so our children could find Muslim friends elsewhere. Attending the ISNA conventions also helped fill the void of absent families. Being surrounded by Muslims, many of whom we have known for years, gives us a feeling of family. Our children aren't able to be close to their own cousins, but they find an *ummah* (community) of brothers and sisters at ISNA (where MYNA has its annual national meeting also). We have been advisors, workshop leaders, transportation providers, parental presence, and whatever else was necessary for our children to be able to go to MYNA activities, including camps and conferences. We took charge of 'Eid parties at the *masjid,* and Muslim parties at our house. We took part in the administration of our *masjid* affairs and contributed our utmost to the weekend school program. Along the way we noticed a very nice fringe benefit—our children had no racial or national prejudices! When I asked my five-year-old to describe his best friend at his new school, he was puzzled. "What color is his hair, what color is his skin?" (I wanted to make sure he was not just making friends with his own racial group.) He told me, "He looks just like me." I was worried until I saw the child with his black curly hair and dark skin. The only looks they had in common were their size and their big smiles as they saw each other.

From 1972 until 1980 I was a stay-at-home mother and a part-time student working on my doctorate. Every year at the AMSS annual convention I would meet Nuri Alam, one of the few women attending this scholarly organization on a regular basis. "Have you finished your PhD yet?" she would ask each year. "No, I'm still working on it," I would reply. It got to be quite a joke, with each year's, "No, not yet" answer. Finally I finished and was anxious to see Nuri at the next convention. I saw her; we talked; she never asked the question. Finally I couldn't take it any longer. "Why don't you ask me how my dissertation is coming?" "Oh," she replied, "After ten years it was getting too embarrassing to hear you say 'not yet!'" and we had a good laugh about it. After getting my doctorate in education in 1980, I put my degree "on the shelf" and continued to raise my children as best as I could. Meanwhile, the AMSS has made a concerted effort to include more women in its activities, and this has borne fruit. By the 1990s, there were many dynamic Muslim women scholars present.[1]

One of the most often repeated words in the Qur'an is *sabr*, patience. So many times during those years did I regret not being able to do anything of real value in the area of Islamic education. I remember visiting in the early 1980s with the late Dr. Lamya al Faruqi. She was a scholar of Islamic art and author of many books on Islamic topics who was murdered in her home in the month of Ramadan, 1986, along with her husband, Dr. Isma'il al Faruqi, may Allah bless their souls. I lamented to her that while she had contributed so much, I had contributed almost nothing. I'll always remember what she answered. She said she hadn't contributed anything while she was raising her children, but now her youngest was in high school and she had the time and opportunity to work on Islamic causes. Thanks to her example, I became more patient. When people exclaimed in shock, "You have a doctorate and you're a stay-at-home mother! Why are you wasting your degree?" I calmly replied that I was not wasting it; I was using the knowledge to do a better job of raising my children, *insha'allah.* I went on to say that after they were grown, I would "take the degree off the shelf, wipe the dust off of it, and proceed to use it." *Alhamdulillah,* I was able to do exactly that.

In 1979 my family and I moved to Riyadh, Saudi Arabia, where we lived for five wonderful years. In Riyadh I started an English-speaking *halaqa* (study group) since there were none in our area. I was also able to write my dissertation and returned to Cincinnati in the summer of 1980 to defend it. The topic was designing an Islamic multicultural social studies course of study. This was the second of my three attempts to design a curriculum for Islamic schools. My first attempt was back in 1973. I had taken a local curriculum as a guide and made an attempt to Islamize it. After writing a segment of it, I asked the MSA education chairman, Dr. Mahmoud Rashdan, to read it, which he kindly did. Later I asked him how he liked it. "It's very nice," he replied politely, "but you know it's not Islamic." He went on to explain that my entire curriculum was focused on the individual and individualized instruction, while in the Islamic ideology, the family is the center of society, not the individual.

Five or six years later, while working toward my doctorate, I was able to take three courses on Islam, via correspondence, with Dr. Isma'il al Faruqi at Temple University in Philadelphia. He continued where Dr. Rashdan had left off. It is necessary to start with an Islamic framework, he maintained.

After establishing the Islamic parameters, then look at American education and see where it fits into the Islamic model, not vice versa, as I had done before. The Islamic framework included the underlying concept that Allah has created us to be His vicegerents on earth. He has given us minds so that we can learn how to come closer to Him, and how to act as His vicegerent. In history, for example, we start with the Qur'anic injunction to study the peoples of the past in order to learn from their mistakes.

I tried to take this advice while developing a social studies curriculum for the Manaret Al Riyadh English medium school in Riyadh. Having a general idea of the Islamic framework was necessary, but unfortunately not sufficient, and this curriculum was also unsuccessful. I had access to school administration, teachers, parents, and students, but due to the fact that I couldn't speak or read Arabic, I had no access to Islamic scholars or scholarly works about the Islamic parameters and concepts of history. Another problem was related to the school administration, which didn't realize the importance of knowing more than you will teach the students. There was no school library, even for teachers. The result reflected the needs and wants of the school population, but it was not based on Islamic principles of history (such as the role of cause-and-effect or the spiral progression of a people).

By 1995, when our family moved from Ohio so my husband could help at the International Islamic University in Malaysia, only the last of our five children was still in elementary school. With no children at home during the day, I was ready for a real commitment to an Islamic curriculum. The university set up an office to work on establishing an international Islamic school with a totally new curriculum, one in which every subject was based on Islamic ideology. On the university campus we had access to Muslim scholars in many areas of the curriculum, including religious studies and history. Furthermore, these scholars represented every area of the Muslim world and they were seriously committed to working on an Islamic-based curriculum. I was able to work on this curriculum for three years before I had to return to the United States. You might think that three years of work would be sufficient, but we were only able to work on three or four subject areas, and we didn't fully complete any. Having known for a long time that this new from-scratch curriculum would eat up hours and years, I wasn't surprised by the lack of completion. What did surprise me was the real difference it made to have Muslim scholars who think from an Islamic perspective. The most important outcome of this attempt at developing an Islamic curriculum was the growing awareness of which Islamic principles needed to be included from the conceptual stage.

Freda Shamma

In 1998 we returned to America. At about
the same time, the International Islamic
University changed its direction and lost interest in that curriculum. I brought it to the attention of FADEL (Foundation for the Advancement and Development of
Education and Learning), a Muslim organization whose name, FADEL, is
an Arabic word referring to the bounty of Allah, and thus was able to continue to develop this innovative curriculum. Some have commented that the
project is too large and will never be finished. They are probably right. I don't
consider that it's my job to finish the curriculum. It's my job to contribute
as much as I can, and encourage others to join in so the work continues.

One person cannot make a curriculum or start a school, but one person
can persist in reminding others of the need, and a person can be patient, and
prepare, and be ready when the opportunity arises. A wise friend of mine said,
"Everyone has the same twenty-four hours in a day. Whether we acknowledge it or not, we make choices about how we will use that time." Our problem is not that we don't have the time; it is that we don't take time to think
about our actual priorities, as opposed to our wishful priorities. We also need
to be available wherever help is needed. My field is education. I offered to
teach at the weekend school and I was refused. Eleven years later I offered
again, and this time, I was accepted.

My field is education, but when it is necessary I speak about Islam to
churches and public schools. I have participated in various sessions at ISNA
conventions, and have written articles for Muslim journals on women in
Islam and raising children in North America as well as on education.

In the course of my Islamic activity, I have also given weekly rides to the
grocery store, babysat, listened to people who needed someone to listen, and
edited books. One of the most pleasant moments of my life was when I met
a young lady I hadn't seen since she was a child in Indianapolis. She said she
remembered me because I had been the first person to let her see that it can
be fun to be a Muslim. I was really grateful to have been of benefit to this girl
in particular, because her mother had been a wonderful role model for me.

Allah does not give us a burden greater than we can bear. He tells us that
if we walk toward Him, He will come running to us. Allah also tells us that

He does not hold us accountable for the success of our endeavors. He only asks that we try, and when we try, we find that Allah makes it easy for us. When I look back I can see that I often did too little, and sometimes I did nothing at all when I could have done something. And even my best has been of minor importance. But I have tried, and in the trying I have been blessed with knowing so many wonderful people, and my life has been full and rewarding. And the most rewarding of all is the five Islamically active young people that Allah has blessed my husband and me with, *alhamdulillah,* all thanks be to Allah.

Notes

1   Indeed, Dr. Katherine Bullock served as the AMSS program chair for the thirty-second annual conference in 2003.

16

Taking the Bus to the World of Islamic Activism

Samana Siddiqui

I trudged up the slushy steps of the city bus, flashed my pass at the driver, and proceeded on a quest for a seat to settle my weary, sixteen-year-old bones into. I was going to be late for school. Again.

The next move I made changed me forever.

It was winter 1991, during the Gulf War, and on this particular day, I was wearing a black *hijab* (headscarf). It wasn't a political statement, this choice of black. Maybe I just threw it on because it was the first thing I could find. Or maybe it was because black was one of my favorite colors. Whatever the reason, I probably looked very, very "Muslim."

As I turned away from the bus driver and started walking down the aisle, the looks on people's faces caught me off guard. Instead of the usual mild curiosity or obliviousness when they saw me, I could feel hostility in the air, like electricity during a lightning storm. One particular woman's expression remains imprinted on my brain to this day: narrowed, angry eyes looking straight into mine. She frowned at me, offering me a hard, grim expression.

As far as I recall, no one offered me a seat.

I had gotten off pretty lightly during the Gulf War compared to other Muslims in Canada and the United States. No one crank-called my house, CSIS didn't come to visit, I wasn't beaten up in school, and no one pointed a gun at me or even taunted me. I don't even think our phone was wired.

But the incident on the bus unnerved me. Why did people look at me so hatefully? I was normal, wasn't I, a teenager catching the (late) bus to school? Did those who stared think I was going to blow up the bus or kill somebody? Did they think I was related to Saddam Hussein?

"Perception is reality," my first political science teacher taught me. In other words, a person's perceptions become his/her understanding of reality. The incident on the bus made it very clear that some people's perceptions about who Muslims are and what they represent had allowed them to assume that I was the "other" in this war of the "good guys" (Canada, the United States, NATO, etc.) versus Saddam Hussein. Stereotypes about Muslims as terrorists, among other things, aren't new. But this was the first time I fully understood their repercussions. The media was reporting on the war in such a way that a line was clearly drawn between who "us" and "them" were. I was clearly the "them," at least visually.

The bus incident propelled me into what is called "Islamic activism." It was the desire to stand up for my beliefs and make it clear that Islam is not what prevailing "wisdom" in the West says it is. No, I'm not a terrorist. No, Islam is not a murderous, violent religion bent on destroying and suppressing life, beauty, and the good. The vision behind my activism was simple: to clear up misunderstandings and refute lies against Islam. Creating a utopian Islamic society didn't really come into the picture. How could we establish such a society when our beliefs and ideals were so misunderstood, sometimes even by Muslims? Although I do hope someday such a society will exist, I strongly doubt it will be in my lifetime. The transition from apathetic teenager to "activist" was sudden but seamless. I had no doubts about my need and desire to get involved in working for Islam within my capacity. It was something I had to do.

My initial career goal had been to become a genetic engineer. But after taking chemistry, I never wanted to set foot in another lab again. Journalism, my second career choice, was fun and I loved to write. But after the incident on the bus, I realized that journalism could not simply become my cash cow. It had the power to transform perceptions and interpret reality. I was not going to sit by as these perceptions smeared my beliefs and obfuscated the truth. Journalism, for me, would be to present "just the facts ma'am" about Islam.

The seeds of my activism were actually planted many years before this bus incident in different ways. One of them was how my parents, especially my mother, made a point to teach me that I am a Muslim, I'm different, and that this is not something I should be ashamed of. Growing up in Canada in the 1980s, and attending a public school where my brother and I were among barely a handful of Muslims, this message needed to be reinforced regularly. Our worthiness, our "different-ness" was not something to be embarrassed about. Being a minority because of my beliefs and skin color also made me acutely aware of how futile "fitting in" eventually was. You could dress and talk like everyone else, but when push came to shove, you were never like everyone else. You would still be called a "Paki," a "terrorist," or be excluded at some level. With this realization, standing up for my beliefs became easier. So did being who I really was, instead of kowtowing to the majority.

Activism's seeds were also planted when I started wearing *hijab* (head-cover) in grade nine. This was a turning point. I had finally decided during a hot shower on a cold November day that I would start wearing *hijab,* despite expected (and later on, experienced) taunts and hostility. That was, perhaps, the point of no return. I could no longer try to hide myself and deny who I was. *Hijab* set me apart. It was a marker that indicated I was no longer embarrassed by my "different-ness." My activism really took off when I started CEGEP (the equivalent of grades twelve and thirteen in some school systems, pre-university education in others) at Vanier College in Montreal. In a new school, away from the pressures of high school, and in an environment where diversity was encouraged, I plunged into writing and working for the Muslim Students' Association (MSA).

My parents fully supported me in my new role as "activist." Whether it was driving me places, letting me call during odd hours of the night to prepare MSA work, or letting me stay late when I needed to attend meetings or gatherings, their support was always there. It was a significant turnaround from high school, when coming home late would never have been tolerated. But for Islam, their hearts and their resources were always there for me.

Phoenix, Vanier College's campus newspaper, was where I learned to hone my skills as a writer, and to put my thoughts about Islam on paper. Oddly enough, it was perhaps more for me than anyone else, that I wrote about Islam when I did. It was like a catharsis. All that pent-up frustration, as well as the desire to clarify and to be understood, channeled into what some considered a newspaper to line their birdcages with rather than to read.

Looking back, I sometimes cringe when I read my own writings from those days. How immaturely ideas were put forth. How badly sentences were structured. But little did I know that, *alhamdulillah* (thanks be to God), my efforts were having a small but significant impact. A woman

Samana Siddiqui

named Sonia put it into perspective for me. I actually met her when I was in university and she was conducting an interesting experiment: wearing *hijab* and acting "Muslim" for a class project. After a couple of meetings with her, she said something that surprised me.

"Those articles you used to write in the paper at Vanier really changed the way I saw Islam and Muslims," she told me. "They helped me develop a more open mind."

Really? Wow. *Alhamdulillah*. And here I was thinking no one read them—or at least dismissed them as the ravings of a religious fanatic.

I experienced something similar sitting one day at a booth set up by the Vanier Muslim Students' Association. A tall, burly student came over and started telling me how horribly Muslim women were treated in his native Morocco. He was of Moroccan Jewish background. After explaining the role cultural traditions antithetical to Islam play in how Muslim women are often treated, he said to me, "You know, it takes a lot of guts to do what you guys are doing by explaining your faith. I really admire that. Thanks."

That was another "Really? Wow, *alhamdulillah*" moment for me.

Through activism, I met many of my mentors. In particular, Dr. Sheema Khan (director of the Council of American-Islamic Relations, Canada) played a critical role in connecting me with a number of worthy projects and organizations. But more importantly, she was a role model of a Muslim woman activist for me. I have great respect for her drive and dedication to serve Allah and to use her many talents and skills for Islam, *masha'allah*. I have also learned a tremendous amount about my faith from her in personal interactions, as well as in the weekly Islamic study circle for young women she used to conduct in Montreal.

The plunge into activism continued at Concordia University (in Montreal), where I completed a bachelor's degree in journalism. My staple activities, the school paper and the Muslim Students' Association, continued. There were, of course, times when attending seemingly endless meetings drove me up the wall, and covering another story about mundane university affairs was a drag. But I never thought of really quitting—until the end of my last year at the university when I realized it was time to come up for air after plunging into the waters of activism.

There were a lot of different reasons for this, but perhaps the bottom line was, I was burned out. After five years of being involved, I needed a break. Little did I know that this desire would soon plunge me into something else. confusion. After finishing school and then completing a three-month summer internship as a journalist for the *Montreal Gazette,* my city's daily newspaper, I no longer knew what I was going to do with my life. The internship made me realize that working in the mainstream media was definitely not for me. At the *Gazette,* I felt like a cog in a wheel, a drudge expected to churn out stories by deadline, with fleeting attachment to the story I was working on and the people involved in it. That's not the *Gazette*'s fault; that's just the nature of most mainstream journalism. I didn't want to do a master's degree right away either. I needed time off.

I took Arabic for a year at McGill University, wrote a little bit for one of the campus newspapers, and got involved in some volunteer work for Muslim youth and the local mosque; but I was confused and lost. I still wanted to use journalism to present a clearer picture of Islam, but I wasn't sure how and in what venue. *Now what?* That was the question I kept asking myself for three years as I dealt with story ideas rejected by editors, my own incompetence at freelancing, and a fear that there was nothing more I could do with my journalism. The ideal job, I had finally decided, was something that would merge my love of Islam with my love of writing.

The "break" came, *alhamdulillah,* in 1999, when I was offered a job by the Chicago-based Sound Vision Foundation, to write articles for their website. Being a neo-Luddite, I was initially intimidated by the whole idea of "the web." I was scared, but then remembered: I'm being hired to write, not tinker with computers. I was expected to write practical articles aimed at helping Muslims, especially in North America, live Islam. That meant, for instance, interviewing experts and offering tips about how to prepare an in-class presentation about Ramadan, writing up a sample letter to get time off for 'Eid, advising parents how to work with their children's teachers, and more. *Alhamdulillah,* this was my dream job. It still is.

I've come to realize that activism is not something we can simply do on the side, apart from our other daily activities. The early Muslims did not compartmentalize their lives into the "mundane" and the "activist-oriented activities." This was reflected by their drive to serve Islam in any way, with whatever their capacities, because they loved Allah and wanted to establish the truth. They were all activists.

And maybe one day, *insha'allah,* I'll be one too.

17

Is the Reward for Good Other than Good?

Shahina Siddiqui

Let there arise among you a band of people enjoining what is right and forbidding what is wrong...

(Qur'an 3:104)

I grew up in Pakistan, in an extended family system where uncles, aunts, siblings, and grandparents lived as one unit. This enhanced my nurturing and provided various parental figures that contributed to a secure and extremely loving environment. In addition, the schooling I received at a Roman Catholic convent school exposed me to other faiths and a strong, intellectually challenging, and academically satisfying environment.

Along with my many teachers, the one person that shaped, influenced, and inspired me the most was my paternal grandmother. Her name, Najmunissa (star among women), literally defines her character. She never received any formal education, but was well read and had been blessed with deep insight. She taught me all I know about dealing with people; her insights into human nature and her philosophy of life were profound. Her close relationship with God animated and transfused every aspect of her life. She may not be considered a scholar by normal standards, but her deep understanding of what it is to be a Muslim influenced me and has guided me throughout my life.

I was brought up to believe that to work toward helping others and to devote one's time, efforts, and energy in relieving people's distress was not a matter of choice but a duty and a privilege. My father's undying service to his family and his selfless service to the community further reinforced my commitment to be an active participant in society.

I migrated to Canada in 1976 with my husband and son. This is where I had the opportunity to start learning Islam without the cultural influences that had stunted my intellectual understanding and academic knowledge of Islam. The firm grounding in spirituality instilled in me by my grandmother needed nurturing through pursuit of Islamic knowledge and study of the Qur'an, and this I undertook with passion and determination. *Insha'allah* (God willing), this pursuit will continue till the day I die.

My involvement in the Muslim community did not start till 1984—after the death of my firstborn. During the long illness of my child I had come to recognize the lack of services within the Muslim community and the lack of support, resources, and motivation needed to reach out and help members who were in need. I thus made a silent commitment to Allah, that God willing, I would try and make a difference. Having made this commitment, I turned to the Qur'an for inspiration and guidance, and sincerely prayed to Allah to use me in whatever way He saw fit.

The first barrier that I needed to overcome was to understand what my role as a Muslim woman was. Was it the culturally jaded view that prevailed in the community? Or was it the inspiring role that my grandmother personified? And thus my study of the Qur'an led me to the firm understanding that in addition to my responsibilities to my family, my duty to forbid evil and to promote good compels me to be involved in the affairs of society. Language was not a barrier, and the exposure to Christianity in my schooling provided me with the confidence to charter a course for myself that has led me in many directions but with a singular goal: to worship the Creator through service to His creation.

A lesson I learned as a child was that as long as you do things for the sake of Allah, He will make it easy and open doors for you. This belief has empowered me to overcome many obstacles and to withstand many trials. As a *muhajjabah* (wearing a head-cover) Muslim woman activist, I am always conscious that every time I enter the public forum there are three strikes against me: (1) I am a visible minority; (2) I am Muslim; and (3) I am a woman. One would think these would only apply as barriers in the mainstream community, but the fact is that even within the Muslim community there have been hurdles that women activists encounter to this day, albeit at a lesser frequency. However, by the grace of Allah, instead of weakening my

Shahina Siddiqui.
*Photo courtesy of
Shahina Siddiqui*

resolve, these challenges have strengthened my character and dismantled my fears. Being a visible minority has given me empathy for those who are discriminated against, and insight into the culture of fear and racism. Being a Muslim has given me a spirit that is undaunted and a soul that is fearless. And as a woman, I appreciate my unique understanding and perspective, which enhances public discourse, and I celebrate my strengths as a mother, a wife, and a daughter.

Ironically, what many see as a symbol of gender seclusion became my initiation into community activism: it was in the kitchen of our Islamic center that I recognized where the power and control over our communities lie. This may sound facetious. But it is the simple truth, considering that our community was very young and very chauvinist at the time (and the chauvinism persists). While many sisters resented our relegation to the kitchen, I recalled that my grandmother had taught me to look beyond the obvious; I was able to see that any program in the *masjid* depended on how timely and well organized the food services were. The brothers were too busy taking the podium to take responsibility for actually running the programs, be they seminars or conferences. Thus I took advantage of this and along with one other sister, soon became active in program committees, which consequently enabled us to have a say in topics and speakers.

I have noticed that in general women do not crave as much limelight as our brothers do. And of course we all know, in our quiet unassuming manner, it is usually sisters who actually hold and run the Islamic centers and *masjid*. What we need to do is assert that role in a constructive manner and not be doormats and be patronized by statements such as *"subhan'allah* sisters, what you do is for the sake of Allah and you should leave the community to 'Us,' the men, as we know what is good for you."

I remember the first time attempts were being made to block off the sisters' section in the *masjid* by black glass and peepholes. I headed a campaign along with some younger sisters to block this move, with threats of taking a hammer to the divider. We were not successful in removing the barrier altogether, but got blinds (that can be opened part way) instead of the ugly black glass, the kind the Taliban had placed on the windows of the women's area in Afghanistan. Yes, this was way back in the 1980s, and in Canada.

Shahina Siddiqui

My second battle came when another sister and I were elected by acclamation to the Islamic Centre executive committee, but were barred by the other members of the executive committee from attending meetings. Thus started the battles of the fatwas: Can sisters sit on executive bodies of Islamic organizations? And so to and fro we went. The group barring us resorted to writing to Saudi Arabia for a fatwa regarding this issue. The answer that came back was a clear *no*. The community also consulted the Fiqh Council of North America, who responded with a unanimous *yes*. With their fatwa being read at *jumu'ah* prayers, the *khateeb* of the day decided to attack the two sisters for causing *fitna* (division in the community). *Alhamdulillah,* on closer scrutiny it was discovered that the question posed to Saudi Arabia was not "can sisters sit on the executive" but rather "can sisters, if they want to, act as the imam of a community." In the end, we were successful; the executive apologized and invited us to join the committee, at which point we resigned. Our objective was to set a precedent, and also we wanted the younger sisters to know that it is the responsibility of all members of society regardless of their gender and age to stand up for what is right.

This was a trying time and a truly grueling training for me. My resolve was tested and my faith challenged but, *alhamdulillah,* with the support of some brothers and our husbands (most of the sisters did not support us through this and, in fact, tried to coerce us into withdrawing), I coped. It must be stated in all fairness that sisters had been members of our executive prior to that particular committee and that our constitution neither prohibits nor bars women from voting or holding office. But for some years a new puritan attitude had been developing within the Muslim communities and many changes were being introduced under the guise of purifying Islam that were meant to restrict women's participation. This trend was not particular to our community but was rampant all over North America in the 1980s.

I state this incidence as an inspiration for younger sisters. You must understand, first, that we should never take anything for granted because things can change in our communities if unscrupulous people take hold of office. Second, never give up on your God-given rights. What may seem like a little thing may develop into something big and out of control.

I see a worrying trend among younger Muslims, both male and female, of isolating women from community involvement, relegating them to "sisters' groups" and promoting the idea that the best women are those who stay home and raise children to the exclusion of all else. Too much time and energy is wasted debating whether or not women can hold office, men should wear beards, or women can speak at mixed gatherings. All these debates are spiritually exhausting and emotionally draining. They leave little time for concrete activism and practical work to make this society a safer place for our children. To assume that a woman who is isolated and indifferent to what is out there can be an effective mother is naive at best and criminal at worst. How can she immunize her children against societal ills if she does not know what they are and does not struggle to change things for the better?

Prophet Muhammad *(pbuh)* stated, "Help the oppressor and the oppressed." When he was asked what he meant by helping the oppressor, he stated, "Restrain them from inflicting oppression." I have taken this as a guide for my activism within the Muslim and non-Muslim community. When we approach working in society from this holistic mind-set, we are addressing the cause rather than applying a band-aid treatment to symptoms. Our quest for peace and justice as Muslim activists should not just target the victims of injustice and war but must be extended to helping the perpetrators of injustice through education and other means.

My media activism started with my first letter being published in the *Winnipeg Free Press* in 1990 as a response to an editorial on Muslim women. Having being born into a family of journalists, I have felt most natural and comfortable in this area of my activist career. I have since published numerous articles, editorials, and letters in local, national, and international papers and magazines. One would think this would be a smooth undertaking. It is expected that people will disagree with your analysis or point of view, and as a writer I welcome honest critique or discussion. However, what I was not expecting was an open attack on my right to write and express my views by some men in the community, not because they necessarily disagreed with what I have written, but because I am a woman. One even had the audacity to suggest that I can write as long as I put a brother's name on my articles. By the grace of God, these are the voices of a very few ignorant people that have been drowned out by the overwhelming endorsement and support that I have received from my Muslim and non-Muslim readers. It is heartwarming when you get calls from people who have been living in Canada for over thirty years and who have never practiced their faith saying they were inspired by your articles and are reclaiming their Islamic roots.

Prophet Muhammad *(pbuh)* has stated that when a believer sees some wrong or injustice being committed, s/he should first try to stop it with his/her hands, and if not, then speak up against it, and if s/he is not able to do either, then should at least disapprove of it in his/her heart, and this, he said, was the weakest kind of faith. Many young Muslims are disheartened by the state of affairs in Muslim countries or in the Muslim community in North America. Yet they should be reminded of this *hadith,* so they can fulfill their duty by speaking and writing against injustice. For this very reason, in spite of my many commitments, I am honored to be part of the Council of American-Islamic Relations in Canada (CAIR-CAN) and to be serving on their board of directors. This organization is devoted to serving the Muslim community in a nonpartisan manner and to be a media watchdog and a Muslim advocacy group.

My role as paraprofessional in the field of social work was dictated more by the need of the Muslim community than by any conscious decision on my part. Before I knew it, I found myself writing and publishing brochures to help mainstream service providers understand their Muslim clients, patients, and students. Invitations to give cultural sensitivity workshops started to pour in from all directions, both private and governmental. This inspired me to organize the first weeklong training program for Muslim volunteers in social work and counseling. For this, by the grace of Allah, I was able to secure funds from the Department of Canadian Heritage, and the program received rave reviews from its participants, who came from across North America.

My dream of organizing and developing a continent-wide social services association for Muslims was realized in 1999 when the Islamic Social Services Association (ISSA) was founded in Washington at the conference of the Muslim Social Service Providers. I was fortunate to be one of the founding members along with three other sisters from the United States. It has since been incorporated in both the United States and Canada. Praise be to Allah. This has been a long and arduous journey but one that has been fulfilling and rewarding. The enthusiastic contributions of the young people in ISSA represent the most satisfying and hopeful sign for the viability and long life of this organization. Since ISSA's incorporation, we have done many training programs in Islamic social work and counseling for the Muslim community as well as organizing conferences and publishing many handbooks for service providers to help them better serve their Muslim clients.

Also, recognizing that Muslim marriages were in trouble, I compiled the Marriage Preparation Course for Muslims, based on the model used in churches and customizing it to our needs. This program is slowly receiving recognition by imams and is sought after by young couples.

Spiritual counseling is also an area that I have ventured into. Having counseled hundreds of people as a nonprofessional volunteer, by the mercy of God, I have now developed a spiritual counseling manual that is perpetually a work in progress and that has been recognized by Muslim professionals as an essential and effective tool in their practice. In December 2002 it was introduced to mainstream professionals when it was presented at the First International Conference on Spirituality and Mental Health in Ottawa.

I have served at Hospice and Palliative Care Manitoba for two years and have been an informal pastoral consultant for Muslim patients for a decade. I give regular workshops to nurses, medical students, and other health care professionals on Muslim patient care and on the Islamic concept of death and dying. I have now developed a training manual for this for both Muslim and non-Muslim health care workers.

My other passion is interfaith dialogue and activism. Currently I sit on the Interfaith Roundtable of Winnipeg. Post–September 11, 2001, I have done hundreds of speaking engagements about Islam and Muslims, mostly at schools and churches, and also in both the private and public sectors and at government departments and agencies, both provincial and federal. This humble effort was recognized by YWCA/YMCA (Winnipeg), who awarded me their Canada Peace Medal in 2002.

I have been a speaker and workshop facilitator for over a decade and travel across North America quite frequently presenting on Islamic, social, and gender issues. In 1997 I organized the first monthlong educational retreat in North America, for Muslim youths. By the grace of God, it was a success. The setup was based on our traditional style of learning, where forty carefully chosen young people had the opportunity to learn and socialize with the scholars. For one month we created a sample of what a true Muslim society would be like—peaceful and just.

My work continues and my passion for activism remains constant if not stronger than when I was younger and a lot more naive. My faith has sustained me through the hard times and the good times. I always remind myself that Allah will only hold us responsible for what good we tried to accomplish, and not only if we are successful in doing so—for the results are in Allah's hands alone.

My work with the mainstream in human rights, poverty, and social justice issues has given me a unique opportunity to appreciate what wealth of ideas and solutions Islam offers. I have also learned a great deal about organization and mutual cooperation by observing and taking notes on how other

Shahina Siddiqui

communities have developed or are struggling. I believe that we cannot be isolationist in our activism since the world is one, humanity is one, and what affects others affects me as well.

It is the fear of losing our faith and being assimilated that paralyzes Muslims from getting involved in the mainstream community and to work toward improving society in general. This fear stems from ignorance of our faith and lack of confidence in the truth of our *deen* (religious way of life); it does not, as is mistakenly assumed by some, spring from high level of religiosity. Our *deen* is about living and contributing, as is evident from the *seerah* (life) of our beloved Prophet Muhammad (pbuh), who came to bestow mercy on humanity. It is interesting to note that the Prophet used to retreat to the mountains for reflection, but once the message came, he had the courage and the fortitude to proclaim it to all of humanity. Islam meant work, involvement, change, and service to humanity. If this is not activism, what is?

In conclusion, I humbly suggest the following before embarking on the path of activism:

ך Make sincere supplication to Allah to clean your intention of any ego-centric leanings, as ego will destroy sincerity just as vinegar spoils honey.

ך Read and attempt to understand the Qur'an on a daily basis.

ך Study the life of our beloved Prophet and stories of all other prophets, as this will inspire you through hard and difficult times.

ך Clean your heart of grudges every day and forgive those who hurt you.

ך Seek out sincere friends; those who love and fear the Creator will always counsel you to the truth and will counsel you to perseverance.

ך Ask people to make *du'a* (prayer) for you often, especially those who feel obliged to you and want to do something for you.

ך Remind yourself constantly and consistently that you are merely an instrument through which Allah chooses to help others and that Allah has blessed you by choosing you to do His work. Understand that His work will continue whether you are there or not.

ך Thank Allah (swt) all the time for this favor of allowing you to serve IHm and IHs creation.

- Have a support network—parents, spouse, or a friend—on whose shoulder you can cry and who will be there for you.

- Get training and continue to educate yourself; keep an open mind and do not make difficulties in your religion.

- Do not despair. Difficulties only make us stronger; challenges enhance our resolve, and opposition makes our faith grow and blossom.

- Be merciful, compassionate, and forgiving to all.

- Care about people sincerely and selflessly.

- Finally, keep a sense of humor. Eat well, rest, and exercise.

May Allah strengthen our resolve, make firm our hearts, unite us, forgive us, and purify our efforts and actions such that all we do and work toward is solely to seek Allah's pleasure and reward.

Shahina Siddiqui

18

Undoing Internalized Inferiority

Tayyibah Taylor

The first time I resolved to change the world, I was seven. Having just emigrated from the Caribbean to Canada, I stepped from an earthy world with warm sea breezes and carefree childishness into a new world of snow, ice, and adult caution. Caution because I was now different from those around me.

Admonished by my loving parents, I was encouraged always to behave perfectly, speak eloquently, and dress impressively so that as a person of color, others would deem me acceptable. For a free-spirited, inquisitive, candid seven-year-old that was a tall order. I decided that I would change the world so that the snow people would accept the earth people without the rigid demands of cashmere socks and patent leather loafers, diction devoid of singsong accents and continuously constrained comportment.

I didn't change the world. Instead, I skillfully mastered the art of acquiescence for all those who required me to be twice as good in order to be treated half as well. As I grew, I impressed others with intellectual acrobatics, eclectic clothes, and impeccable public decorum. Still, beneath it all, I internalized a sense of inferiority, a sense that something was wrong with us as a people, and the glaring absence of positive images of people like us in the media exacerbated the conviction that somehow we were not quite good enough.

The first time I read *Ebony* magazine, I saw media images of people of color that were positive. Instead of visuals of black people in race riots being hosed down by police, there were photos of people of color in positions of authority. Instead of news stories of people being arrested with the aid of police dogs, there were articles about black people accomplishing amazing feats in science, education, and business. It seemed that the earth people were really OK, after all—an epiphany.

While at the University of Toronto, between studies of philosophy and microbiology, I questioned the universe and everything in it. Trying to find my place and purpose in existence, I escaped back to the beaches of Barbados. There, I chose Islam as my spiritual path and resolved once again to transform the world so that everyone could experience the joy and tranquility I gained from Islam.

The lukewarm reception I received from others dampened that enthusiasm, and so I decided to concentrate on changing myself. With the tools of Islam, I began my own metamorphosis.

A pivotal time of my life was the six years I lived with simultaneous legal claim to residency in five different countries. Trinidad, the country of my birth; Barbados, the country of my parents' birth; Canada, then the country of my citizenship; United States, where I was a legal alien; and Saudi Arabia, where I was living and had a resident's visa. This experience gave me a unique lens through which to view the world, and I witnessed how ethnocentricity can often cloud one's view of humanity.

Wherever I went, I could never be counted as part of the dominant culture. I began to see how easily inferiority can be internalized by those who are not of the dominant culture, especially when they are marginalized or stereotyped in the media. Perhaps this was when the seed of *Azizah* planted itself in my mind.

After helping to found the Islamic School of Seattle, teaching there and serving as its administrator, I decided to shift gears and do something about a void that had been bothering me for such a long time. I decided to create a magazine for Muslim women that would be a vehicle for their voices and issues.

I began working with a publisher as the editorial director and created a publication called *Sisters!* magazine. After four issues the publisher made a business decision to discontinue publication and I found myself without a job. Still I had the desire to publish a magazine that would express the authentic voice of the Muslim American woman and accurately reflect her. Two years later, I moved to Atlanta, Georgia, and determinedly set about doing just that.

Learning as much as I could about business and the publishing industry through classes, seminars, and conferences, I drafted a debt-free business plan. I incorporated the business as WOW Publishing, Inc., and set up the first office of *Azizah* in the corner of the family room. With my life savings and a loan from a family member, the business operation and magazine production began. With business partner Marlina Soerakoesoemah in Seattle handling all the layout and graphics, and Nadia Hassouneh in Portland managing editorial copy, our cyber office was rounded out with freelance editors, writers, artists, and designers from all over the country.

Azizah is for the woman who doesn't apologize for being a Muslim and doesn't apologize for being a woman. It is a magazine that presents the issues and accomplishments of the Muslim American woman in her voice, from her perspective. Unlike other Muslim publications, *Azizah* is not focused on a particular ethnic group, one school of thought, or on an Islamic organization or mosque. Instead it reflects all Muslim women in their diversity, thus speaking to the polycentric nature of Islam. Interestingly enough, you can find a woman named Azizah in any Muslim country. It is a name that transcends ethnic and cultural borders, as does the magazine. In classical Arabic, the name Azizah means "dear, strong, and noble." So, we defined the *Azizah* woman as the one who is dear to herself and others, with noble strength and dignity, boldly reclaiming our attribute of strength.

Eleven issues and three years later, we are operating from an office building in midtown Atlanta and selling subscriptions and single magazines on our website, www.azizahmagazine.com. *Azizah* can be found now in university and public libraries across the country and in many homes and businesses.

Creating the magazine and running the business has been challenging intellectually, financially, and physically. There have been many obstacles and numerous surprises. Managing a family and a startup business at the same time is always difficult, and the support of my family has been pivotal to the success of the magazine. The tasks and troubles have been many, but they are far outweighed by the great pleasure the magazine brings. Along the way, I have met many phenomenal women—talented, inspirational, and powerful.

I marvel at the comments Muslim women make when they flip through the pages of *Azizah* for the first time.

Tayyibah Taylor, editor-in-chief, *Azizah* magazine.
Photo © Sumayah Clarke, courtesy of Azizah *magazine*

Tayyibah at her desk.
*Photo © Sumayah Clarke,
courtesy of* Azizah *magazine*

Usually, it is their first experience seeing themselves portrayed positively in the media. They are amazed by the beautiful depiction and diverse representation of themselves. Through their reactions, I see my own experience with the *Ebony* magazine and I witness the wheels turning, undoing the internalization of inferiority.

Absence, marginalization, or stereotyping of a group of people has a profound affect, not only on the group portrayed, but also on the people of the dominant culture. Thus, when people who are not of the faith tradition of Islam pick up a copy of *Azizah,* the wheels of internalization quickly begin turning as well. Stereotypes are smashed, myths debunked, and intellects stimulated.

Indeed, *Azizah* might surprise anyone captivated by counterfeit images or ideas. Those Muslim men who have formulated ideas about Muslim women's ability or inability to contribute to society may also experience a subtle shift in paradigm when reading a publication that depicts the Muslim woman with all her spirituality, intelligence, and beauty.

One of the slogans of the magazine is, *"Azizah* is more than a magazine. It is a catalyst for empowerment." Scores of women have shared the inspiration received from *Azizah*—things they were inspired to do, or not do. Energized by seeing positive representations of themselves and motivated by the validation of self, they set about accomplishing that which they had dismissed as impossible.

We have heard many times—"To those whom much is given, much is expected." I believe that as Muslims we have been given much; as believers we have been given much; as women we have been given much. Removing the emotional blindfolds and undoing the internalized inferiority give us the impetus to use all that we have been given to start and complete work on our communities, our world, and ourselves.

Every activist hopes to make a change—a microscopic one or a momentous change that impacts lives. While many hope to change the world, some are content to change minds, believing everything begins within the mind. There the shackles of internalized inferiority paralyze us, keeping us from realizing our capacities and living full lives.

As an Islamic activist concerned with women's affairs, I have chosen to change minds about Muslim women through *Azizah* magazine. Perhaps, those transformed minds will change the world.

Glossary

'abaya	Arabic name for traditional silk cloak, usually black, used by Iraqi, Saudi, and most Arabian Gulf women
Allah	Arabic name for God, used also by Christian and Jewish Arabs
Allahu Akbar	God is Great
alhamdulillah	Thanks be to God
'awra	that part of the woman that should be covered in front of unrelated men
chadoor	Persian name for traditional cloak, often black, used by Iranian women
da'wa	spreading the news about Islam
deen	way of life
'Eid Al Fitr	the festival of ending the monthlong Ramadan fast
'Eid Al Adha	the festival to commemorate Prophet Abraham's willingness to sacrifice his son, Ismail. Celebrated at the end of the religious pilgrimage, the hajj
fiqh	Islamic law
fitna	chaos, disruption
hajj	religious pilgrimage to the Kaba, in Mecca, Saudi Arabia, an obligation of Muslims who can afford it, once in their lifetime
halaqa	a religious study group
itjihad	to derive new rulings of Islamic law using approved methodology
istikhara	special prayer seeking the guidance of God

jumu'ah	Friday, the day of special communal worship, like Sunday church service
khateeb	the one who delivers the sermon on Friday
Khilaafa	the institution for governing the Muslim community, whose ruler is the Caliph, and which was formally disbanded by Attaturk, Turkey's ruler in 1923
masjid	Arabic term for mosque
muhajjabah	a woman who wears a head-cover
pbuh	"Peace be upon Him," an expression of respect, said after the name of any prophet
Ramadan	the month of fasting
seerah	the study of the life of the Prophet Muhammad (pbuh)
shari'ah	the collective name for the body of Islamic laws, including religious, liturgical, jurisprudential, and ethical systems
Sunnah	the example of the Prophet Muhammad's (pbuh) life, words, and deeds, as recorded by his companions
swt (Subhaanahu wa ta'ala)	"May God be praised and may His transcendence be affirmed"
ummah	global Muslim community
usul-ul-fiqh	source methodology for Islamic law

Bibliography

Banna, H. Al. *Al Mar'a al Muslimah,* compiled and edited by Muhammad Nasir al-Diin Al Albani. Cairo: Daar al Kutub al Salafaiyah, 1983.

Barazangi, Nimat Hafez. "Domestic Democracy: The Road to National and International Democracy." *Center for the Study of Islam and Democracy, Fourth Annual Conference Proceedings.* Washington, D.C., May 16, 2003, http://www.islam-democracy.org/4th_Annual_Conference-Barazangi_paper.asp. Accessed September 16, 2003.

————. "Islam and Early Childhood Education: Implications for Women's Education." *Al-Ittihad* (Journal of Islamic Studies) 17, no. 1 (January–March 1980): 33–38.

————. *Women's Identity and the Qur'an: A New Reading.* Gainsville: University Press of Florida, forthcoming.

Bewley, Aisha. Islam: *The Empowering of Women.* London: Ta-ha, 1999.

Boddy, Janice. *Women, Men, and the Zar Cult in Northern Sudan.* Madison: University of Wisconsin Press, 1989.

Khan, Shahnaz. *Muslim Women: Crafting a North American Identity.* Gainsville: University Press of Florida, 2000.

Maudoodi, Syed Abul A'la. *Al-Hijaab.* Beirut: Daar al-Fikr, 1967.

McCloud, Aminah Beverly. African American Islam. New York: Routledge, 1995.

Siddiqi, Muhammad Zubayr. *Hadith Literature: Its Origins, Development and Special Features.* Cambridge, U.K.: Islamic Texts Society, 1993.

United Nations. *Covenant for the New Millennium: The Beijing Declaration and Platform for Action.* Fourth World Conference on Women. Santa Rosa, CA: Free Hand, 1996.

Webb, Gisela, ed. *Windows of Faith: Muslim Women Scholar-Activists in North America.* Syracuse: Syracuse University Press, 2000.

Wikan, Uni. *Behind the Veil: Women in Oman.* Baltimore: Johns Hopkins University Press, 1982.

About the Contributors

Nimat Hafez Barazangi, PhD

Nimat Hafez Barazangi, PhD, is a research fellow in the Women's Studies Program (the name of the program became, in the fall of 2003, Feminist, Gender, and Sexuality Studies) and the Cornell Participatory Action Research Network at Cornell University. She specializes in curriculum and instruction, Islamic and Arabic studies, and adult and community education. She has received several awards for her participatory action research, including the Glock Award for her 1988 PhD dissertation from the Department of Education at Cornell, a visiting fellowship from Oxford University, a scholarship from the International Council for Adult Education, a three-year Serial Fulbright Scholarship, and the United Nations Development Program Fellowships in 1999 and 2002. She has published the anthology *Islamic Identity and the Struggle for Justice* (1996) as well as over twenty-five articles and essays (see her website: <http://www.arts.cornell.edu/womens/barazangi.htm>); her most recent essay is "Understanding Muslim Women's Self-Identity and Resistance to Feminism and Participatory Action Research," in *Traveling Companions: Feminism, Teaching, and Action Research* (2004): 21–39.

Born and raised in Damascus, Syria, she is an Arab American citizen of the United States. Her thirty-five years of voluntary work with Arabs and

Muslims has been intertwined with her scholarly research. She has worked extensively on building a curricular foundation for Muslims in North America, working with both parents and youth to understand and integrate Islam into the American educational system. This work led to her being invited to serve as the guest editor of the 1998 edition of *Religion and Education,* the first journal volume on Islamic education in the United States, used by Islamic schools and multicultural training for teachers in public and private schools. She can be contacted via e-mail (nhb2@cornell.edu) or mail (Feminist, Gender, and Sexuality Studies, 391 Uris Hall, Cornell University, Ithaca, NY 14853).

Ekram Beshir, MD

Ekram Beshir, MD, graduated from Alexandria University Medical School in 1973. She has made Canada her home since 1975. It was when she was volunteering for field trips and activity days while her children were in school that she became aware of the pressures her children faced in the North American school system. With Dr. Mohamed R. Beshir (her husband), she coauthored two books on parenting Muslim children in the West: *Meeting the Challenge of Parenting in the West: An Islamic Perspective* (Amana Publications, 1998) and *Muslim Teens: Today's Worry, Tomorrow's Hope* (Amana Publications, 2001). Dr. Beshir is a founding member of Rahma School, a weekend school, and Abraar School, a full-time Islamic school, both in Ottawa.

Mariam Bhabha

Mariam Bhabha is the founding president of the Federation of Muslim Women. She has been active in the Muslim community and in the community at large for many years. She has served in a variety of volunteer positions, from being president of a political riding association to serving on the board of directors of the Children's Aid Society.

During the Bosnian war she was a founding member and the first president of the Bosnian Canadian Relief Association (BCRA). She made four trips to war-ravaged Bosnia and waged public relations campaigns at home to promote peace efforts. In recognition of her work during the Bosnian war she received, in 1996, the Woman of the Year Award from the Toronto-based Women's Intercultural Network.

In Canada she works tirelessly to promote interfaith and interracial understanding and tolerance. In the summer of 2002 she joined the newly formed London-based International Women's Peace Service (IWPS) because she felt that ordinary people needed to do what world political leaders were unwilling to do, namely, to protect the lives and human rights of civilians living under Israeli occupation in Palestine. For more information about IWPS please visit www.womenspeacepalestine.org.

Katherine Bullock

Katherine Bullock completed her PhD in political science at the University of Toronto in 1999. She has taught and lectured on Islamic civilization and Middle East politics in California and Toronto. Her publications include *Rethinking Muslim Women and the Veil: Challenging Historical and Modern Stereotypes* (Herndon, Va.: IIIT Press, 2003). Currently, Dr. Bullock is the executive director of Education, Media, and Community Outreach for the Islamic Society of North America (ISNA), Canada. She is also the editor of the *American Journal of Islamic Social Sciences.* She was a founder and board member of the Federation of Muslim Women, a grassroots nonprofit organization based in Toronto. She was very involved with the local *masjid* in California, from running a youth group, to teaching at the weekend Islamic school, to working at the *masjid* library. Originally from Australia and of Anglo-Saxon roots, she now lives in Toronto, Canada, with her husband and two sons.

Muniza Farooqi

Muniza Farooqi graduated from Livermore High School, California, in the year 2002. She is currently attending Las Positas College in Livermore. She has been involved in her community in many ways. At Livermore High, she was a member of the Art Club, Afghan Club, and the Muslim Club. She was the cofounder and vice-president of the Muslim Club in 2001. In 2002, she cofounded and became the vice-president of the Muslim Student Association at Las Positas College. She is also involved in the Islamic Center of Livermore. She has volunteered at the Islamic center's Sunday school and library. She was born in Kabul, Afghanistan. She came to the United States in the year 1999. She currently lives in Livermore, California, with her parents, three sisters, and a brother.

Khadija Haffajee

Khadija Haffajee is a retired elementary school teacher in Ottawa, Canada. She was born in a small town in South Africa, where Muslim girls were not typically educated. Khadija fought the local customs and became a teacher. In 1966 she moved to Canada, where she found a home with the Muslim community in Ottawa. She became active in the Ottawa Muslim Women's Auxiliary, and after many years of activist work she was elected to the Majlis ash-Shura of the Islamic Society of North America. She was the first woman elected to the board. She lives in Ottawa with her husband.

Rose Hamid

Rose Hamid was born in Buffalo, New York, of Palestinian-Latino heritage. Rose was a flight attendant for twelve years and was nearly fired when she started to wear the Muslim women's head-cover. With the help of the Council on American Islamic Relations, she fought back, and was awarded a new position as a flight attendant instructor. She has been very involved in the Girl Scouts as a troop leader since 1995 as well as serving as a member of the district team and leader trainer. She was instrumental in revamping the weekend Islamic school curriculum at the Islamic Center of Greater Charlotte. She lives in Charlotte, North Carolina, with her husband and three children.

Gul Joya Jafri

Gul Joya Jafri (MA, anthropology) is a former director of sponsorship with the Canadian Palestinian Educational Exchange (CEPAL) and has volunteered with the International Development and Relief Foundation (IDRF). She has worked for the UN in Amman, Jordan, and in New York city. She now lives in Ottawa, where—when she is not at protests on Parliament Hill—she works with the Canadian International Development Agency (CIDA). She is coauthor, with Katherine Bullock, of "Media (Mis)Representations: Muslim Women in the Canadian Nation" (*Canadian Woman Studies,* Summer 2000). She was born in Lahore, Pakistan, and grew up in Toronto, Canada.

Laila Al-Marayati, MD

Laila Al-Marayati, MD, an obstetrician-gynecologist, is the spokesperson and past president of the Muslim Women's League (MWL), a Los Angeles-based organization dedicated to disseminating accurate information about Islam and women and to strengthening the role of Muslim women in society. Dr. Al-Marayati has written articles and participated in numerous conferences addressing issues of concern to Muslim women ranging from basic women's rights in Islam to reproductive health and sexuality. She spearheaded the MWL's efforts on behalf of rape survivors from the war in Bosnia in 1993, and she was a member of the official U.S. delegation to the UN Conference on Women in Beijing in 1995.

Dr. Al-Marayati served as a presidential appointee to the Commission on International Religious Freedom from 1999 to 2001. Prior to that, she was a member of the State Department Advisory Committee on Religious Freedom Abroad. She has testified before Congress and as part of the U.S. delegation to the OSCE Human Dimensions meeting in Poland regarding religious intolerance against Muslims in Europe.

As an American of Palestinian descent, Dr. Al-Marayati frequently speaks about the rights of Palestinians. She is a member of the board of directors of KinderUSA, a newly formed charity whose primary focus at this time is on addressing the health and educational needs of Palestinian children living in the West Bank and Gaza.

Olivia Monem

Olivia Monem is Canadian-born and of Egyptian heritage. She has a bachelor's of arts degree (with honors) in French and English linguistics, and a bachelor's of education degree from Queen's University in Kingston, Ontario, Canada. In Canada, she was an active member of the Islamic Society of Kingston (ISK), a member of Kingston Muslim Youth, and then a member of the Queen's University Muslim Students' Association (MSA) member. Later she became the education coordinator for the ISK and the principal of the weekend Islamic school. After moving to the United States in 1997, she completed a web-based teachers' manual on Islam and became an active member of the Islamic Society of the New River Valley (ISNRV). Later she became the chair of the ISNRV Ladies Committee and a member of the Virginia Tech MSA. Currently she is working on her master's in instructional technology at Virginia Tech, and is the principal of the weekend Islamic school in Blacksburg.

Nadira Mustapha

Nadira Mustapha was born in Winnipeg, Canada, of Caribbean heritage. She has been active with the Muslim Youth Council and the Muslim Students' Association in Winnipeg, Manitoba, for over ten years, both as a member and in leadership positions. She has been a summer camp counselor for many years in several cities across western Canada, and has organized and directed conferences, sporting events, and *halaqas*. She moved to Montreal, Canada, to pursue a master's and then a PhD in Islamic law from McGill University. She is currently a cofounder and chairperson of Canadian Muslims for Peace and Justice and hopes to inaugurate Canadian Muslims for Jerusalem in the near future.

Samadah Raquibah Amatul Nur

Samadah Raquibah Amatul Nur is the president/founder of AN-NUR Creations, a unique line of educational products for children and for those who work with children in the home, schools, community, and office settings. Samadah holds a degree in early childhood education, social science, and technical engineering; she is also certified in sign language. She has been involved in the field of education for more than twenty-five years. Her products at AN-NUR are diversified and are for all children, of all ages, including adults, with special features geared toward the African American, Muslim, and the hearing and visual impaired (see www.an-nur.com.) The Islamic motivational stickers and the Allahu Akbar puzzles are on display at the International Museum of Muslim Cultures in Jackson, Mississippi, and on the office walls of Imam W. Deen Mohammed and the Honorable Minister Louis Farrakhan.

Samadah Nur was the president of the Early Childhood Club at Erie Community College in Buffalo, New York. She has conducted education workshops for the National Black Arts Festival in Atlanta, Georgia, as well as for the San Jose Black Studies and Women's Studies departments.

Samadah is a member of the National Black Herstory Conference Task Force, the National Black Child Development Institute, the Metro Atlanta Kwanzaa Association, the Buffalo Kwanzaa Committee, the Baitul Salaam Network, Inc., the Islamic Crisis Emergency Response System, Inc. (ICERS), and Grass Roots Institute, and the Muslimah Consultation Group, just to name a few.

Samadah Nur is the daughter of Willie Mae Clanton Johnson (Nur) and Raymond Johnson. She is the proud mother of Edward Welch, Abdul Zahir Nur, and Tauhid K. Nur, and the proud *grandumie* (grandmother) of six grandchildren who are the joy of her life. Allah has been her guiding light.

Mona Rahman, PhD

Mona Rahman, PhD, was born and raised in Kingston, Ontario, Canada, where she has been involved in the activities of the Islamic Society of Kingston for most of her life. Recently, she has participated in the Muslim Kids' Club and served as advisor for the Kingston Muslim Youth, as well as serving as a teacher at the weekend Islamic school, a member of the education committee, a writer for the community newsletter, and a member of the Committee in Support of the Palestinian People. She has been involved with the Muslim Students' Association (MSA) on a local level (with the Queen's University MSA or QUMSA) as well as doing some work on the continental level, and on the Internet as Sisters Net administrator. She also served on the Interfaith Council at Queen's University and was involved, as an advisor, in the Multifaith Youth Group in Kingston. Currently she is the network coordinator for Canadian Muslims for Peace and Justice (CMPJ). She obtained her BSc (Honours) and her PhD in biochemistry from Queen's University, and is currently doing a postdoctoral fellowship at the Robarts Research Institute in London, Ontario.

Academic achievements include the Governor General's Silver Medal upon graduating with her BSc (Honours) from Queen's University, and the Merck Frosst Award, a national award given to ten students in Canada in third-year chemistry or biochemistry. She was awarded a Medical Research Council scholarship for her graduate studies.

Margaret Sabir-Gillette

Margaret Sabir-Gillette was born in Clayton, Alabama, to parents of African American descent. Margaret has been married fifty years and is mother of four and grandmother of two. She joined the Nation of Islam in 1958, and in 1975, she embraced the universal teachings of Islam under the leadership of Imam W. Deen Mohammed.

Margaret received her certification in secretarial and office practice from Bryant and Stratton Business School in Buffalo. She retired in 1994, after twenty-four years as an administrative assistant in the Department of African American Studies at the State University of New York at Buffalo.

Margaret is the president of the Buffalo chapter of the International League of Muslim Women. She also serves as special assistant to the international president, Sahirah Muhammad, and is responsible for overseeing the chapters in the Northeast region. Margaret also serves on the Family Life Team of the American Society of Muslims. She has become well known in the city of Buffalo for the work she has done over the past ten years with the Somali refugee families who have been resettled in the city. In 1999 she was the recipient of the United Way's J. C. Penney "Golden Rule Award" for Outstanding Adult Volunteer of the year for the city of Buffalo.

Freda Shamma

Freda Shamma was born in California, of English-German ancestry. She embraced Islam in 1969. She was awarded her PhD in education from the University of Cincinnati and has been active in the area of education ever since. She has been a teacher at her local Islamic weekend school for years, and has lectured and published articles about education and raising children in several journals and magazines. Dr. Shamma has reviewed and edited books about education and/or children for American Trust Publications. She was a founding member of the Association of Muslim Social Scientists (AMSS).

For the past seven years Dr. Shamma has been the director of a worldwide curriculum development project to produce a curriculum based on an Islamic worldview for all subjects taught in Islamic schools. Begun in Malaysia, the project is now centered at FADEL (Foundation for the Advancement and Development of Education and Learning), in Cincinnati, Ohio. Using her pen name, Freda Crane, she and Sarah Conover are co-authors of *Ayat Jamilah/Beautiful Signs: A Treasury of Islamic Wisdom for Children and Parents* (Spokane: Eastern Washington University Press, 2004).

Samana Siddiqui

Samana Siddiqui was born in Montreal, Canada. She was always aware of being "different," but it was the reaction to her head-cover after the Gulf War in 1991 that propelled her into journalism, as an attempt to alter the negative stereotypes of Muslims. A stint in a mainstream newspaper disillusioned her for a while, until her dream job arrived when Sound Vision, an Islamic multimedia organization based in Chicago, offered her a job in 1999. Samana's heritage is Pakistani. She is married and has two children.

Shahina Siddiqui

Shahina Siddiqui is the founding member and executive director of the Islamic Social Services Association, Inc.. She is the founding member and on the board of directors of the first Islamic school in Winnipeg. She is senior director at the Council of American Islamic Relations (Canada). She is also a member of the Manitoba Coalition for Human Equality, the interfaith roundtable, and the Winnipeg Coalition for Peace. She is past director of the board for Hospice and Palliative Care Manitoba. Shahina is a freelance writer and has authored many newspaper and magazine articles as well as book chapters. She has presented papers at conferences and works in the field of human rights, minority issues, social work, media, community relations, and palliative care. She is also a volunteer counselor.

Tayyibah Taylor

Tayyibah Taylor is an Islamic activist passionately concerned with spirituality, women's issues, and communication. She seeks to foster sisterhood between women of all backgrounds and perspectives through her work and her publication, *Azizah,* for which she is editor-in-chief. *Azizah* magazine presents the accomplishments, aspirations, and issues of the diverse community of Muslim American women, dispelling myths and speaking to the joy of the Muslim woman's experience.

Tayyibah founded and worked as the administrator of the Islamic School of Seattle over twenty years ago. While in Seattle she was also active in prison ministry and Seattle's Islamic Sisterhood—a women's group that coordinated social services, *da'wah* materials, 'Eid activities, and Islamic seminars.

Born on the island of Trinidad in the Caribbean, Tayyibah grew up in Toronto, Canada, and studied biology and philosophy at the University of Toronto. She lived in Jeddah, Saudi Arabia, for six and a half years and while there, attended school for Arabic and Islamic studies. During this time Tayyibah had simultaneous legal claim to residency in five different countries, giving her a unique lens through which to view the universe. She performed *hajj* three times. She is the mother of five children.